Jeremy Black is one of the UK's most respected and prolific historians. He is Emeritus Professor of History at the University of Exeter and a renowned expert on the history of war. He is a Senior Fellow at the Foreign Policy Research Institute. His recent books include *Military Strategy: A Global History, A History of the Second World War in 100 Maps, Tank Warfare* and *The World of James Bond*. He appears regularly on TV and radio.

T0003402

Other titles in this series

A Brief History of the British Monarchy
Jeremy Black

A Brief History of Portugal
Jeremy Black

A Brief History of the Caribbean
Jeremy Black

A Brief History of the Mediterranean
Jeremy Black

A Brief History of Britain 1851–2021
Jeremy Black

A Brief History of France
Cecil Jenkins

A Brief History of Germany
Jeremy Black

A Brief History of Italy
Jeremy Black

A Brief History of Spain
Jeremy Black

A Brief History of Medieval Warfare
Peter Reid

A Brief History of the Normans
Francois Neveux

A Brief History of Slavery
Jeremy Black

A BRIEF HISTORY OF

The Pacific:

The Great Ocean

JEREMY BLACK

ROBINSON

ROBINSON

First published in Great Britain in 2023 by Robinson

1 3 5 7 9 10 8 6 4 2

Copyright © Jeremy Black, 2023

The moral right of the author has been asserted.

All rights reserved.
No part of this publication may be reproduced, stored in a retrieval system, or
transmitted, in any form, or by any means, without the prior permission in
writing of the publisher, nor be otherwise circulated in any form of binding or
cover other than that in which it is published and without a similar condition
including this condition being imposed on the subsequent purchaser.

A CIP catalogue record for this book
is available from the British Library.

ISBN: 978-1-47214-673-1

Typeset in Scala by Hewer Text UK Ltd, Edinburgh
Printed and bound in Great Britain by Clays Ltd, Elcograf S.p.A.

Papers used by Robinson are from well-managed
forests and other responsible sources.

MIX
Paper from
responsible sources
FSC® C104740

Robinson
An imprint of
Little, Brown Book Group
Carmelite House
50 Victoria Embankment
London EC4Y 0DZ

An Hachette UK Company
www.hachette.co.uk

www.littlebrown.co.uk

For David Abulafia

Contents

Preface

....

Making the mighty Atlantic appear small, the Pacific is the great ocean, indeed the greatest on Earth. The time it takes to cross remains different to that of other oceans, and the psychological weight of the Pacific is more profound and more challenging to both imagination and experience.

There are many problems in writing the history of the Pacific. Scale is one, but another is that the model of Atlantic history, a history that is more developed than that of the Pacific, is not really helpful. In part this is a matter of scale and the related problem with offering a narrative of convergence. Related to this, the idea of unrelated parallel developments on widely separate shores is only so helpful. In comparison to the Atlantic, the 'timetables', in the shape both of indigenous presence on the far more numerous islands in the Pacific, and of Western control or influence over the islands and shores, are very different. As a consequence, there is a bigger 'overlap' of these societies. The Western coastal and oceanic presence began in the sixteenth century with the Spanish takeover of the coasts of Central America, Colombia, Ecuador, Peru and part of the Philippines, but, despite a Russian presence from the 1630s, there was no subsequent advance for European power in the Pacific until the late eighteenth century. As a result, there was a considerable overlap between the Western presence and the continued vitality of indigenous societies.

The Pacific can be divided between the four quadrants of the ocean which, if the meridian was seen to go through Honolulu with the top at the North Pole, would accordingly be North-East toward North America, South-East toward South America,

North-West toward Asia, and South-West toward Australasia; and this designation will be adopted. There is also the conventional grouping with reference to regions devised in the nineteenth century, that of Melanesia, Micronesia and Polynesia, which in practice do not cover all of the ocean, notably much of the North Pacific.

All three regions, alongside Australasia, are regarded as part of Oceania, and Oceania is usually taken to extend as far east as Easter Island, but the United Nations has excluded from its definition the possessions of non-Oceania states, thus, for example, leaving out the Bonin Islands, Hawai'i, Easter Island and the Juan Fernández Islands, which belong to Japan, the United States, Chile and Chile again respectively.

Recent organisations repeatedly reflect the tensions of commission and omission. Thus, the World Rugby Pacific Nations Cup was first held in 2006 as the Pacific Five Nations. It included New Zealand, Fiji, Japan, Samoa and Tonga. But the composition has been far from fixed. Australia only played in 2007–8, and New Zealand has not participated since 2009. In turn, Canada and America joined in 2013.

Like other oceans, there is the question repeatedly not only of the islands within the ocean but also of the coasts. In this respect, furthermore, there is the question of how far the Pacific should be subordinated to differences based on the land masses to each side, as when the pro-Japanese German geopolitician Karl Haushofer presented the leading 'pan-regions' as *PanEuropa*, *PanAsien*, and *PanAmerika*, the second designated for Japan with an extension into the southern hemisphere. The Pacific therefore became a sphere of struggle between Japan and America, prefiguring the current emphasis on China and America.

At all events, there is a considerable difference between treating the Pacific in terms of islands, or islands and coastlines, and, if only islands, which are to be included. For example, Japan and the Philippines each contrast greatly not only within and between each other, but also with those in Polynesia. All too often, the idea of the Pacific is one of Polynesia, with possibly a concession to Micronesia and even Melanesia, but there are many other islands in the Pacific, notably in the North Pacific. They provide different ideas, not least with the realities of cold seas. This issue is much more of a challenge than in the case of the Atlantic.

In the case of the Pacific, the 'coasts' includes 'coastal' islands such as the Aleutians, Japan and New Zealand, each of which is an archipelago, as well as continental coastlines on the ocean, such as those of North and South America and Asia. There is a separate problem in the south-west quadrant as both Indonesia and Australia are composed of islands, but, particularly the former, are peripheral to the Pacific, not least with an important presence on the Indian Ocean. As far as this book is concerned, there will not be a history of Japan or California or Peru or Australia, but an engagement with their interaction with the Pacific, notably in terms of migration, trade, fishing and power-projection.

Aside from these issues of span, there is also the conceptual one, and as the Fijian academic Epeli Hau'ofa pointed out, there is a difference between the Pacific as 'islands in a far sea' and, on the other hand, 'a sea of islands', the second appearing both more holistic and with more of an emphasis on the islands and the links between them created by voyaging, rather than the surrounding powers.

Although there was the earlier link in the shape of Bounty bars, 'The Taste of Paradise', I would like to thank all those who sponsored my visits from 1992 to the Pacific and those who travelled with me. It has been very stimulating and great fun, but, as the Pacific so often is, a reminder of other voyages that could have been taken. After four trips to Hawai'i in 2003–5, during one of which, in a memorable occasion for me, I lectured on the deck of the *Missouri* in Pearl Harbor on why the Allies won World War Two, I was offered a job. I considered it, but knew that it would not have worked for the family; however, I often wonder 'What if?'

I owe a great debt to Steven Roger Fischer, Peter Hoffenberg, Patrick Manning, Paul Moon, Valerie Munt, Geoff Rice and Mark Stocker who kindly commented on an earlier draft. Gregory Cushman, Bill Gibson, Robert Guyver, Carlos Tromben and Jon Wise answered questions. Zoe Bohm has been a most supportive editor and Alison Griffiths a very helpful copy editor.

This book is dedicated to David Abulafia, the world's leading maritime historian. I first heard him lecture when an undergraduate in the 1970s and, many years later, was fortunate enough to lecture with him on a cruise. We are fellow members of the Athenaeum, and his acceptance of the dedication has given me great pleasure.

Beveridge Reef

Any visitor to an ocean has their favourite memory. Mine is of Beveridge Reef, which is really in the middle of nowhere, about 130 miles from Niue (within the Exclusive Economic Zone of which it lies) and 600 from the Cook Islands. Named after the ship that first reported it in 1847, it is submerged other than at low tide when a very small part is visible and on that portion, smaller than my study at home, a few of us stood savouring the sheer surprise of the experience. The remains of a fishing vessel that had run aground on the submerged reef were visible, and otherwise nothing. Ocean and sky stretched for what seemed millennia.

Palmerston Atoll

A visit to a tiny sandy islet on a coral atoll in the Cook Islands is an encounter with the progeny of William Marsters (1831–99), a ship's carpenter from inland Leicestershire who arrived at the uninhabited atoll in 1863 with two Polynesian wives, to whom he subsequently added a third, all from Tongareva. Masters had at least twenty-three children, and their descendants own and govern the island which was annexed by Britain in 1891 and has been under New Zealand from 1901. Most of his descendants live in New Zealand or on Rarotonga, but others on Home Island, the only inhabited part of Palmerston Atoll. There are issues with past inbreeding, but also a sense of distinctive anglophile community on the other side of the world, one a long way away in an extraordinarily beautiful and only infrequently visited setting.

Introduction

....

A visit to Rabaul, its volcano observatory, and the devastation wreaked by successive earthquakes, is a stark reminder that the Pacific is a play of potential physical forces. Storms, earthquakes and volcanoes have long contrived to make navigation and settlement variously fatal, hazardous and difficult. The Rim of Fire is a reminder in language of this drama of new outcomes.

As an area to sail, the ocean has other challenges. The scale, not least the mismatch between distances and specks of land, ensures that many areas can only be sailed to, or between, by those outside such a sight; and some of these distances are very great, notably so in the northern and south-east Pacific. This poses major challenges for navigation and ship supplies, of both food and water.

There is also the cultural challenge of the Pacific. There was often bitter rivalry within islands and island groups, but, separately, the very isolation of the ocean helped ensure the development of different cultures, and this isolation and these differences posed particular issues of comprehension and acceptance.

Geology provides a long distinctive history, with the Pacific developing in the Mesozoic era (252–66 million years ago) from the Panthalassic Ocean, the super-ocean that surrounded the super-continent Pangaea. The Pacific originated about 190 million years ago from the centre of this ocean, with the origins of the Pacific Plate east of the Mariana Trench. The plate expanded at the expense of the three plates that met in this area, each of which then subducted (moved underneath) surrounding continents, where they helped to cause volcanic instability, as with the Aleutian Islands where the Pacific Plate moves under the North America Plate. These processes continue. The Coast Miwok people of Pacific California believe that the Earth started with land from the Pacific.

Mariana Trench

First sounded in 1875 by the *Challenger* expedition, and echo-sounded by *Challenger II* in 1951, the deepest oceanic trench on Earth is 200 kilometres (125 miles) east of the Mariana Islands. About 2,500 kilometres long, the trench has a confirmed depth of up to 11,000 metres in the Challenger Deep, which is greater than the height of Mount Everest. The water pressure at that depth ensures a far greater atmospheric pressure than at sea level. Microbial lifeforms have been observed including large single-celled amoebas. Snailfish have also been found. However, microplastics have been found, as well as carbon-14 from nuclear bomb testing. The depth of the Trench has encouraged its being featured in imaginative fiction. A British warship, the *Challenger* was loaned to the Royal Society of London for scientific purposes, and from 1872 to 1876 it sailed the oceans, surveying and investigating. The *Challenger* entered the Pacific in June 1874, leaving the ocean in January 1876, in what was an oceanographic cruise that helped develop the subject as a scientific discipline, as well as providing many biological specimens. It had been assumed that the deep sea would provide instances of missing links in the evolutionary process, not least acellular protoplasms, but this did not prove the case. Professor Challenger was the name Arthur Conan Doyle gave to his resolute scientific explorer.

Volcanic action in a variety of forms was responsible for the Pacific islands, including mantle plumes, as with Hawai'i, Samoa and Easter Island. In the case of Hawai'i, the plume of magma from the hot spot remains stationary, but, due to continental drift north-westward, a chain of islands is created as the Pacific plate moves over the spot. To a degree, there is a continuation in the submarine Emperor Seamounts. Prominent volcanic peaks in Polynesia include those on Mo'orea, Bora Bora, and Ua Huka in the Marquesas.

Very differently, volcanic action was responsible for atolls, where coral growth – that of coral polyps, animals that secrete calcium carbonate – leads to reefs after volcanoes sink, as in the Cook, Solomon and Tahiti archipelagos, for example Tupai in the last. Their low relief makes them very vulnerable to changes in sea level, and thus to climate warming.

Coral contributes to the hazards posed to inshore navigation. Coastal approaches to many islands are treacherous, partly due to reefs, but with sandbars also not helpful. Thus, the *Pandora* sank in 1791 on the Great Barrier Reef when bringing back the *Bounty* mutineers who had been captured on Tahiti. Limited information on these hazards was frequently also a problem. So also with the limited docking that ensured a reliance on beach-side lighterage.

Major volcanic eruptions have included those in Niuafo'ou in the Tongan archipelago in 1946 and on Ambrym in the New Hebrides in 1951. In 2020, the Calabarzon region of the Philippines was hit by the Taal volcano which led tens of thousands to flee. On Hokkaido, the Showa-Shinzan volcano was formed in 1943–5. Volcanic eruptions in the eastern Pacific include that on the island of Socorro off Mexico in 1993. The Pacific has also seen the deepest undersea eruption yet recorded, the West Mata submarine volcano north of Tonga erupting in 2009 at over 1,100 metres deep. In 2018, a tsunami hit Palau in Sulawesi after an earthquake, causing great devastation. So also with Japan with a submarine earthquake in 2011, which moved the main island 2.4 metres to the east and caused a tsunami that led to a catastrophe at the Fukushima nuclear plant. Earthquakes are a major threat to California, where tectonic plates join. One in 1906 destroyed over 80 per cent of San Francisco, killing about 3,000 people and making about 300,000 homeless. Another major one is in prospect. In 1906, there were also major earthquakes in the Aleutian Islands and Chile, while, in 1939, an earthquake in the Chilean port of Concepción killed about 28,000 people. Another earthquake and subsequent tsunami there in 2010 left many homeless in the city, but relatively few casualties.

The Pacific Plate does not cover the entire ocean, which contributes greatly to the geological complexity of the area. So also with the relationship between plates and continents, so that, for example, Zealandia, a largely submerged mass of continental crust nearly as big as Australia, leaves, above sea level, New Zealand, New Caledonia, the Lord Howe Island group, and Norfolk Island.

The complex geology of the Pacific is partly responsible for often difficult conditions near its coasts, especially shoals, which were a particular problem for those unfamiliar with their waters. The situation did not really improve for Westerners until the mid-nineteenth century. Not only were surveys important but also the construction of lighthouses, for example that on the Farallon Islands off San Francisco in 1853.

We have already visited the question of definition in the Preface, and that helps explain differences in the accounts of the scale of the Pacific. Yet, there is no doubt of role: the Pacific indeed is the dominant central ocean in Athelstan Spilhaus's three-lobed 'Composite Shoreline Map', which was first devised in 1942. It is safe to see the Pacific as covering one-third of the world's surface, and to note its great distances such as over 10,000 miles between Manila and Panama. To the north, there is a clear divide, in the Bering Strait, into the Arctic. In addition, South America's southwards length ensures that there are restricted entrances into the South Atlantic, and there are restricted passages north of Australia between the Pacific and Indian Oceans. However, in the south there is no clear divide between the Pacific and the Southern Ocean.

The last factor adds to the problem of describing the climate. It is overly easy to focus on that of the tropics, not least if commenting on Polynesia, and to ignore the far more difficult cases of the non-tropical North and South Pacific where cold temperatures and strong westerly (from the west) winds are to the fore, notably the Roaring Forties and Furious Fifties in the southern hemisphere. This could make entry into the Pacific from the South Atlantic difficult. William Bligh tried this course en route to Tahiti with the *Bounty* in 1787, but was repulsed by winds and storms and, instead, had to go by the lengthy route via the Cape of Good Hope.

Komandorski Islands

The Pacific includes many islands that are far from Polynesia and very different to it. The Komandorski or Commander Islands, named after Commander Vitus Bering, are Russian, but geographically the westernmost of the Aleutian Islands, otherwise an American chain.

With a maritime climate that involves high rainfall, which contributes to the large number of lichens and mosses, the islands have only a small human population, but there is a very large animal presence, notably of birds and sealife.

In the tropics, in contrast, the trade winds blow for much of the year – from the east or north-east north of the Equator, and from the east or south-east to the south of the Equator. They usually provide a relatively equable climate and consistent sailing conditions to which navigators had to adapt. Thus, beginning in the late sixteenth century, the eastbound voyage of Spanish galleons from Manila to Acapulco took a great circle route, but the westbound voyage saw a more southerly track in order to take advantage of the trade winds.

However, if the trade winds are weak, an El Niño event arises, because warm waters can spread east from the western Pacific and limit the movement of cold deep water northward along the Pacific coast of South America. This has a broader impact on global climate, as in 1997–8. El Niño events see the water temperature off Peru rise considerably, and are linked to changes in weather pattern. More generally, El Niño events interact with global warming, not least in causing drought in the western Pacific, as in Fiji and Samoa.

Moby Ducks – a Tale of Currents

In January 1992, 28,800 Friendly Floatees – yellow ducks, red beavers, blue turtles and green frogs – were washed overboard from a container ship en route from Hong Kong to Tacoma during a Pacific storm near the International Date Line. Lacking holes, unlike the 61,000 Nike running shoes that went overboard in 1990, the Floatees did not sink and have become a way to study oceanic surface currents. Many came ashore on the north-west Pacific coast of North America, as a result of the North Pacific gylp, or circular current, but others turned south, going to Indonesia, Australia or, less frequently, Hawai'i and Chile. Some travelled, via the Bering Strait and Arctic pack ice, into the North Atlantic.

The trade winds provide breezes that counter high temperatures, and also rain when they hit high slopes, for example on O'ahu in the Hawaiian group, where the rainfall on the windward eastern slopes contrasts with the drier, leeward, rain-shadow of the slopes. When the trade winds fail, humidity is acute, and there is much convection rainfall, both at sea and on the islands. The length of the wet season, however, varies, being longer, for example, on the Solomons than New Caledonia. The windward side of New Guinea has annual rainfall of up to 300 inches, particularly in the monsoon, which helps make rivers impassable and feeds large mangrove swamps. The situation is exacerbated by forest clearance, notably for tropical hardwoods. The rainy season can bring hurricanes and floods, as well as more insistent soil erosion, leaching and landslides. In contrast, the leeward side of New Guinea around the capital, Port Moresby, is dry from May to December.

Voyaging was affected by storms, as with the private Japanese attempt to conquer Taiwan in 1616: thirteen junks filled with warriors were wrecked by a storm, only one ship reached the island, and the local population killed the crew.

Hurricanes are known as typhoons in the Pacific. A typhoon hitting between Manila and Yokohama in 1908 badly disrupted and delayed the American 'Great White Fleet' on its circumnavigation (see page 167). In December 1944, Typhoon Cobra hit Task Force 38 east of Luzon in the Philippines, sinking three American destroyers; Lieutenant Thompson Webb on the carrier *Nehenta Bay* reported gusts of well over 100 miles per hour, waves rising to 70 feet and lifting the screws clear of the water, the barometer falling to 29.12, aircraft and many men lost overboard, seams on the ships opening, and fear. At the end: 'Of the hundred or more that had been together, single vessels were scattered in all directions,' with some ships that had rolled over as much as

72 degrees; 'I believed that I was seeing the wrath in the face of God.'

In 2013, Typhoon Haiyan killed over 7,000 in the Philippines, Pam in 2015 was a real hazard in the South Pacific, and, in 2018, Typhoon Mangkhut had gusts of up to 255 kilometres per hour in Luzon. In 2020, Typhoon Harold hit Vanuatu, damaging 21,000 houses. There was massive disruption in each case. Hurricanes tend to be less dramatic in the eastern Pacific, but Nora hit the Mexican coast hard in 1997.

Rainfall is linked to vegetation, not least regeneration after felling and cropping. High rainfall indeed ensures tropical forest, plant diversity, and large and old plants on the Solomons, and the Fiji, Samoa and Hawaiian groups. However, geology is also significant, with volcanic islands sometimes providing a poor habitat for vegetation, not least if there is also no fresh water. Isolated islands that are short of fresh water have less vegetation. A shortage of fresh water is a problem, for example, in the lowland parts of the Islands. The small population on the Mexican island of Guadalupe depends on water brought in by tanker.

The spread of animals and plant species was affected by isolation. As a result, animals and vegetation are often specific to individual islands, as in the Galápagos, the Bonin Islands, New Caledonia and Norfolk Island, the last a particular instance of a Pacific temperate ecosystem. Wildlife is also very specific, for example coconut crabs, the largest land-invertebrates in the world. They are exported as food from the Polynesian island of Makatea. Birds were the animals that spread most easily to other islands, and the sole mammal in Polynesia, Micronesia and Melanesia prior to the arrival of humans was the flying fox. In contrast, there were dingoes in Australia, while Hokkaido has the brown bear and the red fox.

Steller's Sea Cow

An extinct sirenian (sea cow), like the manatee, this mammal could be up to 33 feet (10 metres) in length. Observed in 1741 on the Komandorski Islands, on Bering's last expedition, by the naturalist Georg Wilhelm Steller (after whom a sea eagle, jay, eider and sealion are also named), the animal was hunted to extinction for food. It was possibly extinct by 1768, although there were alleged later sightings, such sightings being an aspect of the Pacific as a world of report and rumour. The hunting of animals for such purposes was also seen with whalers killing large numbers of turtles on the Galápagos Islands.

A more benign consequence of isolation was the more limited spread of tropical diseases, notably malaria, than would otherwise have occurred, while yellow fever is absent. In World War Two, however, non-local forces, both Allied and Japanese, were hit hard by disease. The most serious was malaria, especially on New Guinea, but dysentery, scrub typhus, dengue fever, ringworm, hookworm and blackwater fever all posed major problems. In 1943, Brigadier-General Carroll of the American army reported:

Malaria is the most potent enemy we have so far had to contend with in the South West Pacific Area. It causes more losses and non-effectives than all other causes combined. Not only does it cause the actual loss of personnel for prolonged periods of time, but it also causes a great loss of efficiency of troops remaining with their organisations.

Parasitic illnesses have been a persistent problem for islanders. Indeed, lymphatic filariasis or elephantiasis was eliminated only in the late 2010s in the Cook and Marshall islands, Niue, and Vanuatu.

There are about 25,000 islands in the Pacific, but, again, this depends on definitions of the ocean. Following a Western early nineteenth-century designation that left out much of the northern Pacific, the islands are generally grouped in terms of Micronesia, Melanesia, and Polynesia. Micronesia – the Palau, Caroline, Mariana and Marshall islands of the north-west Pacific – has close to 1,500 islands, but a land area of fewer than 1,000 square miles. Its people are ethnically similar to Polynesians. Melanesia, in the western Pacific, notably Fiji, New Caledonia, the New Hebrides, and the Solomons, contains islands of contrasting sizes, as well as differing ethnic populations. Far-flung Polynesia in the southern and central Pacific, which includes Samoa, Tahiti and Tonga, is particularly engaged with the ocean, with fishing more important to its traditional culture than in Melanesia.

Mineral Resources

Although coal is worked in Australia, the Pacific is rich rather in mineral resources, especially nickel on New Caledonia (which also has chrome, cobalt, iron, gold, silver and copper), and copper on New Guinea, where the remote Ok Tedi mine was opened in 1988, and where Panguna on Bougainville has the world's largest reserves. Despite potential oil and natural gas, notably in New Guinea, where oil is produced near Lake Kutubu, production is not much developed; but New Zealand benefits from geothermal energy. On the ocean edges, there is oil and gas extraction off California, Alaska, and the Russian Far East, as well as considerable potential for more extraction.

Much of the ocean is deep, and, as a result, the lowering of water levels during the freezing of the Ice Age did not lead to any significant extension of the coastline into the ocean. Lower California in Mexico, and southern California in the United States, were modest exceptions, while the North and South Islands of New Zealand were joined, and there was a substantial land bridge between New Guinea and Australia, which was then linked to Tasmania. With the exception of Australasia, the principal differences in coastline were close to Asia, with Asia, Borneo, Sumatra, and South-East Asia all joined, the Philippines likewise, the Japanese islands linked to the Asian mainland via Sakhalin, and both the Yellow Sea and the South China Sea land. There was no comparable case in the islands of Polynesia, Micronesia and Melanesia, and thus, aside from the sea level falling, far less change there in the period at the close of the Ice Age. Nor did the Ice Age provide an opportunity for the movement of plants, animals or humans into these Pacific islands, as occurred between Asia and North America.

The Threat to Whales

In May 2021, HMAS *Sydney*, a guided missile destroyer, exercising off San Diego, California, returned to harbour with bodies of two fin whales stuck to the hull. Indeed, up to fifty fin whales are struck by vessels annually off the West Coast of the United States. The fin whales are vulnerable because they are large and also rest and sometimes feed near the surface.

Oceans absorb most of the excess heat and much of the carbon dioxide from the Earth. As the largest ocean, the Pacific is both crucial to this process and also greatly affected by the warming of the climate. The warming of the Pacific makes it harder for cold and warm layers of water to mix and, as a result, the supply of oxygen and nutrients is greatly diminished. Indeed, the Pacific is losing oxygen and taking on excess carbon dioxide in its upper layers. This more acidic ocean is then an issue for lifeforms such as coral.

More extreme climatic variations within this deteriorating pattern have also had an impact, and, crucially, are becoming more frequent. Thus, acute heat in Pacific North America in 2021 was linked to the death of hundreds of millions of marine creatures, including salmon. The physical environment, therefore, is not unstable only due to continental drift.

International Date Line

An agreed line through the Pacific that serves as the boundary between one calendar day and the next, the line runs roughly along the antemeridian, the 180° line of longitude, but has detours to accord with particular territorial interests, thus swinging to the east to include Kiribati. Movements in the line have included Alaska, when it was purchased from Russia by America in 1867, while Samoa moved back to the west in 2011, in order to be in line with Australia and New Zealand.

An Atlantic Comparison

Size alone does not explain the differences between Atlantic and Pacific, differences that have interacted with human action to create the major contrasts between the two oceans. In large part, this is a matter of the interaction of the middle latitudes and the pace of settlement. By 1400, the islands in the middle latitudes of the Pacific were settled, and these societies were able to continue largely undisturbed by Westerners until the late eighteenth century. In contrast, in the Atlantic, there were fewer islands, some were not settled prior to the arrival of Europeans, notably Madeira, the Azores, Bermuda, St Helena and Ascension, and they were all more subject to Western pressure. In addition, Atlantic islands that were extensively settled, notably the Canaries and those in the Caribbean, were conquered and there was a demographic revolution on them: disease savaged indigenous populations, and the use of imported slaves to create a new workforce linked to provision for the new Western-run Atlantic economy ensured a European-African demographic world. This was different to that on the American landmass where indigenous Americans continued to predominate, albeit with a significant Hispanic element and (in Brazil) an enslaved African dimension.

There was no equivalent in the Pacific until the widespread arrival of Western settlers in the nineteenth century, either overland as in North America, or by sea, as in Australasia and to a degree in North America. This demographic movement from the West helped create a perception of the Pacific as those areas not settled by outsiders, but that approach was misleading, both as far as the situation then was concerned and also, more generally, because that account underplays the role of Asia, both historically in terms of the origins of the movements of people into the area and in terms of the continuing impact of Asian peoples and powers.

This impact, moreover, remained an element despite the size of the ocean, as with trans-Pacific population movements from the nineteenth century. At the same time, the very size of the Pacific ensured different links and also gradations of linkage within it, both to a degree not seen in the Atlantic.

2

The Indigenous World to 1513

The extent to which the Pacific saw significant development prior to the arrival of Europeans can be presented in different perspectives. This arrival is generally dated to the entry of Magellan's expedition in late 1520, but Vasco Núñez de Balboa, a Spanish explorer, in 1513, had already crossed the Isthmus of Panama to the Pacific, defeating the divided indigenous peoples and claiming what he called 'Mar del Sur' and the adjoining lands for Ferdinand and Isabella of Spain. He then used canoes to reach the Isla del Rey in a search for pearls. Subsequently, after his overthrow by Spanish rivals in 1514, Balboa was rehabilitated and named Governor of the South Seas. In 1519, he built four ships on the Rio Balsas and sailed nearby Pacific waters, but his efforts were cut short that year when Spanish rivals overthrew and executed him. Although these rivals used his ships, they did not sail any great distance.

In contrast, non-Europeans had been doing so for many years, although, for a long time, this was not apparent at all to the arriving Europeans. Indeed, the Polynesians had crossed vast tracts of the Pacific, an ocean whose distances put the Atlantic into the shade. The settling of the Pacific, including the movement into it of peoples from further west, was a complex process that has been illuminated by archaeological work, but there is much that is still open to debate, and discussion will doubtless continue as new research and fresh insights are assessed.

As elsewhere in the world, the major change in sea levels during the Ice Ages played an important role in creating possibilities, although outcomes were not inevitable, a position that very much remains the case. The movement of Archaic

Papuans (sometimes referred to as Australoids), probably from the Andaman Islands in the Indian Ocean and then Sunda, the region of most of modern Indonesia, to Sahul, that of New Guinea, Australia and Tasmania, possibly occurred up to 60,000 years ago, with a short sea crossing from Timor, which was then part of the mainland of Sunda. The Sydney area was settled about 40–45,000 years ago. There was also movement from Sunda into New Guinea; although that was probably also settled by Archaic Papuans who had already crossed from Timor to Australia.

The subsequent pattern of population movements is unclear, not least because the later rise of the sea level when the Ice Ages ended led to the loss of archaeological material, and notably so in coastal areas. Nevertheless, the settlers moved around the coastal areas of both Australia and New Guinea, for example the Huon Peninsula on New Guinea; although there were also settlements inland in both. From about 40,000 years ago, although the nature of their watercraft is unclear, the Archaic Papuans pressed on to islands east of New Guinea, first New Britain and Ireland and then, from about 24000 BCE, to Bougainville in the Solomon Islands. This remained an axis for the later movement of Austronesian peoples, although the pace of movement varied.

Moreover, aside from this 'forward' expansion of Archaic Papuans which attracts most attention, there was also much movement within Australia and New Guinea. The latter, indeed, showed a pattern of agricultural development that was to be repeated elsewhere. The clearing of dense forests by the Archaic Papuans ensured that hunter-gathering could be supplemented by later Austronesians who brought crop-cultivation, notably of taro from about 4000 BCE, and then by the domestication of pigs and dogs from about 3000 BCE. This represented an expansion of Asian agricultural and domestic techniques. The warmth and rainfall of New Guinea proved very good for crop cultivation.

Separately, the rising sea level was part of the transformation of the geography of Sahul, a transformation that forced the need

to respond to more coastlines, separated Tasmania about 9000
BCE, and cut the wide land bridge with Australia from about 8000
BCE. In the resulting Torres Strait Islands, an Archaic Papuan
culture based on the cultivation of yams and on fishing devel-
oped. Ground-down mollusc shells were used for fish-hooks.
They were also employed in mainland Australia, as was spearing.
The maritime legacy is covered in the National Maritime Museum
in Sydney.

Originally from South-East Asia, extending up to Taiwan,
and probably spreading from Taiwan via the Philippines, the
Austronesians assimilated earlier peoples and were to press on
from the Bismarck Archipelago, from about 1000 BCE, to the
Caroline Islands, where taro, cassava, sweet potato, bananas and
coconuts were cultivated. From the eastern tip of New Guinea,
in about 2000, there was a move across the generally benign
Coral Sea to New Caledonia. There, taro, cassava, yams and
sweet potato were cultivated. From about 1500 BCE, there was
movement along the Solomons to the Santa Cruz Islands, northern Vanuatu, and Fiji. For example, the far-flung Northern
Vanuatan islands were settled between 1100 and 700 BCE. In
what was a long crossing, a separate movement from the
Philippines reached the Marianas from about 1500 BCE, where
taro, cassava, rice, bananas and coconuts were cultivated. This
was the basis for the Chamorro people with their *sakmans*, sailing outriggers.

Polynesian society emerged from about 1000 CE in Fiji, Tonga
and Samoa. This society proved extremely dynamic, and able,
both psychologically and practically, to overcome vast distances.
Although there has been extensive debate on these points, the
Lapita pottery that was used makes it possible to suggest both a
distinctive culture and a chronology of spreading settlement.
Probably from the Samoa group, in about 830 CE, there was,
genetic sequencing published in 2021 would suggest, a migration
to Rarotonga, the largest of the Cook Islands, and from there to

Tahiti in about 1050, the South Marquesas in about 1140 and the North Marquesas in about 1330. Archaeological sites include those of the Taipivai Valley on Nuku. Oral traditions, for example that for the Tonga island of 'Ata, present clashes between indigenous aboriginal and later settlers, but it is unclear how widespread this situation was. The tense situation in Borneo in the early 2020s, for example, may be a guide to past circumstances, but the context was different.

Polynesian Knowledge

A map of 1769, Tupaia's Map, was an attempt to present on paper the geographical knowledge of the Tahitian priest Tupaia (c.1725–70). Seventy-four islands were named and depicted, including those of the Austral, Marquesas and Society groups. James Cook and Joseph Banks were very interested in Polynesian navigation and knowledge of the ocean and Banks had a map made of the list provided by Tupaia, who joined Cook's first voyage and provided navigational and linguistic help. Tupaia died of dysentery in Djakarta en route to London.

Nearly half of the islands in the list have not been identified, probably due to difficulties in understanding the Tahitian language and locations, while Tupaia's knowledge was presumably weaker for more distant islands. Conversely, the Cartesian grid of the Europeans could make little of the space-time complexities of Polynesian understanding with their roles for the relationships between human ancestors, and environmental elements.

The genetic sequencing indicates that the Pallisers were settled in about 1110, Mangareva in about 1130, and Rapa Iti, Aitutaki and Ma'uke in about 1190. Mangareva proved the base for a move, presumably via the Pitcairn Islands possibly in the twelfth century or about 1210 CE, to Rapa Nui (Easter Island), although pollen and linguistic evidence has also been used to argue for 600 or 700 CE. The Cooks were the basis for migration to New Zealand, whence the Chatham Islands were settled. The Kermadec Islands were probably settled from Tahiti. There may have been at least one voyage from New Zealand to the Ross Ice Shelf in Antarctica as in Māori fable, but this is based solely on oral lore, the legend of Ui-te-Rangiora located in about 650, which speaks of 'a place of bitter cold where rock-like structures arose from a solid white sea', and also speaks of snow. Although the Māori visited the sub-Antarctic islands, there is no physical or archaeological evidence to confirm this story, and it is highly dubious. However, what the legend may preserve is the sight of a large detached iceberg surrounded by sea ice. These have certainly come far north in recent decades, while voyaging far south may not have been cold during the medieval temperature optimum.

In separate migrations, the Hawaiian group was reached in about 400 CE, while the Fiji group was the basis for an advance, by 500 CE, via Kiribati, to the Marshall Islands, while there was an earlier move from New Ireland to the Caroline Islands. As a result of these voyages and, crucially, settlements, by 1350 CE, many of the Pacific islands, or at least island groups, were inhabited. Hawai'i, New Zealand and Easter Island were the apparent extremes of the Polynesian triangle.

Sources for Ancient Polynesia

The human history of Polynesia is shorter than that for other regions, as, bar Antarctica, it was the last area on Earth to be reached by humans. This proximity to the present should make the history easier to assess, but that is not the case due to the lack of a written language and therefore any written records. Oral stories are important and have been used with particular effect in work on Māori history, while archaeology expanded most as a source in recent decades, before the development of genomic research. Archaeology is a matter not only of the direct human trace, but also of impact in the sense of evidence from pollen, skeleton remains, tree trunks and pond sediments. Radiocarbon dating has helped provide enhanced data on settlement dates. The radiocarbon dating of the pollen layers of sediment cores in O'ahu in the Hawaiian group reveals the early presence of the *loulu*, a tall palm with edible nuts, only for this indigenous palm (as well as other indigenous trees) to decline, possibly because of human deforestation, the transformation of forests into taro farms, and the eating of the palm nuts by the Polynesian rats that accompanied the settlers. These settlers were presumably responsible for the marked decline of creatures whose habitats were in the forests that were cleared, notably indigenous snails and flightless geese and ducks, which also would have provided a source of food. Archaeological work, however, can also lead in different directions, as in very different evaluations of the start of settlement on the Tongan island of 'Ata.

Designed by the Norwegian Thor Heyerdahl to show that Easter Island (Rapa Nui) could have been settled from South America and therefore that Polynesia could have been settled from the east rather than the west as suggested above, the *Kon-Tiki* expedition of 1947 indicated that such links were indeed possible. Named after the Inca god Viracocha (also known as Kon-Tiki), the raft was built out of balsa logs, and set out from Callao in Peru, although it had to be towed from the coast in order to escape the powerful Humboldt currents. The raft travelled about 4,340 miles, mostly drifting, before beaching in the Tuamotus. Yet, as genetic and linguistic research have established, the settlement was certainly from the west, with Polynesia looking to the Malay world for language, crops, animals, tools and canoes. The expedition, however, contributed to the role of the ocean as a focus for stories.

Knowledge of trans-Pacific contacts comes from several major sources. The key ones are archaeological evidence, the reconstruction of genetic lineages, linguistic and technological indicators, and oral tradition, including the reconstruction of traditions and technologies of long-distance voyaging. Archaeological evidence solidly suggests that the very early colonisation and settlement by sea in the western Pacific, and along the Pacific shore of the Americas, started as far back as at least 19,000 years ago on the eastern shore (from where humans moved south as far as Chile), and upwards of 50,000 years ago in the southwest Pacific.

For Polynesia, genetic patterning caused by the founder effect, in which genetic diversity becomes less marked with each successive colonisation, has helped to establish the sequence of settlement, although the timing is necessarily by generations, not years. The reasons for Polynesian expansion are suggestive rather than definitive. The obvious factor may appear to be the need for land, and, in particular, for good land; as opposed to the marginal opportunities that might have been all that was on offer to those seeking to establish themselves in islands under population pressure. Equally, existing settlements might have been affected by a reduction in soil fertility arising in part from a lack of fertiliser, from rainwater-produced leaching on lands cleared of vegetation, and from the heavy demands for nutrients of crops. Most societies responded accordingly with slash-and-burn practices, but the opportunities for these were limited on many islands, as well as by slopes and soils that were inappropriate for cultivation.

Deforestation on Easter Island (Rapa Nui)

Easter Island appears to have demonstrated the precarious nature of Pacific environments, a nature that could stem from a variety of often overlapping causes, including low rainfall, little fresh water, and poor soils. Vulnerability to human action, and to animals, plants and pathogens introduced by outsiders could also be a factor, and was increased by both population rises and greater connectivity. On Easter Island, the increase in the human population may have been a major cause of deforestation, although that has also been linked to religious practices. At any rate, less timber affected the availability of boats for fishing, putting pressure on agriculture as a source of food, with control over land becoming a more significant cause of clan feuds.

Origin Traditions

The British missionary William Ellis, who spent 1816–24 in the Tahiti and Hawai'i groups, noted the tradition that the first inhabitants of the South Sea Islands originally came from 'a country in the direction of the setting sun, to which they say several names were given, though none of them are remembered by the present inhabitants'.

In turn, the genetic lineages of the sweet potato (*Ipomoea batatas*) cultivars, and archaeological remnants around the Pacific strongly suggest that Polynesian voyages brought at least one sweet potato lineage from the Americas back to the Pacific islands, and eventually all the way to New Zealand, around 1,000 years ago, with a rapid diversification therefore on the various islands of Polynesia. That was Heyerdahl's hypothesis, but the circumstantial evidence suggests that Polynesian voyagers made the contacts, and not Andean voyagers. Meanwhile, recent research has indicated that the hypothesis that the sweet potato sailed on its own on rafts of vegetation, or was derived from wild *Ipomoea* species on the Pacific Islands, is highly unlikely. As a separate instance of diffusion, Spanish voyagers brought another lineage of sweet potato west across the Pacific in the late sixteenth century. It then made its way via exchange all the way into the highlands of New Guinea and Taiwan within two centuries. The ancient DNA of Amerindians from what is now Colombia has been found in Polynesians from the Marquesas, which suggests direct human interchange and sex between these two regions, again about 1,000 years ago. This is the strongest piece of evidence for inter-hemispheric exchange before the voyage of Magellan in 1519-21.

No Polynesian objects and settlements have been yet found in the Americas analogous to the Norse objects and settlements discovered in Labrador; or vice versa. However, the presence of the sweet potato in archaeological deposits, plus the new human genetic evidence, is very difficult to explain without presuming ancient trans-hemispheric contact. It is also highly implausible that Polynesian voyagers, as skilled and adventurous as they were, would stop at Easter Island (Rapa Nui) or the Chatham Islands and fail to venture on, however briefly, to the continental coasts of South America and Australia, when they had already sailed so far. There are apparently linguistic remnants of Polynesian visitors in Amerindian languages.

The migrations posed formidable challenges, not least of navigation, seamanship, and supply. There is an extensive scholarly literature now on ancient voyaging between the islands. It is supported by archaeological evidence and some fascinating sailing experiments using traditional techniques between the Pacific Islands. Drawing on the role of the maritime cultures of

Southeast Asia in the confluence of ideas about shipbuilding, the Polynesians used double-hulled canoes that could carry up to seventy people, and supplied themselves with fish they caught and rainwater, while also having supplies in the shape of the food they took with them, including pigs (a prime source of protein), chickens, and dogs. The boats with their parallel hulls linked by cross beams or platforms were flexible, and could be propelled by rowing, sail, or a combination of the two. There were differences in boats between particular areas. For example, Fijian plank-built *druas*, with their second hulls rather than outriggers, were particularly large and were regarded as valuable on Tonga. The largest ships were those built in Fiji.

The sail was mastless, being supported by light spars on each side, the spars being braced with guy ropes, and the sail v-shaped as the spars come together at the base in the canoe's hull. Such a sail could threaten instability but the latter was offset by the use of the outrigger. With time, one of the sail-supporting spars became thicker, taller and more vertical, and the other more similar to a slanted boom. Variants included the development of 'claw' sails in the Marquesas and Tahiti groups. V-shaped sails gave way to the lateen in the seventeenth and eighteenth centuries, while there were also hull modifications.

These boats were more impressive than the *Kon-Tiki*, which can be seen in the *Kon-Tiki* Museum in Oslo. Thus, the new Humboldt Forum Museum in Berlin contains a Melanesian wooden sailing boat built on the island of Luf, one of the Hermit Islands, in about 1890, but seized by the rapacious German company Hernsheim and Company, that, founded in 1875, was important in the copra trade. Fifteen metres long, and made from a single tree trunk, the boat was designed to carry about fifty people, and was rather like that depicted in the Disney animated film *Moana* (2016).

Sharks and whales use magnetic fields in order to find their way to breeding grounds to feed and give birth, even in the absence of underwater landmarks such as coral. This throws an interesting light on the skills that human navigators were to show.

Navigation was an issue for the Polynesians not least as there was a need to find often infrequent islands in the vast ocean where, in addition, visibility from the boats was limited by their lack of height which affected the ability to see over the curvature of the Earth. The Polynesians presumably used the trial-and-success method of following particular winds and currents until they succeeded, benefiting from an understanding in particular of the currents, while star sequences on the horizon helped set bearings. They also proved adept at following the signs of island life, notably birdlife, but also weather conditions, as clouds, which could be seen at a great distance, frequently indicated the presence of islands, above which hot air rises. So also with swells. Cook was impressed by the Polynesians' ability to sail across the ocean.

There has been extensive debate about the navigational methods and knowledge of Polynesians and other Pacific islanders, and how far these permitted navigation across hundreds of miles of open ocean with no land in sight. Attempts to re-enact Polynesian sea voyages suggest that navigational errors that resulted from the islanders' methods may have cancelled each other out. In other words, the navigator's sense of where his craft was may not have been too far from where it actually was. Furthermore, more positively, it has been argued that their use of the star compass to establish a position by dead reckoning meant that they did not need to concern themselves unduly over distance. Use of the star compass meant the need to gain amazingly complex knowledge.

Recording journeys, so that return and repeat voyages could be made, was a major task. When sailing offshore, the Polynesian sailors could read the changes in swell patterns caused by islands, such as the Marshalls, and thereby fix their position. They recorded this pilotage information in the form of charts (notably the midribs of coconut fronds), and of shells which were studied by mariners before undertaking their journeys.

Adrift in the Ocean

In 1966, Peter Warner, the master of *Just David*, a Tasmanian crayfish boat, saw a burnt-out patch on the uninhabited island of 'Ata. He found six 13- to 16-year-old Tongan boys who had been there for fifteen months having left their boarding school one night, 'borrowed' a longboat for illicit fishing, and had the anchor line snap in a squall. After drifting for eight days, surviving on raw fish, and sharing a single bottle of drinking water, while baling seawater from the boat, they landed and established a settlement, including a food garden, a crude thatched hut, a permanent fire, and hollowed-out tree trunks to store rainwater, although there was little of that. They ate wild taro, coconuts and bananas, caught seabirds to eat with their bare hands, and discovered wild chickens which they kept in chicken pens. Not the Polynesian voyagers of old, but an instance of adaptability on the ocean and its islands.

In 1793, the British persuaded two Māori whom they had abducted to draw a map of New Zealand. This was very different to Western maps of the period, as scale depended not on a geometric representation of distance, but rather reflected the interest of the mapmaker. Thus, the North Island was shown at a larger scale than the South Island in which the source of greenstone, the most important item for North Islanders, was similarly emphasised. The Māori did not, in fact, produce maps such as this prior to contact with Westerners; but this map demonstrated the attitudes that conditioned their mental mapping.

As with the indigenous Australians and those of other indigenous peoples, Māori mental maps embodied abstract, mythological, and religious concepts; a strong tradition of storytelling was also based on an understanding of geography and landscape.

Many Māori names could only be understood through their connection with other names and places. Such connections commemorated events such as journeys and related to an oral world of stories. The relationship between people and the natural world was central to the understanding of space.

Journeys were considered as astral, as well as on land and sea, and their interrelationship was central to the engagement with meaning as well as distance. Thus, in New Caledonia, the entrance to the Underworld, the subterranean country of the dead, was regarded as of particular importance. The mental and physical geography on New Caledonia also included the mythological place in which man originated, while, as in New Zealand, society was organised into spatially differentiated clans with reference to mythical ancestors.

The Polynesians understood their world; but its scope was not that of the oceans of the Earth or even of the whole of the Pacific. As a result, Western explorers were able to make genuine discoveries about the Pacific, notably the northern Pacific. Indeed, while fit-for-purpose, which is the key criterion, Polynesian navigational techniques and shipping were not suited to the temperate zone, to cold climates, or to carrying much cargo. In contrast, Western navigators took their ships across the Pacific from the sixteenth century, and Western mapmakers stored, incorporated and reproduced the resulting information.

The societies that migrated can to a degree be recovered through anthropology, archaeology and oral memory, with evidence obviously most plentiful for recent times. There is the danger that a changeless society is assumed, and that was not the case. For example, Māori society was very fluid and constantly evolving, notably as a result of conflict and migrations. The concept of *tapu* meant that access to locations was constantly changing, a situation that was probably what proved fatal to Cook.

On the other hand, there were limits arising from environmental factors. Thus, food availability, disease and the state of medical skills limited average lifespan; whereas now high birth rates affect the age pyramid, such that in 2018, Indonesia's median age was 28. Māori relied heavily on shellfish. The sand wore down their teeth, as seen in skeletons, and the rapid loss of teeth might have left an older person unable to eat hard foods, such that they starved to death.

The possibilities of cultivation were a key element in settlement, with both geology and climate important to them. The coconut palm does not tolerate height, which helps explain why it is found on low-lying coasts, with the population distributed accordingly, as on Tahiti. In contrast, where the coconut is less important, as on New Guinea, Vanuatu and the Solomons, there is a greater emphasis on root crops, including taro, yams and sweet potatoes, and they can be grown in the interior where the land is better drained. The ability of agriculture to keep up with population growth was an issue, and this growth may well have led to the spread of farming areas that, in turn, contributed to conflict between families and clans.

Moai

Carved from soft volcanic rock, *moai* are huge stone statues with overly large heads, the living faces of deified ancestors, on Easter Island that were erected between 1250 and 1500 CE, their movement from the quarry a matter of considerable effort. They were possibly moved upright using wooden rollers and a rocking motion guided by guy ropes. They face inland, presumably to protect clan and/or family lands. William Hodges' painting *Monuments on Easter Island* recorded his visit on Cook's second voyage in 1774, showing a number of *moai*, some of them with hat-shaped stone 'topknots.' Hodges depicted most of the *moai* standing upright on stone platforms, known as *ahu*, although some had been toppled. In 1722, Jacob Roggeveen had seen the inhabitants lighting fires before the *moai* and thus honouring them. All had been toppled by 1868, possibly due to earthquakes and conflict, although the relative significance of each is unclear. Some have since been restored.

The British Museum has a *moai* referred to as *Hoa Hakananai'a,,* meaning 'Stolen or Hidden Friend'. Estimated to weigh about four tonnes, it is made of dark grey basalt, a hard dense fine-grained volcanic rock. The surface of the rock is rough and pitted, and tiny crystals glint in it. Basalt is hard to carve and unforgiving of errors.

The British Museum example is a monumental carving of the head and torso of a man – the head one third of total height, proportions which are typical for *moai*. It is almost twice life-size. This example was probably first displayed outside on a stone platform, before being moved into a stone house at the ritual centre of Orongo. It was collected by the crew of the British ship *Topaze*, under the command of Richard Ashmore Powell, on their visit to Easter Island in 1868 to carry out surveying work. Islanders helped the crew to move the statue to the beach. It was then taken to the *Topaze* by raft. The figure was originally painted red and white, though the pigment washed off in the sea. The crew recorded the islanders' name for the statue, and also acquired another, smaller basalt statue, known as *Moai Hava*, which is also in the collections of the British Museum.

Hoa Hakananai'a is similar in appearance to a number of Easter Island *moai*. Its head tilts back as if scanning a distant horizon, and it has a heavy eyebrow ridge and empty eye sockets, once filled with coral and stone eyeballs. The nose is long and straight, ending in large oval nostrils, while the lips are thin and set into a downwards curve, giving it a stern, uncompromising expression. The jaw line is well-defined and massive. The clavicle is emphasised, and the nipples protrude. The arms are thin and lie tightly against the body; the hands are rudimentary, carved in low relief, hardly indicated. Elongated ears end in large lobes.

The back of the figure is carved with ceremonial designs, some in low relief, some incised, believed to have been added at a later date. These images relate to the Birdman cult of the island, which developed after about 1400. The key Birdman cult ritual was an annual trial of strength and endurance in which chiefs and followers competed to capture the first sooty-tern egg of the season. The birds nest on three tiny rocky islets off the coast of the Orongo crater. The victorious chief then represented the creator god for the following year, shaving his hair and growing his nails like talons.

In the centre of the figure's head is a small fledging bird with open beak, flanked by ceremonial dance paddles, with faces carved on to them. The centre of the back is carved with a 'ring and girdle' motif that is carved on many wooden figures from Easter Island.

As with much of the world, the Pacific islands were in the Stone Age, with metallic ores not worked. Pottery played a role, but the appropriate clay was not widespread. As in the Americas, there were not the changes linked to horses and oxen, but nor were there draught animals such as llamas, camels or elephants; although, on Mocha Island off Chile, chilihueque, which are related to llama, were used, not least as plough animals. Human skulls with Polynesian features have apparently been found on the island.

Prior to the arrival of Westerners, the spread of human settlement greatly affected ecosystems, notably in New Zealand with the extinction of birds, particularly large, flightless birds known as moa. About twenty-eight land bird species became extinct on New Zealand after the arrival of the Māori, as they were a major source of food and tools, notably in the fifteenth century. However, their extinction created a serious issue for the sustainability of

Māori society, one that prefigured the damage done in the nineteenth century by Western sealers and whalers.

Offering continuity, but also changeable, ritual was important to society, with ancestor cults playing a major role. Ritual served to bond households, extended kinships, and villages. It was also seen in social relations between the prominent and others, relations that were feudal, with high chiefs playing the directing role, and their kin often a type of nobility. Ritual was also important in the relationship with nature, notably in propitiating storms and in hunting.

Marae

These temples, the larger ones run by priests, were centres of ritual and social cohesion. These open-air places of worship were used for a range of ceremonies, including human sacrifices. A *marae* included an altar (*ahu*) and, sometimes, upright stones. *Marae* were destroyed in conflict and have been damaged by agriculture, but many surviving ones can be visited, for example Marae Taputapuatea on Ra'iatea in the Tahiti group, a seventeenth-century foundation dedicated to 'Oro, the god of war. On Huahine in the group, there is a god house where images of gods were kept, as well as many *marae*.

Tiki

The most famous statues in the Pacific are the *moai* on Easter Island, but the *tiki* on the Marquesas, notably at Iipona on Hiva Oa, deserve attention. Shorter than the *moai*, the *tiki* appear to have had a religious purpose with *Tiki Takaii* commemorating a great warrior chief. Women are also commemorated.

CONFLICT

The overlap between hunting animals and fighting other tribes typical of hunter-gatherer societies was particularly the case across Australasia and Oceania, with, at the same time, adaptation to specific physical and human environments. The former included the nature of the terrain and vegetation, and the proximity of other islands. The latter included the size and geographical range of tribes, with population density an important overall factor. Alongside the absence of gunpowder, horses, beasts of burden and wheeled transport, there was variation in both weaponry and fortification, although there can be problems with the dating of archaeological finds.

As far as weaponry was concerned, there was an important distinction between the use of projectiles, such as slings and stones, and contact weaponry. The Hawaiians tended to use the former, but the Tongans and Māori employed contact weapons, including clubs of whalebone and jade timber, and adzes were also made from jade. In a typical utilisation of the animal and plant environment, shark teeth were used to edge swords, spears and daggers. Coconut fibre could be employed for armour, as on Kiribati where it was worn by the key warriors.

War canoes, often with their two parallel hulls, were a formidable sight for William Hodges when, accompanying Cook as an artist, he saw them at Tahiti in 1776. They also came out to challenge Cook off New Zealand. Canoes could have shields, as with the Iatmul of Papua New Guinea where the shields protected the lead warriors, but were also part of the symbolism in which the shield itself was part of a prow representing the ancestral crocodile.

In New Zealand, fortified *pā* settlements, as opposed to *kāinga* or open settlements, spread, especially on the North Island, and their number suggests serious competition for the resources of land and sea. They were fortified with wooden palisades. Many would not have been occupied at the same time, but over 6,000 *pā* sites have been found, and it has been suggested that there may have been about twice that number. In contrast, the Samoans adopted forts with high stone walls and a protective ditch or moat. The remains of a fortification wall can be seen on Matairea Hill on Huahine in the Tahiti group. Hawaiians did not build fortified villages, but relied mainly on natural features for defence.

Conflict was seen at a number of levels. At the highest, there were empires that rose and fell. Samoa's Tui Manu'a empire had control over much of Polynesia, but was largely replaced by the Tu'i Tonga empire from about 950 CE, which, in turn, declined from the thirteenth century in the face of opposition, notably from Samoa. Western visitors later could find themselves drawn into conflict between indigenous groups, as in 1783 when the British *Antelope*, shipwrecked in the Palau islands, became involved in warfare there with one of its cannon used with success.

War greatly affected social relationships, bringing status or the stigma of defeat, with the weak seeking shelter with stronger kinsmen or, if captured, being incorporated into the victors' kinship network. In the Tahitian archipelago, 'Oro, the god of fertility and war, was a formidable figure who received offerings of dead men. Overpopulation there and elsewhere was linked to conflict, with rival clans competing over farming areas. The defeated could expect slaughter and the destruction of their traditional temples or *marae*. The clan war of 1768 over who would be paramount chief led to genocide for the defeated and a wall of skulls built by the victor. The association of war and food was seen on the Tahitian island of Huahine, where Tāne was god of war and fishing.

As part of a more general and wide-ranging engagement with natural and supernatural entities, Māori mythology focused on the demigod Māui, under whom the islands of New Zealand allegedly originated. Māui was also important to origin myths of other Polynesian islands such as Tonga, Samoa, Tahiti and

Hawai'i. The assertion of a relationship to Māui was important as part of a process of winning and asserting divine support in the frequent conflicts between tribes. War dances and priestly incantations celebrated the power of gods and ancestors, and the latter, in turn, were also seen in war. There are some similarities with Japanese Shinto. Indigenous Australians emphasised the creative role of ancestor spirits such as Daramulan.

Understanding Māori history is not simply a matter of learning about different events and places, but also that they reflect a specific view of the connectedness of the past and of the relationship of past and present. Many Māori names can only be understood through their connection to other names and places; for example, connections commemorating historic events such as journeys recorded in oral histories that can be cartographically depicted because they sought to explain and appropriate particular landscapes. As with the significance of certain shrines and religious sites in Japan, for example Takachiho mountain on the island of Kyushu, Māori oral history is very specific geographically, with great attention being devoted to the rivers, lakes and mountains of particular tribes. The Māori oral tradition is accessible, both from nineteenth-century European records and because it is still alive today, although oral accounts have nothing to do with history (as defined in the West) and everything to do with contemporary power, prestige and possessions. The situation is less favourable in Latin America, although differences in national sensitivity to indigenous peoples are also a factor, as in Chile and Peru.

Explanations for development can be contentious and, while detailed research can throw light on more general principles, it can also highlight differences. For example, on East Timor in 1100–1700, there was a major shift toward fortified settlement sites in the shape of stone-walled structures on hilltops and clifftops. Research has linked this to climate change in the shape of the El Niño climatic oscillation, with decreasing and unpredictable rainfall the key context leading to an emphasis on granaries and their defence.

At the same time, as a reminder of the dynamic nature of research, there also has been scepticism about climate-based accounts. Instead, there has been an argument for the redating of sites and for the possibility that the profits of sandalwood exports from East Timor and other external factors were crucial in the process of fortification. This underlines the difficulties of developing and adopting global models, and, more generally, of the problematic nature of supposedly definitive accounts. Thus, in contrast to East Timor, the focus in the Pacific Northwest of North America was on control over coastal positions where salmon congregated. This reflected both livelihood and divine purpose.

SOUTH AMERICAN LINKS

Alongside the Malay origins of Polynesia, there were links with South America. In particular, the sweet potato appears to have arrived at the Marquesas from South America, while chickens appear to have been transported from Easter Island to Chile in about 1400 CE. At any rate, the cultures on the South American coast are longstanding, with temple mounds in Peru by about 2500 BCE, and farming not only for high-altitude crops in the Andes, notably maize, but also for crops near the Pacific coast, including sweet potatoes, sunflowers, and cacao. Settlements in the Andean region tended to be inland, as with the Chavin culture (c.850–200 BCE), the Nazca (c.350 BCE–450 CE), and the Moche (c.1–600 CE). Organised for public works and conflict, these societies, however, did not have a maritime equivalent. Instead, irrigated river valleys were important in coastal areas, as with the Huari empire (500–800 CE), the Chimu empire, also of northern Peru (c.700–1476 CE), and its Inca nemesis (1438–1532 CE). To the north and south of these empires, there were chiefdoms which lacked the resources or organisation for significant power-projection.

Environmental factors were significant in explaining the emphasis on inland rather than coastal settlement. The coastal region was drier, often arid, as in the Atacama and Sechura deserts of Chile and Peru respectively, which affected the prospects for agriculture. The llama, the animal of the region, was an upland beast, while supplies of fish and shellfish from the Pacific may well have been affected by climatic shifts such as the El Niño effect.

There were, however, links with the islands off Peru, notably the Chincha Islands, as guano (the accumulated excrement of seabirds that can be used as fertiliser) was collected for over 1,500 years and possibly for up to 5,000. The Inca appear to have appreciated the value of the guano and controlled access to it.

More recent archaeological work, including radiocarbon dating, has undermined earlier claims of Inca visits to the Galápagos Islands. It is not easy to assess Inca views of the Pacific, because all Inca history derives from oral accounts written down in the Spanish colonial era. The available accounts have gone through several filters: translation, cultural misunderstandings, and major differences in the conception of time and space between indigenous people and Europeans. Moreover, the Inca treated their histories as statements of sociopolitical hierarchy and cosmology, rather than as event-based histories, with past acts therefore recast in terms of contemporaneous political power structures. Spanish chroniclers complained about the variety of accounts they were told, while it is also difficult, as with the Aztecs, to reconstruct Inca history spatially, not least as military, political, economic and cultural perimeters did not match well. Empire did not begin with the Europeans.

Indigenous people remain important on some South American Pacific coasts. Moreover, there is growing interest in them, as in Chile, where in the 2012 census two million people declared having indigenous origins. There, recognised by the government in 2020, the Changos are descended from nomads on the coast, notably in northern Chile, over ten thousand years ago who fished, ate molluscs, had sealion-skin rafts, and mummified the dead earlier than the process started in Egypt. They were part of the Chinchorro culture of hunter-gatherers, and shell middens and bone chemistry reveals that about 90 per cent of their diet was seafood. At least one mummy shows tattooing in the period about 2600–1900 BCE. Other indigenous people in Chile include the numerous Mapuche and the Diaguitas, the latter recognised by the government in 2006.

The Chiloé archipelago

The many trajectories of Pacific island life are suggested by this archipelago off southern Chile, an archipelago very much dominated by the forested and mountainous Chiloé Island, which is 3,241 square miles. Illustrating the problem of the inaccessible coasts (see below), that of Chiloé on the Pacific is rocky, and the more accessible and populous coast is that on the east, being a submerged part of Chile's Central Valley. The waters off the island have extensive whale, dolphin, sealion, sea otter and penguin life. In about 5000 BCE, humans arrived, and middens (rubbish remains) indicate that nomads fed off mussels and clams, hunted, fished and had stone tools. The people used boats called *dalcas*, which were a reminder of the variety of fit-for-purpose vessels employed by Pacific peoples. These boats were essentially for navigation in the archipelago. Spanish explorers in the mid-sixteenth century were followed by Spain laying claim to the island.

CENTRAL AND NORTH AMERICA

In Central America, there were civilisations with a reach to the Pacific, notably the Olmecs who, while based near the Gulf of Mexico, had a site at Pijijiapan, and the Maya, who had others at Finca Arizona and Salinas La Blanca. Zanja, La Victoria and La Blanca were other early sites. However, the Pacific coast had far less development than either that of the Gulf of Mexico or in the uplands. In Mexico, the centres of development were in the interior, notably the Valleys of Mexico and Oxaca, and the Gulf of Mexico, although there were Toltec sites at Petatlán and Zacatollan, while Acapulco saw development linked to the Valley of Mexico. However, the dryness of much of the Pacific coast was a major issue, as was the impact on accessibility from the interior due to the mountains of the Sierra Madre del Sur. Aridity was also a factor elsewhere, for example the Mohave desert of California. At any rate, there are no signs of exploration into the Pacific. Now Mexican, the Revillagigedo Islands, 434–679 miles west of Manzanillo in Mexico, contain no evidence of human habitation or visits prior to Spanish exploration from 1533.

On the sub-Arctic coast of Pacific North America, there were indigenous peoples who took to the water, notably the South Alaskan Inuit, who established themselves on Kodiak Island, and the Aleuts whose sites included Chaluka. These peoples were active fishermen, and also fed off shellfish and pursued sea mammals such as sea otter. To the south of these people, there was also extensive fishing and trade, for example of the volcanic glass obsidian which was valued for its use for cutting. There were not, however, any lasting links across the North Pacific. So also with the indigenous peoples of North-East Asia. Moreover, indigenous bands did not acknowledge overarching authority.

The Pacific Northwest

On the coast of modern Canada, tribes such as the Kwakiutl, Bella Coola, Haida, Tahltan, Tlingit, Stó:lo, and Salish combined the benefits of the Pacific – notably shellfish, such as mussels and sea urchins, and fishing – with hunting. Maritime life was helped by the warm-water Japanese Current and grey, humpback and killer whales were frequent, as were seal, salmon, sealion, and sea otters. Supernatural animals served as tribal ancestors. Dugout canoes were used. Tribes had scant unity, but it is unclear how far conflict was endemic. The Museum of Anthropology in Vancouver is an excellent guide to the sophistication of the indigenous peoples, notably their creative skills, including totem poles, armour, and the masks for the tribal masked dances.

JAPAN AND CHINA

In contrast, Japan did develop a state capable of deploying fleets, as, helped greatly by typhoons, in successfully resisting Mongol invasions from nearby China in 1274 and 1281. Khubilai Khan, having established his rule over northern China, had turned towards his eastern borders. He inherited significant naval resources from the coastal areas of China, and the Mongols had always been good at assimilating the military methods and assets of those they conquered. He therefore decided to attack Japan. The ships Khubilai Khan had access to were the result of generations of Chinese engineering and development, and were possibly the most advanced warships of the medieval period, some with combinations of oars and sail, ideal for amphibious attacks; but Chinese ships were more riverine than suitable for the high seas.

Khubilai sent his first invasion force to Japan in 1274, and part of his strategic design was to cut trade links between Japan and the Song empire of southern China, which was still resisting the Mongols. The attack on Japan was limited in size, and consisted of Mongol and Korean troops with Chinese and Korean seamen. Their initial attacks were against weakly held islands, but the invasion force then arrived at Hakata Bay in northern Kyushu on 19 October and was fiercely resisted. Superior Mongol firepower, both arrows and catapults firing explosive pots, established a beachhead, but, due to the severity of the fighting, the Mongols withdrew to their ships to rest and to replace their weaponry, especially their arrows. The ships then appear to have been disrupted by a storm and returned to Korea.

The second invasion, launched after the Song empire was finally conquered in 1279, was significantly larger than the first, and well organised. Khubilai even established an 'Office for the Chastisement of Japan' to oversee the logistical and administrative arrangements for a massive seaborne assault. Korea possessed the resources and knowledge to build another fleet and the manpower to crew the ships. The ambitious plan called for a Korean-led force, with a Mongol army, of nearly 1,000 ships and 40,000 troops, to rendezvous with a force of South Chinese ships, the old Song navy, with a further 100,000 South Chinese troops engaged. The build-up was delayed as Khubilai demanded that additional ships be impressed. The forces were to meet and coordinate their attack, but, instead, the Korean/Mongol force left Pusan in southern Korea in 1281 and followed the same route as the previous invasion force. This proved to be a bad mistake as the Japanese had prepared a defensive stone wall from which to guard the beach. This proved effective in stalling the attackers who withdrew to their ships after hard fighting. They seized a neighbouring island to act as a base.

The Japanese took the initiative in attacking the Mongol fleet at anchor, and achieved considerable success. They also attacked the island base, and compelled the invasion fleet to weigh anchor and retreat to Iki Island, across the straits from Hakata Bay. The second Chinese fleet had meanwhile made the 480-mile passage with 3,500 ships and 100,000 men. They avoided Hakata Bay and landed 30 miles to the south. The fleet had been spotted, however, and the Japanese opposed the landing by the second force, causing heavy casualties. Although the invaders established a beachhead, fighting ashore continued for two months. The Japanese used fireships to attack the Mongol fleet, but it was a typhoon which finally destroyed the invasion force. Marco Polo described the disaster, and modern archaeology confirms his account.

The two invasions highlight the logistical difficulty of mounting such massive assaults from the sea, and their vulnerability both to determined opposition at the point of landing, and to the vagaries of the weather. These were attempts that dwarfed anything attempted in the Western world during this period.

There was no equivalent to the unification of the Hawaiian archipelago by Kamehameha in the 1790s–1810s, although the context was very different. The failure of the 1281 invasion squandered the massive navy that Khubilai had inherited from the Song, and the one created by the Koreans. Khubilai reacted by ordering the construction of more ships, but the effort caused widespread unrest, especially in southern China. The Korean ships, which were simpler, but smaller, than their Chinese counterparts, seemed to have survived the *kamikaze* wind better than the Chinese. Yuan court records reveal that many eventually returned to Korea, along with a number of their troops, providing the fighting core of a new navy, but the cost of the failed invasions of Japan had drained the Mongol finances. Khubilai abandoned his plans for a third invasion of Japan in 1286, and turned his attention to the lucrative trade routes of the South China Sea, and of Vietnam in particular. Money was a key element in such massive combined operations; and he wished to gain control of the rich trading centres of Hanoi and Da Nang.

Khubilai had mounted an amphibious assault on the Champa kingdom, whose capital is present day Da Nang, in 1281. His Japanese commitments, however, limited his resources and although the Mongols captured the capital, guerrilla warfare, disease, and, crucially, a lack of reinforcements and supplies, due to the failure of the first invasion of Japan, led to the disintegration of the invasion force. A much larger invasion, aimed at the northern Dai Viet capital of Hanoi, was mounted in 1286. The Mongols had learnt their lessons from the previous campaign in 1281, and the new one was a two-pronged attack. A land army of Mongols advanced through the border hills from Yunnan province, while an amphibious force assaulted Van Don, the main port of the Dai Viet (present day Haiphong). It was an ambitious operational plan which crucially depended on logistic support, especially rice, from the fleet.

The Dai Viet had learnt the lessons of the first Mongol invasion, and had adopted guerrilla warfare and scorched earth as a pragmatic way of defeating the invaders. After initial Chinese successes, the supply fleet was trapped and destroyed at the battle of Bach Dang. The Mongol fleet was lured into an area of river that had been planted with long sharpened stakes. As the heavy Mongol ships sailed into the stakes, the tide began to fall, trapping the fleet which was then destroyed with fire arrows. The remaining Mongols were forced to retreat overland.

Japan's success was a key episode in Pacific history as it kept its independence and ensured that its expansionism would not reflect Chinese interests and resources. However, although Japanese ships may well have travelled in northern Pacific waters, and its navigators and cartographers had a rather keen interest in the South Pacific from the sixteenth century at the latest, and probably earlier, there was no distant pattern of migration or power-projection. So also with China, which focused its maritime interests southwards, via the South China Sea into the Indian Ocean. There is no reliable evidence for any Chinese trans-Pacific voyaging nor indeed, despite the modern claim to the contrary about 1421, circumnavigation of the world, or of a fleet in 1434 reaching New Zealand.

There are reputable accounts of Zheng-He and the Chinese exploration of India, South-East Asia and East Africa, but apparently he was not interested in the Pacific. The account of the Botanic Garden in Christchurch, New Zealand, being once the site of a Chinese city of 4,000 people is wrong, as are claims that New Zealand was discovered by the Phoenicians, Egyptians, Chinese, Tamils, Vikings and Celts before the Māori and later Tasman arrived. There is reliable testimony from 1836 of a missionary finding a Māori woman near Whangarei cooking potatoes in an upturned ancient bell that had some characters in archaic Tamil script, but this is not proof of any Tamil discovery. It could have been a much-travelled souvenir or been given as an exchange gift in the nineteenth century by a passing European vessel.

However, there was important regional trade in the North-West Pacific. China was particularly significant to the south across the South China Sea, but there was also important trade and fishing from the Japanese islands. This was especially the case with the Ainu of Hokkaido who sailed to Sakhalin, the Kuriles and coastal regions, notably Kamchatka. With the habitual focus on Polynesia, it is far too easy to neglect such voyages, and Ainu culture can be approached through the Ainu Museum in Sapporo.

RETURN TO POLYNESIA

Yet, prior to the arrival of the Europeans, the Polynesians were those who most explored, understood and used the Pacific. No other of the many societies that abutted the ocean did so to anything like the same extent, and the legacy is still very much present in the population of the Pacific islands.

An economic drive for expansion was clearly significant, but so also was the cultural norm in a society that emphasised the ancestral examples, offered by previous activity, and the fame and sign of divine support arising from it. This aspect is one that may be underplayed due to the tendency to focus on economic drives.

Indigenous culture was far from constant. There can be a tendency to adopt that position due to the frequent reference to local cultures as primitive, but such an approach is mistaken as it assumes a continuity that underplays both development and variety. In part, this tendency can be seen in terms of Western condescension. Thus, the preface to the *New School Atlas of Modern History* (1911) by the British academic Ramsay Muir, offered, as the text for the map covering 'The British Settlement of Australasia': 'Happy is the nation that has no history. Apart from the Māori wars in New Zealand, the only noteworthy features of the history of Australasia are the dates of the successive settlements, and the chief stages in the exploration of the region, both of which are shown.'

Yet condescension was more generally present. Thus, Japanese commentators were apt to see both the Okinawa archipelago and Hokkaido in this light. In praçtice, the former in particular was an area of interchange between cultures, as can be glimpsed in the Okinawa Prefectural Museum. Moreover, there were also important variations within the archipelago, with the Miyako Islands displaying their own cultural patterns as well as those from elsewhere in the archipelago.

Linked to this condescension and, specifically, to the mistaken assumption about 'primitive' cultures, there can be an expectation that recent and present circumstances describe and explain earlier conditions; but this approach can be mistaken, as can be the tendency to argue from the examples that are known. In the periods discussed in the following chapters, it should not be assumed that indigenous society was unchanging, both in response to outsiders, and irrespective of that pressure.

Indeed, that had already led to a decline in the Polynesian presence, although the details are obscure. In the south-east Pacific, in what is now the Pitcairns group, there was settlement on Henderson and Pitcairn, as well as Mangareva, the largest island of the Gambier Islands, with the three apparently linked by exchanges of goods that helped them manage in a difficult environment. However, the combination of this difficulty, the depletion of resources, trade declining, and conflict on Mangareva led to the breakage of links, and the populations becoming extinct, possibly as late as the fifteenth century. This was different to the extinction of Viking settlement in Greenland in that, although global cooling, in the shape of the 'Little Ice Age', was probably also an issue, there was not, like Greenland, a hostile human presence in the shape of the Inuit. The 'Little Ice Age' probably caused the collapse of several other voyaging spheres around the Pacific.

3

The Arrival of the Europeans

A change of shift at this point from Polynesians to Europeans is both understandable and yet also misleading. Understandable because the arrival of Europeans from the 1510s was followed by four circumnavigational voyages (the first two Spanish, the next two English), and the development of a Spanish route from Mexico to another colony, the Philippines, as part of an unprecedented spread of Spanish power on both sides of the ocean, one not matched by any other power until the nineteenth century. Indeed, the Europeans appeared to be doing in the Pacific what they had already done in the Atlantic, where Philip II of Spain's accession to the Portuguese throne after his conquest of Portugal in 1580 created an empire on both sides of the ocean that also ruled many of the islands within the Atlantic. That outcome appeared set in prospect for the Pacific, where the Portuguese link brought Spain, which already controlled the Pacific coast from northern Mexico to central Chile, trading bases in China (Macao, 1557) and Japan (Nagasaki, 1570), and territorial bases in the Moluccas, especially Ternate in 1522 and Tidore in 1578, and on the route to the Pacific from the west, notably Malacca in 1511. None of the other Pacific coastal states had become powers across the Pacific, but the situation changed with the establishment of Western bases from the sixteenth century, including Panama, Guayaquil in Ecuador, Lima (understood as including its port of Callao), Valdivia, and Manila; although the main Spanish naval base in Mexico was Veracruz on the Caribbean, and not Acapulco or Panama.

Spain, by 1599, therefore appeared to bestride the maritime entrances to the Pacific from the Atlantic and the Indian Ocean;

and to a degree that was only partly seen when Britain became the great naval power. Indeed, Spain, as a result of the establishment of control over part of the Philippines, was the first empire on which the Sun literally never set.

And yet, this is in part a delusion, for Spain was both the Pacific power and yet also an empire of, at most, potential as far as the ocean was concerned. Most Pacific islanders had never seen, let alone heard of, Spain, or any European power, product, or individual, by 1599. The ships that sailed the ocean were tiny objects on its face, able to see little, still less to control the elements. Navigational methods were flawed and cartographic information limited, which led, for example, to the mis-location of the Solomons by Alvaro de Mendaña on his voyages of 1568 and 1595. The same was to happen with Pitcairn which was charted in 1767 by Philip Carteret 210 miles west of the actual island, due to an error in the recorded longitude by 3°. As a consequence, James Cook could not locate Pitcairn in 1773 and it was not until 1808 that a more accurate location was made, one, in turn, improved in 1814. European ships and armaments were different to those of Polynesians, but that did not equate with power, still less dominance.

Moreover, although Asian states did not project their strength so far, nevertheless, in the waters close to them, they could deploy formidable numbers of ships. In particular, Korea in the 1590s produced potent vessels and had good naval leadership, as it showed in defeating fleets supporting Japanese invading forces. The north Javanese state of Japara also had a significant fleet.

The gradient of naval strength in this case, however, was very different to that of Spain, as the latter had a long-range capability that no East Asian state demonstrated after the Chinese abandoned Indian Ocean expeditions in the 1430s. In contrast, Spain focused its naval strength in nearby Mediterranean and then, from the 1580s, European Atlantic waters, but was also able to deploy warships at much greater distances; and notably so with the addition of Portuguese strength. Despite their East Asian roots in China, firearms came to be far more significant with the Western presence across the Pacific.

Yet, these points can still be misleading, as neither Spain nor Portugal deployed warships to any extent, Portugal not matching in the Pacific the naval forces it sent into the Indian Ocean, nor Spain those dispatched to the Caribbean. For Spain, there was the need to escort bullion from Peru to Panama, and the wish to develop the trade links focused on the Philippines, but there was no comparable attempt to extend territorial power. Furthermore, the pace of Pacific contact with the West did not increase until the late eighteenth century. In this vast region, in the sixteenth and seventeenth centuries, European presence was limited as far as the islands were concerned, although sometimes violent, as in 1595 when a Spanish expedition reached the Marquesas and about 200 islanders were slaughtered.

In his eyes, Christopher Columbus had sailed what would soon be called the Pacific, but, for him, this was not a separate ocean to the Atlantic, but rather the ocean separating Europe from Japan, described by Marco Polo, for which Columbus was aiming in 1492. He had a copy of Polo's account, which had referred to an eastern ocean containing 7,448 islands which was reflected in the Catalan Atlas of 1375. Using Ptolemy's map as a guide, Columbus had expected the voyage from Europe to be a distance of around 2,400 nautical miles. In reality, he would have had to travel some 10,000 to reach his Asian goal.

It was not immediately obvious that the lands that were explored were anything other than outliers of Asia, nor that they prevented further navigation thither. A map of 1504 by the Italian Giovanni Contarini, one that had considerable impact because it was printed as opposed to manuscript, showed Newfoundland and Greenland as parts of a peninsula stretching northeast from China, while, between them and the West Indies, lay a large body of water giving access between Europe and China. In 1520, the *mappa mundi* (world map) of Johannes Schöner depicted the New World as a separate continent between Europe and East Asia, but showed a marine route between North and South America.

The Pacific was displayed by Schöner as far smaller than was subsequently revealed by the first circumnavigation of the world in 1519–22, that begun by Fernão Magalhães (in English, Ferdinand Magellan), a Portuguese pilot who had already travelled to the Portuguese bases in the Moluccas. His measurements of longitude were of interest to the Spanish government in its territorial claims in the western Pacific and East Asia under the Papal partition of the world, and it sent Magellan to confirm them by sailing from east to west, the first such known transit of the Pacific, and the first of several that century.

This expedition was the first (in late 1520) to round the southern point of South America, and, although missing all the major island groups, and the crucial opportunities for resupply they offered, achieved the first recorded crossing of the Pacific, stopping en route at Guam where there was fighting with the Chamorro people. Magellan, however, was killed in 1521, near Cebu in the Philippines, on either Mactan or Poro. This was one of what was to be a series of deadly coastal encounters, encounters that put paid to other explorers, including Cook. Magellan was killed in part as a result of his participation in conflict between local rulers. The *Vittoria*, the remains of the originally five-ship expedition, went on across the Indian and Atlantic oceans, but only eighteen men returned to Seville. With this, and other, expeditions, it was not so much that distance was measured in deaths, but, rather, that voyages saw brief periods of great and often fatal danger.

Navigating the Unknown

For the Europeans to sail to, and in, the Pacific, trial-and-success methods were followed, but it was also necessary to employ astronomical and trigonometric knowledge, notably in order to fix positions accurately. Techniques and equipment were devised accordingly, especially the mariner's astrolabe from the 1480s. Although the ocean proved to be far bigger than he had anticipated, Magellan was able to navigate across the Pacific, judging its width accurately by means of the lunar distance model for longitude. Others were far less successful, but this method was also to be used by Cook who placed the coast of the South Island of New Zealand only 18 miles east of its actual location.

By drawing attention to the size of the Pacific, the circumnavigation also clarified not only the size of the Earth, but also how much more remained to be mapped by Europeans: the larger the Pacific, the more extensive its shores as well as its waters. In what was intended as a crossing, Magellan's expedition, like the voyages across the Atlantic, had taken a route across the ocean; it had not followed its shores. The voyage therefore left open plenty of possibilities that land masses, indeed very large land masses, might lie to the north or south of the route. The latter appeared more plausible in order to help balance the greater-known landmass in the northern hemisphere, a balancing that was (wrongly) assumed to be necessary, an idea repeated by the mapmaker Gerhardus Mercator. Despite not having actually been 'discovered' yet, a Southern continent was depicted on maps, for example that of the Pacific published by Abraham Ortelius, the 1589 version of which showed Magellan's cannon-firing *Vittoria* with its guardian angel. Mapmakers felt that they had to fill in the gaps with what they were certain existed.

In his *Universale*, or world map, of 1546, Giacomo Gastaldi, who, in 1548, became the official cartographer of Venice, captured the eastern seaboard of the Americas and the western seaboard of South America (the location of the newly established Spanish colony of Peru) with some accuracy, yet he had Asia and North

America as a continuous land mass, with the join no mere land bridge, but as wide as Europe. This was an influential model for other maps of the period, although growing knowledge of North Pacific waters, in particular as a result of voyages on from the Indian Ocean to Japan, where the Portuguese and Dutch established trading positions, led to an abandonment of this land link in many Western maps by the late sixteenth century. Indeed, by 1560, even though there had been no explorations to the area yet, a strait was being shown, which in large part reflected the idea of America as a separate continent, an idea with important consequences for the conceptualisation of the Pacific.

Separately, as a valuable admission of a lack of information, and therefore of the expectation that more would be obtained, it was possible to leave the coastlines of the North Pacific blank, as with Edward Wright's map of the world published in the second edition of Richard Hakluyt's *Principal Navigations* (1599). However, it was not until Vitus Bering's voyages on behalf of Russia in the early eighteenth century that the idea of a land link between Asia and North America could be conclusively rejected.

This was not the only source of error, with mistakes far from fixed and gradually receding; but instead sometimes increasing in number. There was the idea of a large northwest passage between Canada and an Arctic land mass to the north. In addition, there was to be a longstanding belief that California was an island. The latter was a common misconception in the seventeenth century, as in the map of 1639 by Johannes Vingboons.

This map included a Lake of Gold near the sea separating California from the mainland, and this belief expressed the economic interest of the ocean. Indeed, gold was to be a key element in the stories that circulated, just as it was to be in the mid- and late nineteenth century, at the time of the 'gold rushes'. Thus, in 1587, an expedition under Pedro de Unamuno, sailing from Macao to Acapulco, not only took Chinese goods to Mexico, but also sought to explore the northern Pacific and, in particular, find the islands of 'Rica de Oro', 'Rica de Plata' and the 'Islas del Armenio'. Reputed to be in the north-west Pacific, these bullion-rich islands were not found. Other imaginary islands in the region included 'Los Jardines' and, later, 'Ganges Island'. Álvaro de Saavedra's voyages in 1528 were partly responsible for these mistakes. He reportedly visited 'Los Jardines' and also named the Schouten Islands the 'Islas de Oro'.

Much of the benefit that was outlined was more mundane and realistic than that of bullion-rich islands. The map of the East Indies designed by Petrus Plancius and published by Cornelis Claesz in 1592, a map which ranged to include New Guinea and the Solomon Islands, drove home the image of commercial value by adding pictures of nutmeg and sandalwood.

European colonial powers were expanding around the Pacific, very rapidly and both to east and (to a lesser extent) west, but they faced the difficulties of operating in these distant waters. Climate and disease were major problems, while the general conditions of service at sea were bleak. Alongside cramped living space and poor sanitation, there was inadequate and monotonous food and, in particular, a lack of fresh fruit and vegetables, and thus vitamin C. As a result, about thirty men died on Magellan's crossing of the Pacific, mostly of scurvy. A shortage of fresh water was also an issue.

Moreover, the unmatched strength of European warships in Pacific waters did not necessarily mean that they could achieve what they wanted. Their limitations, as large, wind-driven wooden warships, included serious problems with operating in shallow waters, and particularly near reefs, to which they were very vulnerable; while their size was such that, in the absence of wind, although they could be towed by rowers in the ships' boats, they lacked the flexibility of the far smaller fighting rowboats seen in Polynesia.

However, in deep water there was no effective opposition to European warships. This tactical advantage was greatly enhanced by the operational range stemming from their size and cargo-carrying capacity, and, linked to that and to the use of sails, a ratio between supplies and sailors that was far more favourable than for ships depending on rowers. Furthermore, the provision of bases on some coasts ensured a relative ease of operation within supply range of those bases.

In territorial terms, the key acquisitions were those by Spain in South and Central America, with Panama a crucial base for Spanish expansion, one that emphasised the significance of inshore or close-shore routes on the ocean. From there, Francisco Pizarro sailed to the coast north of the Inca empire in 1524 and, in turn, to its northern area in 1526. In 1531, he sailed anew from Panama, landed at Tumbres and then marched overland. Benefiting from major divisions among the Incas, often a key element in expansion by both Europeans and others, Pizzaro captured the Inca Emperor, Atahualpa, and then seized the Inca capital, Cuzco, in 1533. Pizarro moved on to the coast, founding Lima in 1535. Separately that year, Tomás de Berlanga, the Bishop of Panama, again sailing from Panama but affected by strong currents, sighted the Galápagos islands en route for Lima. The Pacific had provided a crucial link because, as any visitor readily appreciates, Panama east of the modern canal is very difficult terrain, heavily forested and with many broad waterways, and this situation also continues to be the case in coastal Colombia. Travel overland remains very hard.

The coastal cities founded by the Spaniards in Pacific South America included Trujillo, Paita, Callao and, further south, Arica and Coquimbo in 1537, Valparaiso in 1541, Concepción in 1550 and Valdivia in 1552. There was an expansion even further south than that of the Inca, although some of it was overland. Moreover, northwards from Panama, there were voyages along the coast to Central America, by Gil Gonzales Dávila and Andreas Nino (1522–3) and Francisco Hernández de Córdoba (1524), while the Gulf of California was explored in the 1530s by Hurtado de

Mendoza, San Miguel de Culiacan being founded in 1531 and La Paz in 1535. San Juan Bautista followed in 1564. Sebastian Vizcaino sailed up the Pacific coast of Lower California in 1596, while, in 1592, Juan de la Fuca had found what he thought was a strait into the interior, which, in reality, was Puget Sound.

Voyages along arid coasts were far from easy while the uncertainties of voyaging were also a problem. At the same time, aside from the terrain, resistance from indigenous peoples hindered overland expansion, which could encourage voyages. Yet, it was possible to add information about the Pacific coastlands from the land. Thus, although the southward advance of Spanish rule in Chile was stopped near the Biobio River by the Mapuche, missionaries travelled further south, mapping the coastline, the Franciscans Antonio de Quadramito and Cristobal de Mendo playing a key role in 1574–81. In 1598, the Governor of Chile, Martín Garcia Óñez de Loyola, and his force were surprised by Mapuche under Pelantaro and killed, leading to the driving of the Spaniards back beyond the Bio Bio River which long remained an effective frontier.

A Second Pacific Crossing: the Loaisa expedition

Far less well known than that of Magellan, the crossing of the Pacific by Garcia Jofre de Loaisa reflected the determination of Charles I of Spain (the Emperor Charles V) to exploit the information brought by the Magellan expedition and beat the Portuguese by colonising the Spice Islands, notably the Moluccas. Whereas the Portuguese dominated the route to the region via the Indian Ocean, Loaisa, with seven ships and a total of 450 men, was sent from Corunna in Spain in July 1525 to take the lengthy Pacific route. Three ships did not make it through the Strait of Magellan in 1526, while one more was driven south and was the first to round Cape Horn. Dispersed by bad weather in the Pacific, one ship reached the Pacific coast of Mexico, the first voyage thither from Europe, another disappeared, leading to the modern speculation that it reached New Zealand via Tahiti, a third was beached off Sulawesi with its crew killed or enslaved, and only one, with 105 survivors, reached the Spice Islands, landing in October 1526. Loaisa had already died of scurvy. The Portuguese eventually brought the survivors home in 1536.

From Mexico into the Pacific

A quest for the missing ships of the Loaisa expedition, but, more particularly, to find new lands, led to the dispatch of three ships under Álvaro de Saavedra Cerón from Zihuatenejo, 150 miles northwest of Acapulco in Mexico. The ships had been built by Spanish carpenters using local wood. Setting sail in October 1527, two of the ships were lost in a squall that December, but the survivor, having sighted the Utirik-Toke atoll and charted the Marshalls, and maybe sighting Hawai'i, reached the Philippines in February 1528, Saavedra becoming the first navigator to cross the Pacific having set off from the Americas. The ship sailed on to Tidore, the Spanish stronghold in the Moluccas. In 1528, an attempt to sail back to Mexico led to the discovery of the Nomoi Islands in the Carolines, but the ship was driven back to the Moluccas by the northeast trade winds. Another attempt in 1529 led to discoveries in the Carolines, the Marshalls and Enewetak Atoll, but an absence of westerly winds led to the ship's return to the Moluccas where it was captured by the Portuguese who were then very much rivals.

THE PORTUGUESE AND SPANIARDS AND NEW ZEALAND

There have long been suggestions about Portuguese and Spanish explorers reaching New Zealand, although there is no evidence at all in the archives. Aside from a New Zealand Pohutukawa tree at the Spanish port of Corunna, there are a number of artefacts. The sixteenth-century 'Spanish helmet' found in Wellington Harbour could have been a souvenir or brought back by Māori visiting Britain. Hongi Hika was given a whole suit of armour by George III. The so-called Portuguese helmet dredged up from the Manukau Harbour at Auckland in the 1960s may also have been brought there in the nineteenth century. Timbers in the wreck of a caravel off the coast near Dargaville have been dated as about 500 years old, but could have been recycled into a later vessel.

THE PHILIPPINES

Spanish interest in the Philippines strengthened from the 1540s as a result of another voyage from Mexico, that by Ruy López de Villalobos. Commissioned to sail to the 'Islands of the West,' he left Barra de Navidad, San Juan, with six ships and 370–400 men in November 1542. Sailing via the Revilla Gigedo Islands off Mexico, Wotje Atoll and Kwajalein in the Marshalls, and Fais and Yap in the Carolines, they reached Mindanao, suffering from a shortage of food and the lack of a strong enough supporting wind. Samar, Leyte and the Philippines were named after the king's heir, Philip, later Philip II. Difficulties culminated in imprisonment by the Portuguese on the Moluccas.

Once on the throne in 1556, Philip II became interested in conquest. In 1565, an expedition from Mexico under Miguel López de Legazpi, with five ships and 500 men that had set off from Navidad on 21 November 1564, after landing in Guam and fighting local people there, reached Samar on 13 February, before conquering Cebu. The Spaniards moved on to Panay in 1569.

Poorly defended, Manila was conquered in 1570, and became the Spanish capital.

The vulnerability of the islands to maritime attack and the limited and weak nature of local fortifications were important factors, but this was a conquest that involved relatively little warfare for there was no strong political entity in the Philippines able to mobilise resistance. The *barangay*, a comparatively small kinship group, was the sole significant political unit, and this limited the organisation of resistance. Furthermore, cultural assimilation was aided by the nature of Philippine religion – animist and without an organised ecclesiastical structure – and by the willingness, indeed eagerness, of Spain to encourage effective Catholic missionary activity, which played an important role in consolidating the Spanish position. The cathedral in Manila was built in 1581.

In contrast, it is significant that the Spaniards encountered most serious resistance in the Philippines from those areas where Islam had made an impact: the southern islands of Mindanao and Sulu. The first major Spanish attack on the island of Sulu, begun in 1578, failed; as did a 1596 expedition to Mindanao. Fortunately for the Spaniards, the Philippines were at the edge of the Islamic world, distant from centres that might have provided support for co-religionists. Moreover, there was not a force-projection capability matching that of Spain, which, indeed, had planted its first settlement in the Philippines not from Spain but across the Pacific from Mexico.

The Philippines, nevertheless, were at the intersection of a number of worlds. Thus, the value of the walled settlement built by the Spaniards when they conquered Manila was demonstrated in 1574 when an attack by Lin Feng, a Chinese pirate with sixty-two ships and about 1,000 men, was driven off. Having been defeated, Lin Feng founded a settlement at Pangasinan in Lingayen Bay, but the following year, the Spaniards launched a surprise attack that destroyed most of the pirate ships before laying siege to the fortress. This siege, which ended with the flight of Lin Feng, indicated another strength of the Spanish system as Filipino auxiliaries were deployed alongside Spanish troops. Spanish expansion indeed benefited greatly from the divisions between Philippine rulers and the resulting Spanish ability to win local support.

Tension between Portugal and Spain played a major role in affecting early attempts to develop links across the Pacific from the east. The Treaty of Saragossa of 1529, a demarcation agreement to match that in the Atlantic by the Treaty of Tordesillas of 1494, and an agreement that had encouraged support for early voyages, left the Philippines in the Portuguese sphere, encouraging tension between the two powers. It did not help Spain that Japan and eastern Siberia were in its sphere, but the presence in the Philippines of Spain, a more powerful state than Portugal, proved a key element in determining the situation, as in 1580 did the conquest of Portugal by Philip II, in pursuit of his claim to the throne. The two empires were linked until 1640.

Brought into a wider Pacific system, being governed from Mexico as part of the Vice-Royalty of New Spain, the Philippines were seen as an extension of the Americas by Spain and as a base for further expansion. In, 1589, Philip II instructed its governor to occupy Taiwan, and, in 1598, two warships were sent to seize the harbour of Keelung, only to be thwarted by the weather.

There was an alternative axis of power, a non-European one, one linking the Philippines to Japan, with trade supplemented by the attempt in the 1580s to establish a degree of control, notably by *wokou* or 'pirates' who founded pirate territories at Aparri and Caboloan in the Philippines, only to be driven out by the Spaniards, notably with naval and land clashes in and near the Cagayán River. In the early 1590s, Toyotomi Hideyoshi, who dominated Japan, demanded that Taiwan and the Philippines submit to him, but his failure in Korea rendered these aspirations futile. To the north, there was vigorous Ainu resistance to

Japanese power in Hokkaido, and there was no Japanese focus on moving further north.

The priorities of the Japanese and Chinese states were not in the Pacific, while, in contrast, New Spain devoted a significant, albeit episodic, measure of effort to the military, political, commercial and religious development of the new colonies and of the routes to it. This effort led to an increase in information. In 1697, Paul Klein, a Jesuit in the Philippines, produced a map of Palau based on reports from castaways stranded on Samar who used pebbles to present the information. Another Jesuit, Juan Antonio Cantova, based on Guam, drew in 1722 a chart that was reliant on information from castaways.

The Manila Galleon

Acapulco to Manila became an established trade route that, from 1565 to 1815, played a significant role in both Spanish imperialism and the developing world economy. The first return journey, that in 1565, benefited from Andrés de Urdaneta's suggestion to catch the southwest trade winds and avoid the later typhoons: leaving Cebu on 1 June, Acapulco was reached on 8 October, but scurvy hit hard. Conquest of part of the Philippines enabled Spain to seek to exploit the bullion resources of the New World, notably silver in modern Bolivia and Mexico. This bullion increased liquidity in the Western world and financed trade with Asia. Some trade was via the Indian Ocean, but Spain conducted its trade from Acapulco. Mexican silver was taken to Manila, from where it could be traded for Asian products, notably silk, porcelain and lacquerware, which were shipped to Spain via Mexico. By 1590, the silver shipped to Manila was almost equal in value to that crossing the Atlantic. This trade to China proved much more successful than the Portuguese and Dutch attempts to develop trade via the

East Indies to Japan. The linkages also undermine any sharp differentiation of Pacific from Atlantic history.

Filipinos in and near Manila found the Chinese-Spanish trade useful for their interests. More generally, the Filipinos helped remake Spanish imperialism, notably with the incorporation of pre-Hispanic elements and practices in Catholic rite. This was part of a more general process by which the Spanish Pacific was affected by indigenous practices, being, in particular, more Mexican (and therefore hybrid) than Hispanic. The galleons took over four months for the voyage, but many were shipwrecked, including twenty in the Philippines, and one in Drake's Bay, California in 1595.

There were also far less benign exchanges. European diseases, such as influenza, measles, smallpox, whooping cough and diphtheria, hit New World populations, which had no natural or acquired immunity to them, and, from there, the diseases moved into the Pacific. So also did maize and sweet potatoes, both of which were introduced to East Asia by European traders. The Americas saw the arrival from Europe of horses, pigs, cattle, wheat, grapes, apples, citrus fruits and other species, and these could therefore be moved on into the Pacific.

THE ENGLISH

Instead of from Portugal, the Spanish position in the Pacific was to be challenged from two new directions: by the English and, in the early seventeenth century, the Dutch. Deteriorating relations with England led Sir Richard Grenville to plan for a Pacific expedition and, later, Francis Drake on a raiding circumnavigation in 1577–80. Grenville proposed in 1574 to enter the Pacific in order to seize Spanish treasure, found English colonies, and sail the South Pacific. He approached the Privy Council with a:

Supplication for a new navigation, permission to seek rich and unknown lands, to discover and annex all or any lands, islands, and countries beyond the Equinoxial, or where the Pole Antarctic hath any elevation above the horizon.

Initial support was followed by rejection in 1575 at a time of attempting to ease relations with Spain.

However, in 1577, Elizabeth I sent Drake who had already raided the Spanish Caribbean during which he had seen the Pacific and envisaged later sailing it. Setting off that year, with five ships and 164 men and adding a seized Portuguese ship, Drake, however, lost men in the Atlantic to disease and consolidated the fleet to three ships which set off from southern Argentina, only for one to be wrecked in the Strait of Magellan and another to return.

With his flagship renamed the *Golden Hind*, Drake sailed north along the coast of Chile, being wounded by the indigenous Mapuche on Mocha Island, before raiding Valparaiso, capturing treasure ships off Peru, and landing on what is now northern California which he claimed as New Albion: Drake's Bay is south of Cape Mendocino. After repairing his ship, Drake sailed across the Pacific, via Palau and Mindanao, to the Moluccas. There, he was favourably received by the Sultan of Ternate who was quarrelling with Portugal. Drake returned to Plymouth in September 1580 with only one ship, fifty-nine crew, and a fortune.

Thomas Cavendish followed Drake in 1586–8. A wealthy and well-connected young man, and an MP, Cavendish left Plymouth with three ships and 123 men in July 1586. Sailing through the Straits of Magellan and eating penguins for food, they captured Spanish ships and pillaged coastal towns, before seizing a Manila galleon in November 1587 off Lower California. Picking up supplies in Guam and attacking the only recently founded Spanish settlement of Arevalo on the island of Panay in the Philippines, Cavendish returned to England in September 1588 with one ship, forty-eight men, and a fortune. International competition was helping to drive a process of exploration.

JAPAN

The focus on Western powers ensures that the sixteenth century is seen as a Spanish one, with the stress on developments on the Pacific rim being on the conquest of the Aztec empire and the establishment of power in the Philippines. This approach is understandable, but it can lead to a tendency to downplay the significance of events in Japan which, indeed, was united as a result of campaigning in the period. Competition between warlords there became acute from the 1460s and, more particularly, 1550s, with Ode Nobunaga making the ally shogun in 1568 and, in 1577, becoming the leading ruler, only to be forced to commit suicide in 1582, by one of his rivals.

Toyotomi Hideyoshi, one of Nobunaga's protégés, then won a series of campaigns that left him dominant in central Japan, before, in 1587, mounting the most successful amphibious invasion of the Pacific that century, an invasion of Kyushu, the southernmost of the main islands. Hideyoshi pressed on to conquer Southern Kyushu in 1588, and then, in 1591, the northeast of the main island, Honshu. This was the background to another Japanese amphibious invasion, that of Korea in 1592. The scale of the invasion force, about 168,000 troops, puts into perspective operations elsewhere in the Pacific, both European and non-European. This also looks towards recent and present tensions in the waters off East Asia.

4

The Seventeenth Century

The seventeenth century did not see Pacific exploration of the consequence or scale of the sixteenth and eighteenth. The general route to the Orient remained that via the Indian Ocean, a route that did not encourage much exploration of the Pacific. Moreover, the only regular alternative, the Manila galleon, did not lead ships into the South Pacific.

The most striking developments during this century occurred far distant from Polynesia, the area that repeatedly, but often disproportionally, most focuses attention in the history of the Pacific. Instead, it was the north-west Pacific that witnessed the most important developments. As so often, these were developments of commission and omission. In the former case, the arrival of a Russian explorer, Ivan Moskvitin, with Cossacks and a local guide, at the mouth of the Ulya River in 1639, and the establishment of a position at Okhotsk in 1647, were significant for future developments. In contrast, more immediate importance derived both from Japan's isolationism and from China's pushback in the 1680s against Russian expansion, a pushback that drove the Russians from the Amur Valley to which they did not return until the late 1850s, but, crucially, not from Siberia and the Pacific coast.

RUSSIA

For a long time, the Russian presence on the Sea of Okhotsk and, more generally, on eastern Siberian waters and coasts, was limited. In part, this was due to local opposition. Thus, in 1653, the Lamuts (now called Evens) burned down Okhotsk, which, however, successfully resisted attacks in 1665 and 1677. In Kamchatka, the Russians faced opposition by the Koryaks.

More significantly, although Moskvitin had sailed the local waters, sighting the Shantar Islands, the Russians in the region, while able to build river boats, did not tend to tackle seagoing vessels until 1715, after shipwrights were sent by Peter the Great. As a result, Okhotsk did not become a port, as opposed to a coastal settlement, until then.

Prior to that, Kamchatka was entered overland from the north, itself difficult, and not by sea. Travel there was one of the more formidable tasks of Pacific exploration, and figures such as Mikhail Stadukhin should be better known. Having explored eastern Siberia, reaching the Anadyr River in 1650, he built a boat and sailed along the coast to Okhotsk. There is no support for the report that he sailed completely round Kamchatka. From Anadyrsk, Vladimir Atlasov, a Siberian Cossack, pressed forward the exploration of Kamchatka in 1695–9. He came across a shipwrecked Japanese sailor, and also fought Itelmens, Koryaks and Ainu, exploiting divisions among the first. An official on the edge of empire, his violence and brutality led to his imprisonment, to rebellion by his Cossacks, and to his murder in 1711. The frontiers of empire tended to be uncertain and violent.

The Russian explorers provided an opportunity to redress the flawed interpretation by Maarten Vries who, setting out from Batavia in Java in 1643, had explored the north-western Pacific, presenting Yezo (Hokkaido) and Sakhalin as promontories of Asia, and greatly exaggerated the size of the Kuriles. In 1720, Ivan Yevreinov mapped Kamchatka and the Kuriles, producing the first accurate maps.

JAPAN

The Kuriles represented a move into the area of Japanese interest. The Japanese, indeed, had already explored the islands, which are shown on the Shōhō Era Map of Japan (1644). This was an extension of the Japanese interest in Hokkaido, and, linked to that, in subjugating the Ainu who were seen as barbarians. The Matsumae clan was used by the Japanese government from 1590 to defend the borders in Hokkaido and sought overlordship on the island, including exclusive rights of trade. Relations with the Ainu varied, but Shakushain's Revolt of 1669–72 was suppressed, in large part because the Tokugawa shogunate devoted considerable effort to doing so. Allegedly, the Ainu leaders were murdered after negotiating a peace. An earlier Ainu revolt in 1457, Koshamain's War, had been suppressed, as was the Menashi-Kunashir rebellion in 1789. 'Revolt' and 'rebellion' were very much the views of the Japanese, while the Ainu saw conflict in terms of the defence of their position.

The force and ruthlessness the Tokugawa shogunate was willing to deploy, for example in suppressing opposition within Japan in 1614–15 and 1637–8, highlights the significance of its decision for isolationism, not least as it followed the construction of ships built on the model of Spanish galleons. The first two were built by William Adams, the first Englishman to reach Japan, who had accompanied a Dutch fleet of five ships sent in 1598 of which only one reached Japan in 1600. A third was built in 1613 with Spanish assistance. The last sailed to Acapulco in 1613–14, carrying a Japanese envoy en route to Europe, part of a period of promising development in Japanese-Spanish relations, with trade and technological links in prospect. However, the 'Sakoku' (closed country) policy, introduced under Tokugawa Iemitsu (r. 1623–51) in 1633–9, closed these avenues. In practice, Japan was not so much closed, as accessible only on harsh terms and through restricted channels, notably by the Dutch from 1641. Most Europeans were expelled, and, under an edict of 1635, Japanese were banned from foreign travel, and firm and brutal measures taken against Christianity which was a key means of Western influence, as was seen in the Philippines and, later, in the more distant islands of the Pacific.

Japan did not take advantage of the crisis of Ming power in China in the mid-seventeenth century, in order to resume its attempted 1590s' expansionism into Korea. Nor was there a repetition of the rogue, storm-wrecked attempt by a Japanese merchant-adventurer to conquer Taiwan in 1616. Instead, rather than exploiting the relative loss of Spanish energy, Japan followed a policy of consolidation in frontier zones, notably Hokkaido and the Ryukyu Islands, and not of further expansion. Groups that had maritime interests appeared a threat to Ieyasu, who had founded the Tokugawa shogunate in 1603. Shimaizu, of the powerful Satsuma clan, had obtained permission to restore the profitable trade with China via the Ryukyu Islands, but his conquest, in 1609, of the Ryukyu kingdom, which became a nominally independent vassal state, was seen as a threat by Ieyasu who thereupon ordered the destruction of all large ships in south-west Japan. The kingdom was formally annexed by Japan in 1879. These islands, notably Okinawa, deserve as much attention as those that more conventionally receive attention in discussion of the Pacific.

CHINA

China focused on mainland conflict, bar the eventual establishment of control over Taiwan in 1683. The Dutch bases in Formosa had been conquered in 1661–2 by Zheng Chenggong, known to Europeans as Coxinga, who, with the profits of piracy and trade, had developed a large fleet based in the Chinese coastal province of Fujan, only to be driven out by the conquering Manchu. Instead, he sought control over Taiwan. Dutch attempts to re-establish their position in 1662–4 all failed, and European powers never again established a presence on the island. In contrast, the other areas that had backed the Rebellion of the Three Feudatories against the Manchu had already been conquered. Taiwan surrendered to the Manchu after the fleet of the heirs of Zheng Chenggong was badly defeated in 1682.

THE DUTCH

Although Olivier van Noort sailed through the Magellan Strait and raided the Philippines in 1600, and Joris van Spilbergen sailed through in 1614, attacking Spanish America, the Dutch focused on the route via the Indian Ocean, establishing themselves in the East Indies, where, in 1619, Batavia (Djakarta) on Java became their major base. In 1642, they also captured the Spanish colony in northern Formosa (Taiwan), that had been established in 1626, in part as a defence against Dutch attacks on Spanish trade, attacks based on southern Formosa. Whereas the English presence in the Pacific at this stage was ephemeral, the Dutch, who were the dominant Western power in the spice-rich Moluccas, had a significant and far-flung basis for permanence. Moreover, this provided an opportunity for further expeditions.

The major drive in exploration was that by the Dutch, who hoped, in 'Terra Australis', to discover a land of riches comparable to Latin America. This southern land was believed to lie to the south of Magellan's route. In a process more commonly seen in the eighteenth century, Terra Australis also focused utopian and other aspirations about different ways to organise society, thus fulfilling another role taken by the 'New World'. In turn, utopian ideas conditioned responses to reports of Pacific exploration. This was part of the interplay of fiction and fact involved in exploration, a process that necessarily focused on the search for the unknown and on reports of novelty. Exacerbating the issue, belief that there was disinformation by rivals, especially Spain, as well as undoubted efforts to conceal information, made it more difficult to benefit from the experience of others.

The Portuguese, and, more clearly, the Dutch, both bound for the East Indies and sailing from there, encountered Australia, which the Dutch termed New Holland. The Dutch reached the Cape York peninsula in 1605, landed on the south coast of Australia in 1622, 1623 and 1627, and explored the Gulf of

Carpentaria in 1623. Searching for Terra Australis, Abel Janszoon Tasman in 1642 also touched on Tasmania, New Zealand, Tonga, Fiji and New Guinea, but, as he only sailed up along the west coast of New Zealand, he did not ascertain that it was an island group, rather than the edge of a vast continent. Māori killed four of his crew.

Tasman did not find riches, and his voyage along the north coast of Australia was no more successful. His disappointment, a growing lack of dynamism in Dutch maritime enterprise, serious specific problems for Dutch imperialism from the late 1640s, and the problems of navigation in the South Pacific, all ensured that the voyage was not followed up. Tasman's enduring legacy included naming New Zealand (Nieuw-Zeeland), the oldest non-Māori name in the country. Today's extremely popular Aotearoa for New Zealand was a fanciful 1890s concoction by British New Zealand philologists.

Spain

The early seventeenth century saw Spain discuss abandoning the Philippines in 1609 but that was not pursued. Instead, there was additional Spanish exploration, notably by Pedro Fernandes de Queirós in 1605–7 and Luis Váez de Torres in 1606–16. In particular, there was greater knowledge of the central Pacific. Sailing with proselytising plans from Callao in Peru, Fernandes de Quierós discovered Ducie and Henderson Islands, Hao and Vairaatea. He was an example of Portuguese navigators working for Spain. Having been chief pilot in a violent and unsuccessful, malaria-hit voyage to colonise the Solomon Islands in 1595, Fernandes de Quierós established a settlement at Big Bay on the north side of the island of Espiritu Santo in modern Vanuatu. He named the entire island group 'Australia del Espiritu Santo', as he believed he had arrived at Terra Australis, the great southern continent. He found the indigenous people hostile and his discovery only an island. His Knights of the Holy Ghost had not found a New Jerusalem.

English and Dutch entrance into the Pacific led to plans for the fortification of Acapulco, with the Castle of San Diego, the town's first permanent fortification, built in 1615–16. Pentagonal in shape, it had five bastions. Similarly, there was the fortification of Valparaiso and Concepción that decade, in large part due to the arrival in 1614 of a Dutch fleet under Joris van Spilbergen that attacked Spanish shipping and settlements along the coast from Chile to Mexico, before sailing to the Moluccas in what proved a successful circumnavigation.

Extraneous factors were of major consequence in the pace of exploration, as the seventeenth century witnessed a sustained economic and demographic slowdown, one that lessened the resources and drive available for expansion. Moreover, for Spain there was the loss to rebellion of Portugal and its empire in 1640, the loss to Dutch attack of positions in Formosa (Taiwan) in 1642, and the pressures on New Spain and the Spanish empire as a whole, arising from conflict with the Dutch, English and French. At the same time, there were advances in the Philippines, for example the capture of Zamboanga on the coast of Mindanao in 1635, after which a strong fortress was constructed there under the Jesuit missionary-engineer Melchor do Vera.

The Pacific in the late seventeenth century is usually seen, and with reason, in terms of newfound English expansion, but there was also important activity by others on the Pacific periphery, particularly the Russians and also the Spaniards. Although having to confront Hokan-speaking nomads from the desert coast on the Gulf of California, the establishment of Spanish missions on the coast of Lower California led to the search for a land route from Mexico around the head of the Gulf of California in the 1690s and 1700s. In 1697, in the first clash for control of Lower California, the battle of Loreto-Conchō, a well-armed missionary party fought off an indigenous attack, and victory was followed by the spread of Christianity. As elsewhere, smaller, weaker indigenous groups proved more receptive to conversion.

On the other side of the Pacific, Spain, deploying troops, established a mission on Guam in 1668. Guam had been claimed in 1565 and used to provision the Manila galleons, but 1668 saw a significant change. Initially, the response to Catholic preaching was not hostile, but the Jesuit missionaries sparked tension by destroying the venerated ancestral skulls of the Chamorro. Conflict started in 1670 and missionaries were killed in 1671, notably Diego Luis de San Vitores who was beatified in 1985 by John Paul II but is also criticised today by some modern Chamorro commentators. The Chamorro were hit hard by the warfare which continued until 1683, by a smallpox epidemic in 1688, and by typhoons in 1671 and 1693, and the population fell significantly. Three sieges of the fortified Spanish base of Hagåtña were important in successive conflicts, but none succeeded. The Spaniards also sought to take control of the northern Marianas, conquering and Christianising Rota in 1680–2, and finally gaining control of Saipan, Tinian and the northernmost islands in 1698–9. There was a movement of people to Guam, notably from Tinian, as part of the destructive process of imposing control. The Spaniards burnt villages, executed prisoners and raped women. The island chain was renamed the Marianas, after the Virgin Mary and the Queen-Regent of Spain, to signify the role of religion.

Further south, there was an advance into the Caroline Islands in 1686. They were named after Charles II of Spain. Missionaries from the Philippines reached the Palau Islands in 1710, although a hostile response and storms cut short the opening.

England

By the late 1690s, England had the largest navy in the world, and, although it had no bases on the Pacific periphery, it had already taken up anew the challenge of navigating there. Any voyage across the South Atlantic and round South America into the Pacific, however, was long and risky, with problems of navigation, weather and shipworthiness, compounded by a lack of bases en route, although the development of St Helena greatly eased the position in the South Atlantic, lessening the need to find refuge on the South American coast.

In 1680, a band of English buccaneers under Bartholomew Sharp crossed the Isthmus of Darien from the Atlantic to the Pacific, seized a Spanish vessel off Panama and attacked Spanish shipping, before navigating the waters south of Cape Horn from west to east, a new route, and then returning to England in 1682. The band included Basil Ringrose who wrote a journal of the expedition published in 1685 and compiled a substantial 'waggoner' – a description in the form of sailing directions – for much of the coast he sailed along, as well as for some parts he never visited. This description stemmed from the *derrotero* or set of official manuscript sailing directions, illustrated by a large number of coastal charts, that Sharp seized from a captured Spanish ship in 1681 and that he presented to Charles II in order to win royal favour. Such atlases had been regarded by the Spaniards as too confidential to go into print.

This was a period of pirate attacks on the Pacific coast. Thus, in 1687, Guayaquil, the main Spanish port between Lima and Panama, was looted by a large group of English and French pirates. In 1709, Woodes Rogers and William Dampier, in an English privateering circumnavigation, attacked the town anew, winning a ransom to prevent whole destruction. The privateers took on supplies at Guam.

In Chile, the Mapuche of Mocha Island were transported to the mainland in 1685 by the Spaniards in order to lessen its value as a base for privateers. In the English case, the overlap between buccaneering and official action was shown by Dampier, a former buccaneer, who was given command of an expedition to acquire knowledge about Australia. He sailed along parts of the coast of

Australia and New Guinea, and established that New Britain was an island. Indeed, his voyage in 1700 led to the naming of islands, such as New Britain, New Ireland, New Hanover, and Rooke Island, the last after an admiral, and of features such as Capes St George, King William, Anne, and Orford, St George's Channel and Montagu Harbour. With Cape Dampier, Dampier Strait and Dampier Island, the explorer was not forgotten, although he found nothing of apparent value in Australia. Dampier did not fulfil his plan to sail along its east coast, because to approach Australasia from the east was not easy: the prevailing westerly winds combined with what was to be called the Humboldt Current off South America to push ships north as they entered the South Pacific.

Rather than simply writing an unpublished confidential memorandum, Dampier left a legacy in a series of published works, including the very successful *A New Voyage Round the World* (1698), *A Discourse of Winds* (1699), and *Voyage to New Holland in the Year 1699* (two parts, 1703, 1709). He helped popularise the idea of avoiding the rock-strewn and difficult passage through the Straits of Magellan in favour of the open waters round the more southerly Cape Horn.

Dampier's focus on observation was seen in his reporting on tides, which was highly significant for determining possibilities for landing. Discussion of tides brought together the perception of astronomical influences, the understanding of relations between forces and masses, and the application of knowledge. Similarly, Edmund Halley produced his chart of trade winds in 1689, the first scientific astronomical tables in 1693, and his 'General Chart' of compass variations in 1701, all important tools for navigators. The last, a chart of terrestrial magnetism, was designed to enable navigators to chart the variation between true north and magnetic north (to which compass needles point), and thus to calculate longitude accurately.

At the same time, knowledge could be elusive. In 1674, Joseph Moxon, a member of the Royal Society in London and

Hydrographer to Charles II, published a book, reprinted in 1697, arguing that the Arctic was ice free in the summer at least and that it offered a route from the Atlantic to the Pacific north of Asia. This was part of a long tradition of such misleading assumptions.

In 1687, the buccaneer Edward Davis allegedly discovered 'Davis's Land' in the Southeast Pacific between the Galápagos Islands and South America. The printed account of the expedition spread the news, Davis's Land was recorded on maps, and it was suggested that it was the outlier of Terra Australis. Later explorers searched for 'Davis's Land', which was probably the small island of Sala y Gómez as well as a cloud bank to the west suggesting land. Reports about this and other places led John Green to complain in 1753: 'There are in the *South-Sea* many islands which may be called wandering islands.' In 1766, 'people of an extraordinary size, and hairy' on an island off southern Chile, were described in *The hairy-giants, or, A description of two islands in the South Sea called by the name of Benganga and Coma discovered by Henry Schooten of Harlem; in a voyage began January 1669, and finished October 1671* a work ostensibly translated from the Dutch and published in London in 1671 and, reprinted there in 1766, that was then used for English newspaper reports, for example in the *Leeds Intelligencer* of 25 November 1766.

Spanish Trade

The Manila galleon tends to disappear from mention after its sixteenth-century establishment, but it continued to be very important during the seventeenth century. Indeed, the annual value of the trade has been assessed as two million pesos – over fifty tons of silver – which equalled the value of shipments between Europe and Asia carried by Portugal, the Dutch and Britain together.

Economic Development

The very different geologies and environments of Pacific islands helped ensure contrasting patterns of development, a situation that has considerable relevance for other periods for which information is scanty. The research carried out on both environment and history varies greatly. The presence of major research facilities and funds in Hawai'i ensure that it has received the most attention, but, again, that is most possible for recent centuries. Thus, for example, historical trends in soil quality are not always easy to establish. Taro cultivation was helped by the provision of ponds, which produced irrigation that both intensified and expanded production, thereby increasing surpluses that fostered population growth to probably over 400,000 in the seventeenth century and could be used for other purposes. Population growth increased demand and therefore both agricultural expansion, notably substantial rain-fed fields on volcanic slopes in the seventeenth and eighteenth centuries, as well as state formation, but also stress for the population.

In turn, the disruption of Western conflict, notably economic pressure, was to be related to a major fall in population between 1778 and 1833, due to infections, but, in part, also because of the emphasis from 1811 on sandalwood exports which affected the labour and land available for food.

5

The Early Eighteenth Century

....

The early eighteenth century is an instructive period in Pacific history because of what did not happen. All too often left out in books, and notably so if they have a lot of territory to cover, such periods are in fact of great consequence as they highlight routes not taken, and often, therefore, the far-from-inevitable consolidation of earlier trends instead. Prior to the 1760s, there was a period of what, in comparison, became only modest Western activity. Given the difficulties of navigation to, and in, the Pacific, that may seem harsh, but the Europeans had bases on, or near, the Pacific, notably Acapulco, Callao, Guayaquil, Manila, Batavia and (more modestly) Guam, and had already crossed the ocean on many occasions. Moreover, developments in the early eighteenth century showed what was possible, notably the Dutch arrival at Easter Island, and the Russian in the Aleutians. Yet these were also unusual, and earlier possibilities, such as the Dutch probing of Australasia and the Spanish exploration of Lower California, had little follow-up at this stage.

Moreover, this was despite two factors that might have encouraged such activity. Whereas there had been major wars between the great European powers, notably in 1688–1714, wars that had taken up resources and focused naval attention, France, Britain and Spain, with the exception of an Anglo-Spanish cold war in 1726–7, did not fight each other in 1721–38. Secondly, there was considerable interest in tropical possibilities in the 1710s and, although both the (British) South Sea Company and the (French) Louisiana Company proved speculative bubbles that spectacularly burst, that interest remained.

Instead, the key element was choice. The Western power most strongly represented in the Pacific was Spain. Indeed, it was the only power on both sides of the Pacific until Russia established itself in North America, and Russian strength there and, more generally, in the region was limited. Spain had done badly under Charles II (r. 1665–1700), and then faced a bitter civil war during the War of the Spanish Succession (for Spain 1701–15); but there was a marked revival of strength, capability and energy in the eighteenth century, beginning with the reign of Philip V (1700–46), under whom the navy was revived and became considerably larger.

Philip, however, greatly focused Spanish energy on Europe and did not devote significant attention to the Pacific. His successor, Ferdinand VI (r. 1746–59) similarly lacked attention, while Charles III (r. 1759–88), although very much concerned with Spain's non-European empire, concentrated not on the Philippines, but on the Americas, where international competition appeared more acute. Indeed, there was to be significant expansion on its Pacific coastline during Charles's reign, with an important extension of Spanish settlement in California.

Hoaxing Formosa

Arriving in London in 1703, George Psalmanaazar claimed to be indigenous to Formosa (Taiwan). His *An Historical and Geographical Description of Formosa* (1704) described commonplace cannibalism, a practice that fascinated Europeans, not least as presenting them with apparently self-evident proof of their superiority. Psalmanaazar, who had also invented a Formosan language, which he was asked to teach to missionaries, was discredited in 1708, but his career looked toward the use later in the century of the Pacific as a source of tales.

That there was no equivalent under Philip V provides another way to approach the standard point about a lack of Asian expansion. These were certainly years in which China was a strong and expansionist power. The late seventeenth century had seen the Manchu, who had successfully overrun Ming China in the 1640s and 1650s, confront serious problems in China and more generally, notably the large-scale Revolt of the Three Feudatories (1677–81), but also the rising challenge from the Dzunghars of the Mongolian steppe, a challenge that led to large-scale war in the 1690s. These factors possibly help explain why China did not take forward the naval capability it had shown in conquering Taiwan in 1683. Thus, although a possibility, there was no Chinese attack on the Philippines.

Yet looking for alternative commitments only works so far. In the first half of the eighteenth century, there was renewed conflict with the Dzunghars in the 1730s but, otherwise, no other warfare, let alone the multi-front pressure of which China was capable. Indeed, its strength grew considerably, not least with political stabilisation and economic development. Roughly 150 million people strong in 1650, China had about 300 million in 1800. Thus, the strongest economy and largest population in the world reached to the shores of the Pacific's outlying seas, but did not project its power there.

Strategic culture clearly played a role. Although the Manchu sinicized, there was also a continuance of their earlier culture, not least the emphasis on steppe concerns. The Kangzi and Qianlong emperors were interested in winning glory by victories there, and had particular security anxieties that were only overcome when the forces of the latter finally defeated the Dzunghars in the mid-1750s. The values more generally of the Manchu élite played a key role. They were not associated with maritime activity including exploration. The seizure of Taiwan was seen as an aspect of domestic policy, in the shape of overcoming Ming loyalists, rather than as a base on the route to the Philippines.

Clashes with the Chinese

China had a far greater population than Europe, but, although inland 'colonies' were created, as the Chinese consolidated their successes against the Dzunghars of Xinjiang in the 1690s and the 1750s, the Chinese lacked overseas settlement colonies other than Taiwan, where Chinese rule was followed by a settlement that limited the indigenous Australian population, although leading at times to rebellion. The Lin Shuangwen Rebellion in Taiwan in 1787–8 in part arose from migration from mainland China. This was also the case with the island of Hainan where the original Li people had been driven into the highlands by Han settlers who had arrived from about 100 BCE, but, more particularly, from the sixteenth century. From 1766, the Li increasingly used force against settlers.

European powers took care, sometimes brutally, to prevent the Chinese in ports such as Batavia and Manila from gaining power. The relationship between colonial rulers and non-local inhabitants, such as the Chinese, was sometimes poor. There was often suspicion, as in Dutch-ruled Batavia, where the Chinese were treated harshly from 1722, while they, in turn, evaded immigration quotas. The situation boiled over in 1740 when Dutch fears of a rising, and Chinese fears of expulsion, led to a crisis that got out of hand. About 10,000 Chinese were slaughtered in the ensuing massacre, and the surviving Chinese joined the Javan opponents of the Dutch, provoking fresh massacres. Nevertheless, the crucial role of the Chinese in the economy of Batavia was such that, in subsequent censuses in 1778 and the 1810s, they comprised a large percentage of the population.

There were also severe problems in the Spanish-ruled Philippines: Chinese trade and its impact on that between

Manila and Acapulco was seen as a potential threat to the latter, and thus to the articulation of the Spanish empire in the Pacific. Orders for banishment of the Chinese were issued in 1709, 1747, 1755 and 1769, and there was a massacre in 1763, reputedly of 6,000 Chinese. In practice, the authority of the Spanish state at such a distance was only episodic.

The major movement of Chinese to other continents in the nineteenth and twentieth centuries came not as a result of Chinese conquest, but within a system of state sovereignty and governmental regulation established by Western imperial powers and their successors.

The other non-Western power, Japan, had a different strategic geography, but its isolationism also precluded expansion. The major area of such activity was Hokkaido where, prefiguring the stance of other assimilating societies, whether in Australasia, North America or Polynesia, the Japanese provided goods, in their case ironware, lacquerware, rice, and sake, in return taking fish and fur, with the Ainu correspondingly divided and competitive over how far and how successfully to cooperate with the Japanese.

Separately, the rapidly rising population in Japan put considerable pressure on the limited resources of food and land there, in a pattern probably also seen in many other Pacific islands. This pressure led to an increase in social tension and peasant risings, of which there were more than fifty annually on average in the 1780s. Moreover, their scale, and the level of violence shown, both increased, while, with a degree of social radicalism, the focus shifted from village communities pressing their feudal overlords to cut taxes or provide more rice to attacks on the more prosperous members of the village communities. These uprisings also spread to the towns.

As for the maritime peoples of the East Indies, there was considerable strength in some cases, and, as shown in the sixteenth and seventeenth centuries, East Indies principalities and peoples could deploy considerable numbers for amphibious operations. However, there is no sign of any interest in long-range activity into the Pacific. For Atceh in Sumatra it is understandable that the focus of distant interest looked into the Indian Ocean, but there was no interest into the Pacific from principalities further east, for example those in Java and Sulawesi. In part, that was possibly a product of an absence of any relevant economic or political interest. In particular, New Guinea was not an inviting sphere for activity.

The Sulu Sultanate, an Islamic power that controlled the Sulu Archipelago and parts of Borneo, Palawan and Mindanao, raided elsewhere in the Philippines, notably for slaves, but did not press further into the Pacific. Its ships, particularly the outrigger and well-armed *lanongs* with their shear masts for sails and slave rowers, and the smaller and less heavily armed *garays*, which also relied on slave rowers but lacked outriggers, were able to sail long distances, but focused on nearby waters round the Sulu Sea.

At any rate, the contrast with the situation held to explain earlier Polynesian expansion is instructive, not least with reference to possible land shortage: the islands of the East Indies did not have a shortage comparable to the mostly small islands of the Polynesian expansion. Instead, internal frontiers were more properly the issue in the East Indies, as also in Continental South-East Asia and New Guinea. In all of these, the frontiers were those posed by highland regions and their often different inhabitants, a situation that did not pertain across much of the Pacific.

In this perspective, it is more helpful to consider the relative lack of Western expansion in the Pacific not as an aberration, but as part of a more general pattern. A facile point would be one that linked this to the degree to which, after over a century of decline or stagnation, significant population growth in the West and elsewhere did not begin until the mid-eighteenth century. That is not helpful because there was scant real linkage to Western expansion in terms of Pacific settlement until the nineteenth century. Moreover, there was growing Western interest in the Pacific in the early eighteenth century.

Travel accounts contributed to the information available, presenting it in a readily digestible format. Narratives such as that by Dampier, Lionel Wafer's *A New Voyage and Description of the Isthmus of Panama* (1699), William Funnell's *A Voyage Round the World* (1707), Edward Cooke's *A Voyage to the South Sea and Round the World* (1712), and Woodes Rogers's *A Cruising Voyage Round the World* (1712), helped create a sense of the Pacific as an accessible ocean open to profitable British penetration and one that could be seized from the real and imagined grasp of Spain. This possibility, which was also catered to in the cartographer Herman Moll's *A View of the Coasts, Countries and Islands within the Limits of the South-Sea-Company* (1711), created a context within which the British public was eager for new information. Moreover, the major financial speculation of the 1710s and early 1720s, the South Sea Company, drew on hope for profit from trade to the Pacific.

Contemporary interest in distant seas was seen in Jonathan Swift's novel *Gulliver's Travels* (1726), specifically the fictional Gulliver's voyage to Lilliput, which was located in the South Pacific, as well as Daniel Defoe's novel *Robinson Crusoe* (1726), which was based on the marooning of the Scottish buccaneer Alexander Selkirk on the uninhabited islands of Juan Fernández in 1704–9. He lived on spring lobsters, feral goats, wild turnips, and pink peppercorns, built huts out of pepper trees, and clothed himself from goatskins. Once rescued, Selkirk took part in privateering on and off the coast of Ecuador and Mexico. Fiction played a role in many respects, helping indeed to locate advances in an 'heroic' interpretation of exploration in terms of increased knowledge.

It is pertinent, however, instead of seeing a clear trend, to note a combination of particular political factors and a more general lack of interest. In the case of the first, neither Britain nor France wanted, at least for most of the period, to anger Spain, which both claimed a monopoly of the coastline of South America and sought to keep the route from the Atlantic difficult to others. It is no surprise that, with George Anson's voyage, Britain used the route when the two powers were at war.

Anson's circumnavigation in 1740–4 showed the dangers of such voyages. Although a Spanish attempt to intercept the ships failed, typhus, malaria, dysentery and, in particular, scurvy, hit hard, and there were problems with storms and navigation; of the three ships that prepared to sail from Juan Fernández islands in September 1741, 626 of the 961 crew who had left Britain in 1740 had died. Another two ships had reached the Pacific, but then sailed back; while a sixth, the *Wager*, ran ashore on the Chilean coast and the crew was affected by mutiny, after which thirty-six men from the ship were able, despite many hardships, to return to England. Anson captured Spanish ships off the coast of Peru, as well as the port of Paita. Giant turtles were seized for food on the island of Coiba off Panama. With two ships, Anson set off across the Pacific, but one was badly affected by leaks and abandoned, while, in addition, scurvy hit home. Resupplying on Tinian, the *Centurion*, despite storms, reached Macau and proceeded to capture a Manila galleon, with vast loot, in 1743, before returning with 188 men to England in 1744.

Politics interacted with other factors, and the hopes of trade associated with the South Sea Company and other schemes proved totally naïve. The distance to the Pacific helped ensure that, as yet, despite Spanish fears about Mocha Island, there were no significant concentrations of Western independents or marginals, 'non-state actors', notably pirates, who, in pursuing their own interests, could establish a presence. This concentration had been the case in the Caribbean and Madagascar, with

Mocha Island an equivalent to the latter as an outlier of the world of Atlantic piracy. Non-Western 'non-state actors', such as the *wako*, were seen in East Asian waters, but the extent to which Western trade was regulated, thanks to the role of the British, Dutch and French East India Companies, and of the Portuguese and Spanish governments, affected the opportunities for Western equivalents and contributed to this sparsity of 'independent' actors. So also did the lack, at this stage, of the presence in the Pacific by New England interests that was to develop after American independence.

As both cause and effect, there was also a difference to the economic exploitation that was to be seen a century later. In particular, as yet, there was no commercial interest in whaling or sealing. The distances to markets were too great, but, more particularly, European, North American and Japanese whalers concentrated on local waters which were not yet depleted. Nor had the trade networks yet developed to encourage the exploitation of the vegetation and sea-life of Polynesian islands. The Dutch use of the East Indies, notably Java and the Moluccas, showed that distant products could be worked, and worked hard; but this process had not yet expanded. There appeared neither need nor opportunity to do so. Nor was there any possibility of cooperation with local interests comparable to that seen in the Atlantic slave trade.

Indeed, looping back to consider the hopes expressed about the South Sea, as the British termed the Pacific, it is striking how unrealistic these were in terms of the assumptions of ready economic benefits. The extrapolation onto the Pacific of hopes, ideas, and models developed to deal with the Caribbean was at this point foolish, in terms not only of force-projection but also of the possibilities of the Pacific as opposed to the Atlantic. Yet, this extrapolation was symptomatic of the transfer onto the Pacific of ideas and hopes based on other regions.

EXPLORATION

As with so much else, exploration in the early eighteenth century can be seen rather as a continuation of the previous half-century than as a unit also encompassing the second half of the eighteenth. The first half of the eighteenth century did not see important new explorations in the South Pacific, although, in an expedition sponsored by the Dutch West India Company in 1722, the rival of the East India Company, the Dutch explorer Jacob Roggeveen, having visited the Juan Fernández Islands, 'discovered' Easter Island, and some of the Tuamotus, two of the Tahitian group, and some of the Samoan islands, in a voyage intended to find Terra Australis. One of his three ships was lost on Takapoto Atoll in the Tuamotus, while on Makatea in that group he got involved in conflict on the beach. By sailing further south on his westward route round Cape Horn than earlier navigators, Roggeveen sighted large icebergs that convinced him of the existence of the continent. Indeed, the publication, from 1694 to 1709, of both the earlier Dutch voyages and those of William Dampier, encouraged interest in the identity, extent and character of the land(s) in southern latitudes.

From the voyages of Abel Tasman on, New Holland or Australia was widely understood to be an island that did not extend far further to the east, although in 1714 the map by Guillaume Delisle included in it not only New Guinea to the north but also Espiritu Santo in Vanuatu to the east. A larger New Holland was also a theme in England in the 1740s, notably in the writing of John Campbell and in Emanuel Bowen's *Complete Map of the Southern Continent* (1744).

There was also interest in the idea of an additional large continent, either further to the east or to the south, or both. Belief in such a continent was advanced by Philippe Bauche in France and Alexander Dalrymple in Britain, the latter in his *Historical Collection of the Several Voyages and Discoveries in the South Pacific*

Ocean (1770–1). Whereas Dampier had anticipated 'some fruitful land', Dalrymple, formally an official of the East India Company, was convinced that there might be a population of up to fifty million, and therefore tremendous economic potential.

Easter Island was not the only 'discovery' in the eastern Pacific. In 1711 and 1725, French expeditions visited uninhabited Clipperton Island, named after John Clipperton, who had been on Dampier's expedition in 1703, being captured by the Spaniards. On his second voyage, he used the island as a base for a privateering syndicate, and, in 1721, with his ship running aground for three days, he clashed at Guam with the Spaniards, which led the latter to develop its defences in the 1730s. In 1738, the French East India Company sent Jean-Baptiste Charles Bouvet de Lozier and two ships to make discoveries in the southern hemisphere, but his discoveries were limited to the South Atlantic.

The Spaniards sought to keep other Europeans out of the Pacific, or, more particularly, to thwart attempts to enter the ocean from around South America. In 1749, they objected to British plans for an expedition to the Pacific and the establishment of a British base on the Falkland Islands that would support further voyages in southern latitudes. This was not the route used by Spain, which preferred to rely on cross-isthmus routes in Central America. There would have been a comparable earlier strategic interest in North America had the Northwest Passage been viable for the British. Instead, Spanish defence of the Pacific focused on the Falklands and on attempts to thwart British efforts to develop a presence in Central America, notably on the Mosquito Coast, the Atlantic Coast of modern Nicaragua. Anson had hoped to combine his operation with a British attack on the Panama isthmus from the Caribbean, but the latter proved fruitless.

Interest in the Falklands was focused by the Anson circumnavigation. Much written about, this circumnavigation also encouraged British interest in the Pacific, although only one of his six ships had completed the circumnavigation, and, en route, he had nearly run aground on Tierra del Fuego due to a miscalculation of his position. The voyage had been accompanied by hopes of major commercial gains from the South Sea, the *New Weekly Miscellany* of 8 August 1741 declaring: 'We hear that in every ship of Commodore Anson's squadron there are great quantities of all sorts of European commodities, which must inevitably now produce a vast profit.'

The British were also interested in discovering a navigable Northwest Passage to the Pacific, and made several efforts to find a passage from Hudson Bay. James Knight failed in 1719, but, in 1741, the Admiralty sent the *Discovery* and *Furnace* to Hudson Bay under Christopher Middleton. The following year, he sailed further north along the west coast of the Bay than any previous European explorer, but could not find the entrance to a passage. The naming of Repulse Bay testified to Middleton's frustration. In 1746–7, William Moor, who was sent by the North West Committee organised by Arthur Dobbs, a critic of the Hudson Bay Company, also failed.

Russia

In the North Pacific, the impulse to Russian territorial expansion and scientific development provided by Peter the Great (r. 1689–1725) had borne fruit. In 1725, Peter ordered the Dane Vitus Bering to discover a serviceable sea route from Siberia to North America. Sailing from Okhotsk in 1728, Bering navigated the strait separating Asia from America that now bears his name, although he failed to sight Alaska due to the fog, a situation repeated in 1729. In 1733, Bering was told to follow a different route, sailing across the North Pacific, which he did with Aleksey Chirikov in 1741. The two were separated at sea. They explored the Alaskan coast, and the Aleutians, but storms, scurvy, and an inability to work out his location, led Bering's ship to winter in the Komandorskis, where he died. Pyotr Krenitsyn was sent in 1768 to follow up Bering by surveying the eastern part of the Aleutians. Meanwhile, in 1738–9, Martin Spangberg and William Walton, both in Russian service, sailed from Kamchatka down the Kurile Islands to Japan, 'filling in' the geography of the region. Spanberg produced the first map of the Kuriles. M. S. Gvozdev and I. Fyodorov explored what would later be termed the Bering Strait in 1732. In 1754, a navigation school was founded in Okhotsk. Concern about the Russians encouraged Spanish interest in expansion northward into California.

Meanwhile, vigorous resistance to Western expansion during the century was seen not only in Chile and California, but also on the north-west Pacific coast. Relying on bone or stone-tipped arrows and on slings, the poorly armed Itelmen were brutalised in the inexorable Russian search for furs. They rose in 1706, but were suppressed. In 1731, the Itelmen had some firearms obtained from the Russians and were able to inflict many casualties, but they were eventually crushed, while their numbers were further hit by the diseases that accompanied their adversaries. Largely isolated communities proved especially vulnerable as their immunity was low. Another rising in 1741 was defeated. The Koraks of Kamchatka proved more formidable than the Itelmen, and were effective with bows and captured firearms. The Russians responded brutally and were willing to kill as many Koraks as possible, not least in the war of 1745–56 after which the Koraks submitted. The Chukchi of north-east Siberia were also formidable, defeating a Cossack expedition in Russian service in 1729 and resisting genocidal attacks in 1730–1 and 1744–7. The Russians eventually stopped the war, abandoning their fort at Anadyrsk in 1764, although it had successfully resisted siege as recently as 1762. Trade links developed and the Russians finally recognised Chukchi rights to their territories.

TRAVELLING ON THE PAGE

Travelling on the page became more common as information and speculation about the Pacific increased. *Histoire des navigations aux terres australes* (1756) by Charles de Brosses, a French intellectual who never left Europe, provided an account of what was known of local products and customs, as well as a call for exploration to discover and exploit Australia, and the use of the word *Polynésie*. His work was plagiarised by John Callander in his *Terras Australis Cognita* (1766), which further spread ideas about the Pacific. This situation provided a context for the great amount of information that was to be brought back to Europe from the late 1760s. There were also the fictional travels that made surprising accounts of new worlds appear less disruptive. Thus, *The Life Adventures of John Daniel* (1751; 2nd edition, 1770), possibly by Ralph Morris, included not only a tropical shipwreck near Java, but also a flight to the Moon from which there is a landing to a South Atlantic island in which there are the English-speaking descendants of a human woman and a sea creature.

6

The Age of Cook

....

The Anglocentric title of this chapter might challenge most non-British scholars who do not accept that he dominated the later eighteenth century. This chapter reflects the internationality of Pacific exploration, but Cook was the most prominent individual at the time and in retrospect.

The exploration of the Pacific by European powers did not gather pace until after the Seven Years' War (1756–63) ended. This conflict was important for two reasons. First, British naval success during the war made it difficult for French or Spanish warships to risk voyages. Secondly, the capture of Manila in 1762 increased British interest in the Pacific, even though Manila was returned in 1764. Exploration owed something to scientific interest, but was also driven by the widespread sense that the British maritime dominance recognised by the Peace of Paris of 1763 would be challenged in the future, and that any such war would focus even more on colonial and maritime rivalry than the Seven Years' War had done. At the popular level, there was also widespread interest in Pacific exploration, and this encouraged, and was sustained by, publications such as Alexander Dalrymple's *Historical Collection of the Several Voyages and Discoveries in the South Pacific Ocean* (1770–1). A copy of the first was taken on Cook's first voyage.

Manila Falls, 1762

Mounted from Madras by Colonel William Draper, the daring expedition was helped by Manila's fortifications being weak, the Spanish garrison small, and attack not anticipated. Draper could only dispose of a single battalion of regulars, which, with additional sepoys, pioneers and French deserters, provided a force of only 1,700 men. Fortunately, cooperation with the naval force of eight ships of the line and two East Indiamen was very good, and the fleet landed about 1,000 sailors and marines to help. The breaking of the monsoon was a serious problem as was opposition from Filipino irregulars, but the capture of the well-equipped naval dockyard of Cavite permitted repairs, and Manila fell rapidly, Colonel George Monson recording:

> An eight gun battery was finished about three hundred yards from the wall the 2nd of October at night, and opened the 3rd in the morning on the south west bastion, which immediately silenced the enemy's guns and made a breach in the salient angle of the bastion, the fourth at night batteries were begun to take off the defences of the south east bastion and of the small bastions on the west side of the town; which were opened the fifth by ten o'clock in the morning and had so good an effect, that the general gave out orders for storming the place next day; which was done about seven in the morning, with very little loss, on our side.

This capture however, did not end Spanish resistance and British plans had dangerously exaggerated Filipino cooperation. Pasig was taken but, after initial success, the British were unable to maintain their position in Bulacan.

In 1767, on a voyage organised by the Admiralty rather than by private interests, Samuel Wallis entered the Pacific through the Straits of Magellan on the *Dolphin*. He then sailed on a course different to that of his predecessors, who had followed the route established by the Spaniards. Wallis was able to 'discover' many Pacific islands, including Tahiti, which he called King George the Third's Island. Arriving in 1767, the *Dolphin* clashed with the population and fired grapeshot at menacing canoes from which stones were being fired by means of slings. Wallis went on to complete a circumnavigation of the world. After their ships had passed through the Straits of Magellan, Wallis was separated from Lieutenant Philip Carteret and the *Swallow*. Carteret crossed the Pacific further south than any other explorer and 'discovered' a large number of islands, including Pitcairn's Island.

Wallis and Carteret did not repeat their voyages and their reputation was soon to be overshadowed, but they were important, not least in demonstrating anew that circumnavigations could be successful and could lead to discoveries. Furthermore, the pace of competition hotted up in the late 1760s as Louis Antoine de Bougainville, whose background was in the French army, circumnavigated the globe in 1767–9. The account of his visit to Tahiti helped establish the South Seas in a romantic and ambrosian light in the European consciousness. The presentation of South Sea Islanders as noble savages benefited from the novelty of European contact with them. As the early epicentre for the Europeans visiting Polynesia, and also as a place to consider otherness and self, Tahiti was depicted as an earthly paradise, a Garden of Eden without Christianity. Aside from the beauty of the island, the pleasantness of the climate, the quality and exotic nature of the food, and the sexual freedom of the inhabitants all attracted attention. Tahiti was named New Cythera by Bougainville after the fabled realm of Aphrodite; while his naturalist wanted to call it Utopia. In his *Supplement au Voyage de Bougainville* (1773), the writer Denis Diderot, who had not been there, presented the

Tahitians as noble primitives whose moral openness was a worthy counterpoint to the artificialities of European culture and the restrictive strictures of Christianity. Thus, and this point attracted considerable attention, sex was possible without sin, and promiscuity could be part of a benign moral order.

The seductive portrayal of innocent children of nature was true only in part, but it served to challenge conventional European views and to help in the redefinition of what was considered to be natural behaviour. Expeditions that visited both Alaska and the South Pacific contrasted the inhabitants of the latter favourably with the former. The Pacific islands appeared to offer a primitive, but beneficent, social harmony that challenged civilisation and Christianity and, to those willing to take this view, made a mockery of the notion that the strictures of the latter were moral and necessary. Thus, exploration in overturning earlier fantasies about the Antipodes, provided a site for a new idyll. The Pacific provided a more successful model for primitive virtue than those offered elsewhere, for example by Native Americans.

Bougainville also reached the New Hebrides in 1768, showing that they were not part of *Terra Australis* as Quiros had thought in 1608. However, the outliers of the Great Barrier Reef prevented Bougainville from seeing the east coast of Australia. His *Voyage autour du Monde* (1771) attracted a large readership, and appeared in an English edition in 1772.

In 1769, Captain James Cook, a naval officer who was a skilled navigator, was sent to Tahiti in the *Endeavour* to observe Venus's transit across the Sun, as part of a collaborative international observation which involved 151 observers from the world of European science. Cook's secret orders – to search for the southern continent – helped lead him even further afield. He conducted the first circuit and charting of New Zealand, producing maps of considerable accuracy, and the charting of the east coast of Australia. Here, in 1770, Cook landed in Botany Bay, the first

European to land on the east coast, and claimed the territory for George III. Then, after having run aground on the Great Barrier Reef, and thus had to repair the *Endeavour*, Cook sailed through the Torres Strait, showing that New Guinea and Australia were separate islands, before reaching the Dutch base of Batavia. He had fulfilled his instructions 'to employ yourself diligently in exploring as great an extent of the coast as you can . . . surveying and making charts, and taking views of such bays, harbours and parts of the coast as may be useful to navigation'. He put over 5,000 miles of coastline on the map, and 320 charts and coastal views survive from that voyage, a far larger figure than that of Bougainville.

George III had made a large personal contribution of £4,000 to the Royal Society towards the costs of Cook's first voyage and, in 1771, granted him an hour-long audience on his return. Richard Kaye, the sub-almoner, supplied Cook with George III Maundy coins for burial in newly discovered lands in the name of the king, while Cook presented George with a hei-tiki, or Māori stone embodying the spirits of ancestors, that he had been given in New Zealand in 1769.

On his second voyage, in 1772–5, Cook's repeated efforts to find the southern continent, efforts which included the first passage of the Antarctic circle, failed. He had sailed to 71°10′S, farther than any known voyage hitherto, when he encountered the ice outlier of Antarctica, and reported that it was not a hidden world of balmy fertility. The first known sighting of the Antarctic continent was not until 1820 when Fabian Bellingshausen, the leader of a Russian expedition that was circumnavigating the ice, mapped part of Princess Martha Coast. Nevertheless, New Caledonia, Tonga and the New Hebrides were 'discovered' by Cook. These 'discoveries' overlaid those of other Europeans, for example Bougainville, let alone of Polynesians. European knowledge of the Southern Pacific was increased by Cook, and his energetic determination to keep his men healthy ensured that, as in the other two voyages, no hands were lost to scurvy. The use of chronometers helped in the confirmation of locations, while his extensive voyages were also important to clarification. Just as his first voyage was important to John Hawkesworth's *An Account of the Voyages Undertaken ... for Making Discoveries in the Southern Hemisphere* (1773), so the second led to Cook's *A Voyage towards the South Pole, and Round the World* (1777).

On his third voyage (1776–9), Cook 'discovered' Christmas Island and Hawai'i, while, in 1778, he sailed to a new farthest north – 70° 44'N at Icy Cape, Alaska, and proved that pack ice blocked any possible North-West Passage from the Atlantic to the Pacific to the north of North America. These voyages owed much to technical developments, particularly John Harrison's invention of an accurate chronometer to measure longitude, to an improved ability to keep crews and ships at sea for long periods, not least vanquishing scurvy, and to governmental support. Cook continued the process of British imperial naming, his including the Hervey Islands and Palmerston Atoll. The third voyage was recorded in *A Voyage to the Pacific Ocean* (1784), a copy of which was presented to George III.

The painters who accompanied Cook, such as William Hodges on the second voyage and John Webber on the third, provided a powerful visual image of the South Seas. They were responding both to the desire for pictures in published accounts and to the determination to record biological and ethnographic information accurately. Webber made a large number of water-colour landscapes. His surviving works on public display include *The Death of Captain Cook, View of Huaheine, Poedua ... Society Islands, A Dance in Otaheite, A Chief of the Sandwich Isles, A Night Dance by Men in Hapaee, Tereoboo, King of Owyhee bringing presents to Cook* and *Ship Cove, Queen Charlotte Sound*. He made his reputation and fortune, becoming a full member of the Royal Academy. The Pacific, as in Hodges's *Tahiti Revisited,* offered a vista of paradise, one suffused in light, and of truly noble figures as in Joshua Reynolds's portrait of Omai, a Pacific islander brought back from Cook's second expedition. Omai was presented to George III who treated him courteously and gave him an allowance. At Covent Garden, George subsequently attended several performances of John O'Keeffe's pantomime *Omai, or A Trip Around the World* (1785), being moved to tears by the fate of the protagonist, who had died at a relatively young age. Webber was involved in making the stage scenery and costumes.

There was debate at the time over the accuracy of the pictures, not least with claims that Hodges and, far more, the etchings produced for the Hawkesworth's *Account* had been influenced by neoclassical artistic theory and practice to offer softened, indeed perfect, forms in depicting the Pacific, and notably Polynesia. Hodges' paintings, with their well-lit contrasts, particularly in his views of Tahiti, also to a degree looked to standard artistic presentation of the classical world, notably by French painters, while there was a proto-Romantic quality to some of his works, for example his *A View of Cape Stephens in Cook's Straits New Zealand with Waterspout* (1776).

The voyages also saw the acquisition of botanical and zoological knowledge. An artist had accompanied Dampier's voyage of 1699–1700, his drawings being published in Dampier's *Voyage to New Holland*. Far more information came back as a result of Cook's voyages, which returned with sketches, dried specimens and skins, for example of a kangaroo. The well-connected naturalist Joseph Banks took two artists with him on Cook's first voyage, while the naturalist Daniel Solander and the astronomer Charles Green were also in the party. Having contracted scurvy, Green died of dysentery on the return journey soon after leaving Batavia, a city which proved fatal to many mariners. In a gross instance of depersonalising, Banks purchased tattooed heads in New Zealand.

Cookery and the Pacific

Cook's voyages led to positive accounts of Tahitian barbe-cues in Britain, and 'barbecued pig' was featured in such cookery books as Mason's *Ladies' Assistant for Regulating and Supplying her Table* (1786), Briggs's *English Art of Cookery* (1788), and Farley's *London Art of Cookery* (1792). Elizabeth Raffald in *The Experienced English Housekeeper* (1769) provided a recipe for a 'floating Desert Island'. The pig was not buried, as in Polynesia, but provided an opportunity for the use of spices and fruit.

Alongside benign accounts, alternative readings of the Pacific islanders were at first downplayed. Wallis's expedition had in fact discovered not a primitive utopia but a complex society with rulers, aristocracy, private property, priestcraft and feuding. Cook also stressed the presence of private property, law and social ranks, and thus of a civilisation whose fundamentals were similar to that of Europe, albeit with major differences such as the absence of Christianity. More pointedly, the discovery of human sacrifice, which Europeans found difficult to rationalise, put the stress on savage, and on a savagery without appeal. The killing of Cook, who was presented as an exemplary national hero, in 1779 in Hawai'i further contributed to a sense of brutishness. In practice, Cook had become increasingly angry, even arbitrary, on his third voyage, and, in particular, found it difficult to cope with theft. In the 1780s, one of Jean-François Lapérouse's captains, Paul de Langle, was killed by indigenous people on Samoa, and Lapérouse was sceptical about the notion of the noble savage. A process of mutual disappointment with contact between Europeans and Islanders became more insistent. Contact meant that each had to consider otherness and self, but often in a difficult context and with much mutual incomprehension.

Yet favourable depictions still appeared in print. George Keate's *Account of the Pelew* [Palau] *Islands, from the Journals of Captain Henry Wilson and some of his officers, shipwrecked there in the Antelope in August 1783* (1788) was a considerable success, with five London editions by 1803, and French (1793) and German (1800) translations. This was an indication of the extent to which, as earlier with Dampier, Anson and, even more, Cook, knowledge of British maritime endeavour was widely disseminated. After initial uncertainties, indeed conflict, Wilson and his crew eventually found a friendly reception, and brought back to Britain 'Prince' Lee Boo, who became a celebrity before dying of smallpox in 1784. Wilson's Palau artefacts went into the British Museum.

Whether or not European commentators presented the South Sea Islanders in a benign fashion, they tended to have few doubts about the value of Europe's contact with them. In his *The History of the Decline and Fall of the Roman Empire* (1776–88), Edward Gibbon was convinced of the general benefit of European expansion:

> ... every age of the world has increased and still increases the real wealth, the happiness, the knowledge, and perhaps the virtue of the human race. The merit of discovery has too often been stained with avarice, cruelty and fanaticism; and the intercourse of nations has produced the communication of disease and prejudice. A singular exception is due to the virtue of our own times and country. The five great voyages, successively undertaken by the command of his present Majesty, were inspired by the pure and generous love of science and mankind ... introduced into the islands of the South Sea the vegetables and animals most useful to human life.

In his acceptance of the harshness of 'discovery', Gibbon revealed enlightened susceptibilities, but his account was also Eurocentric: savages were to receive gifts. In practice, Cook introduced pigs and possibly the white potato as well as exotic weeds to New Zealand. Leaving aside the serious issue of ecological imperialism, a present-minded critique of Gibbon's account might emphasize the possibilities of a more multifaceted treatment of human happiness and progress.

The voyages of Cook and others provided much information about what was not and what was. In particular, Cook discredited the belief in *Terra Australis*. More generally, later voyagers benefited from Cook's accumulation of information, Arthur Phillip using Cook's chart when he sailed into Botany Bay in 1788.

However, Cook's voyages tended to provide an outline of coastlines, rather than an exact charting, his mapping of New Zealand incorrectly having Stewart Island as part of the mainland, and, conversely, treating Banks Peninsula inaccurately. The Royal Navy's Hydrographic Office, founded in 1795, was responsible for coordinating much subsequent surveying. Stewart Island itself was charted by William Stewart, a sealer, in 1809, and is still named after him, rather than by the indigenous name of Rakiura. Aside from hydrography, there was also oceanographic research on topics such as tidal ranges and water temperatures.

The foundation of a British settlement in Australia owed much to the loss of America, where many criminals had been sent. In 1786, the British government decided to found New South Wales, in order to provide a penal colony, a course recommended by Banks. Geopolitical advantage was also pursued, both pre-empting the French and providing a base that would project British power into the southern hemisphere (which caused concern to Spain) and provide naval supplies.

The Pacific in Birmingham

For 22 August 1791, the audience at Birmingham's New Street theatre was offered as a 'pantomimical interlude':

> A pantomime exhibition called Botany Bay; or, A Trip to Port Jackson, with entire new scenery, painted for the occasion . . . in which will be introduced a picturesque view of the coast of New South Wales . . . arrival of the Grand Fleet, landing, reception, and employment of the convicts. To conclude with the ceremony of planting the British flag, on taking possession of a new discovered island, with a dance by the convicts, and the grand chorus of 'God Save the King.'

The original Kameygal and Gweagal tribes of what was then called Gwea (later Botany Bay), were not part of the show.

Cook's voyages had a major impact on European opinion, and also encouraged French and Spanish responses, although these are often overshadowed. Jean François de Surville explored the coast of New Zealand and clarified the position of the Solomon Islands, while Marc Joseph Marion du Fresne, having shown that Tasmania was not uninhabited, fell victim to Māori along with twenty-six of his crew while searching for *Terra Australis Incognita* in 1772, although the survivors fought off attacks using firearms. The fate of the crew, which included being eaten, helped undermine the benign portrayal of Pacific islanders.

French activity, which had included in 1772 a voyage to the west coast of Australia, was cut short by entry into the War of American Independence in 1778, but, after peace with Britain was negotiated in 1783, the pace of French activity resumed and in 1784–9, France sent ten naval expeditions into the Indian and Pacific oceans, the most famous being that of Jean-François Lapérouse in 1785–8. This was reported to the British government as Lapérouse intended to establish a base in New Zealand. In fact, Lapérouse, having reached the Pacific, sailed via Easter Island to Alaska and followed the American coast south to Monterey, seeking a river that might lead to Hudson Bay, before crossing to Macao, en route being the first European to discover what he named Necker Island in the Hawaiian group. In 1787, he explored the northwestern Pacific, following the coast of Korea, Sakhalin, Hokkaido and Kamchatka. Like Cook, Lapérouse took with him civilian scientists. By sailing through the Gulf of Tartary, waters uncharted by Cook, he established that Sakhalin was an island. Lapérouse also sailed along the Kurile chain. Only then did he sail via Samoa to Australasia, reaching Botany Bay in Australia on 24 January 1788, six days after the British had arrived to found a penal colony there. Lapérouse's expedition acquired particular renown because it never returned, instead being shipwrecked in the New Hebrides, although that was not to be known for a long time.

An expedition of two ships under Antoine Bruny d'Entrecasteaux set off in 1791 to find Lapérouse, which it failed to do. The expedition circumnavigated Australia and New Guinea, named the Kermadecs, 'discovered' the D'Entrecasteaux Islands, and explored the Solomons, but poor health and a shortage of supplies hit the expedition hard in 1793. Much of the crew, including the commander, his second in command, Huon de Kermadec, and the steward, Louis Giradin (in fact the female stowaway Marie-Louise Victoire Giradin, who was probably Kermadec's lover), all died. Arriving in Java, the survivors divided between republicans and royalists, while as France had gone to war with the Dutch in 1795, the ships were seized and the republicans imprisoned. The energy that had characterised French activity in the mid-1780s was not maintained.

War in Europe also cut short Spanish exploration in the Pacific, which had strengthened in the late eighteenth century. In 1772 and 1775 Spanish missions from Peru under Domingo de Boenechea established a settlement on Tahiti Iti, but there was no follow-up. Later, there was worry about British and Russian activity on the north-west coast of North America. The earlier Spanish policy of attempting to restrict information could no longer suffice. Spanish activity also reflected the determination of Charles III (r. 1759–88) to develop his empire.

The surveying voyage of Bruno de Hezeta, in 1775, led to the sighting of the estuary of the Columbia River, although the currents were too swift for his scurvy-weakened crew to enter the river. Earlier, seven of the crew had been killed by indigenous people when they put ashore for water. Francisco de la Bodega y Quadra, who had sailed on when Hezeta turned back, reached 58°30′N, despite scurvy affecting most of the crew. His surveying voyages led to a far better map of the coast from there to 17°N. Facing the usual problem of deciding how best to interpret and integrate new information, the Viceroy of New Spain, Antonio María de Bucareli, speculated that the Columbia might be the outflow of the inland sea marked on maps, and, in 1793, Revilla Gigedo, his successor, suggested that the river might cross the continent. This led to an unsuccessful Spanish attempt to establish a settlement at the mouth of the Columbia and to penetrate up the river: it was thwarted by the difficulty of the river channel and the hostile attitude of the indigenous people.

Meanwhile, there was a major expansion into California, in large part in order to assuage fears of Russian activity. San Diego was founded in 1769, Monterey in 1770, San Francisco in 1776, and Los Angeles five years later. Spanish expansion was helped by the local availability of Spanish naval power, not least in moving settlers and goods, and thus ensured a ready possibility for economic advantage from expansion. San Blas, Mexico was founded as a port in order to support military activity further north, with a shipyard and a fort part of the new project. Ships built there were used, while the port also provided a stopping point for others. However, California's coastal situation also ensured that other powers could challenge Spanish claims and establish positions, the Russians doing so at Fort Ross in 1812.

In contrast, in Chile, the Spaniards made only minor advances south. Instead, the Mapuche attacked in 1723, 1766 and 1769–70. At the same time, the limited character of Spanish expansion there ensured that warfare decreased. In Peru, a large-scale indigenous uprising, that of Túpac Amaru II in 1780–1, failed, as did the continuing revolts into 1782. These were inland rather than coastal.

Meanwhile, the Spaniards made efforts to discover a North-West Passage between the Atlantic and the Pacific. In 1788, Estéban José Martínez explored what is now the Pacific coast of Canada, and, in 1790, Salvador Fidalgo followed, exploring Prince William Sound and Cook Inlet, while Manuel Quimper explored the Strait of Juan de Fuca. Other Spanish expeditions in 1791, 1792 and 1793 showed that there was no navigable North-West Passage and no river giving access to an inland sea.

The more wide-ranging voyages of Alejandro Malaspina in 1790–3 reflected the energy of Spanish exploration that was cut short by the French Revolutionary Wars. Having already circumnavigated the globe in 1782–4, Malaspina was given command of two frigates in 1789 and sent on a scientific expedition to the Pacific, where he sailed along the Pacific coast of North America to 60°N, searching for the North-West Passage and surveying the coast, before crossing Micronesia to the Philippines, and then Melanesia en route to New Zealand and Sydney, before returning via Tonga. His expedition carried artists including the Italian Fernando Brambila. In 1792, Dionisio Alcala Galiano and Cayetano Valdes surveyed the last unmapped portion of the Pacific coast of North America, part of California. The following year, Spain went to war with France, beginning a conflict that ruined her empire and cut short the drive for exploration. Malaspina died in 1810, his expedition forgotten.

Instead, it was British activity that came to dominate the Pacific, and this reflected British maritime predominance and the relative situation of the leading naval powers. In the waters of the south-west Pacific, the British added to their empire Lord Howe Island (1788), the Chatham Islands (1791), and Pitt Island (1791). Captain William Bligh made intelligible charts of Fiji, the Banks group and Aitutaki in the Cooks, Captain Lever 'discovered' the Kermadecs and Penrhyn Island, and Captains Gilbert and Marshall the islands that bear their names. In 1789, Lieutenant John Shortland coasted the shores of Guadalcanal and San Cristobal.

Running Surveys

An important surveying technique, with observations of major coastal features made from the ship while distances travelled along coastline were measured, the information it yielded was entered on daily survey sheets that then were used for compilation sheets.

Commander George Vancouver, who had been on Cook's second and third voyages, was sent to the Pacific in 1791 in order to carry out survey work and to secure Britain's possession of the Nootka Sound coastline on what is now Vancouver Island. Competition over this coast had nearly led to a major war: in 1789, the commander of a Spanish warship seized the British ships and depot recently established at Nootka Sound and, when the news reached London in 1790, there was a major naval armament. In the event, Spain backed down, in part because it was clear that France could not provide support, and accepted a settlement that established the rights of the British to settle to the north of the areas occupied by Spain prior to the 1789 seizure. British whalers and traders were also to be able to operate 'in the Pacific Ocean or in the South Seas, or in landing on the coasts of those seas in places not already occupied, or for the purpose of carrying on their commerce with the indigenous people of the country or of making establishments there'.

Vancouver explored part of the coast of New Zealand, 'discovered' the Chathams, and charted the Snares to the south of New Zealand, as well as thoroughly surveying the Pacific coastline of modern Canada and Alaska in 1792–5, a survey designed to strengthen the British presence on a coast in which Britain, Spain and Russia were in competition. Showing that there was no water passage between the Atlantic and the Pacific south of the Arctic, Vancouver's expedition also accumulated much information about the areas visited. It was accompanied by a naturalist, Archibald Menzies, who had already visited the Pacific, and brought back a large number of plants as well as the seeds of the Chile Pine (the Monkey Puzzle tree), as well as descriptions of new animals and an account of mountains in Hawai'i. The expedition also collected items of Native American life. The coastlines were scattered with British names by Vancouver, for example Puget Sound, Whidbey Island, Burrard Inlet, Howe Sound, Jervis Inlet, Point Grey, and the Discovery Islands. Named initially after both Vancouver and the local Spanish commander, Quadra and Vancouver Island was to become just Vancouver Island.

The contrast between oceanic exploration by Britain and other powers became even more marked after Britain and France went to war in 1793. The French overseas empire was destroyed and exploration was dominated by the British. George Bass and Matthew Flinders circumnavigated Tasmania in 1798–9, establishing the fact that it was an island, and thus that ships sailing to Sydney from around the Cape of Good Hope did not need to round Tasmania, but could go through Bass Strait, an example of the value of exploration for navigators and one that contrasted with the situation for Ceylon (Sri Lanka). Having returned to England, Flinders was appointed to carry out an accurate survey of Australia's coast. He explored the southern coast of Australia in 1801–2, and was responsible for the first complete circumnavigation of the continent in 1802–3.

Britain and France were briefly at peace in 1802–3, and this enabled Nicolas-Thomas Baudin, the commander of a French scientific expedition, to take on supplies in Port Jackson (Sydney) before exploring all but the north coast. Flinders and Baudin exchanged charts. Allied for much of the period, British mariners also helped guide Russian interest in the South Pacific.

Firearms

Obtained by indigenous people through trade from Europe, the employment of firearms was linked to the use of often sizeable combined forces in order to pursue operational, indeed strategic, goals. One with a lasting effect was the unification of the Hawaiian archipelago. Replacing, or at least supplementing, spears, clubs, daggers, and sling-shots, guns and cannon were used by Kamehameha (c.1736–1819), who dominated the west coast of the island of Hawai'i, a coast frequented by European ships, and whose army increased in size to about 12,000 men, to help win dominance of that island in 1791, and of those of Maui and O'ahu in 1795, with the key engagements, notably Nu'uanu in 1795, occurring on land. Nu'uanu, or in Hawaiian *kaleleka'anae*, which means the leaping mullet, refers to the defended O'ahu army being driven back to a cliff edge where they were pushed over the 1,000 foot drop. In 1796 and 1803, difficult waters and disease ended Kamehameha's plans to invade the island of Kauai, but, in 1810, Kauai submitted rather than risk invasion, although the submission was precarious for most of the decade.

Kamehameha became the first king of the Hawaiian Islands and unified the legal system of the islands. His successor, Kamehameha II (r. 1819–24), visited Britain, only to die there of measles. In turn, Kamehameha II's younger brother, Kamehameha III (r. 1824–54), had to confront both the impact of disease on population numbers and growing Western pressures, including over religion and independence.

This unification was part of the more widespread process of state formation in Oceania. In Tahiti, in the same period, the Pōmares benefited from Western mercenaries and firearms, in order to unify Tahiti in 1788–1815, subordinating the previous independence of the clan chiefs.

Firearms also served Western expansion, as with the Russians in the Aleutian islands in the 1760s, with cannon effective against the Aleut villages. Massacres and Western diseases were also significant. Effective resistance on the Fox Islands had started in 1761 when traders on Ilmnak were killed. However, five years later, Ivan Solovief, a merchant from Okhotsk, organised a fleet that successively overcame resistance. Moreover, mass conversions of the Kodiak Aleutians began in 1794. The Tlingits in the eastern Aleutian Islands proved more formidable as a result of acquiring British and American firearms, and, in 1802, destroyed the Russian settlement of New Archangel on the island of Sitka. It was re-established in 1804 after a long bombardment of the island by Russian warships. Paralleling the situation in north-east Siberia, where resistance long continued, opposition to Russian rule in Alaska did not stop until it was sold to the United States in 1867.

In contrast, the less numerous indigenous Australians proved easier to subjugate after the British had established a penal colony there in 1788. The indigenous Australian used spears against the muskets of British settlers and troops, and learned new tactical methods in order to lessen the dangers posed by the muskets – not least guerrilla warfare, which included raids on farmhouses.

To a degree, ritualised inter-tribal warfare was downplayed in favour of tribal cooperation against the British. Rather than fire-power alone, the latter were helped in Australia by numerical superiority, which was accentuated by the impact of Western diseases on the indigenous Australians, as well as by tactical developments, notably the use of light infantry, especially in night-time encirclements of indigenous Australian camps. The net effect was a total change in control over a large area.

A pattern of dominance was developed that was to be applied elsewhere in the Pacific. This was the case both where settler colonies were established, as by the French in New Caledonia, and where, instead of settlement, sway was sought over local people.

7

Imperial Expansion, 1788–1840

....

Exploration offered the prospect of a new Pacific geopolitics, one of Britain challenging Spain. Suggested in British publications, including a series of London newspapers on 12–14 October 1786 and Sir John Dalrymple's 'Account of an intended expedition into the South Seas,' published in May 1788, this ambition triggered the concern of the Spanish ambassador who reported in June 1788:

> [I]f until now we have seen as the greatest security of our South Sea possessions the circumstance that, having once passed Cape Horn, the enemy would have neither port nor shelter in such a vast extent of coasts ... today I do not believe we should flatter ourselves with such obstacles, for in the many islands which the English have frequented they have found at all times provisions, firewood and all kinds of assistance; they can leave their sick to be cured; form magazines for as much as they require; they will have shelters not only to careen and repair their vessels, but also to construct others.

A different age, that of British power, seemed in prospect. That year, the East India Company drew up a project for an agreement with the Spanish Royal Philippine Company in which Manila was to become a free port, enabling the British to trade indirectly with South America and, as a result, to obtain silver that could be used in the China trade.

Earlier, Australasia had appeared unwelcoming to Dutch explorers, but Cook's account of his visit in 1770 suggested that it was fertile and could support settlements. In contrast, New Zealand was not settled by Europeans until the following century. Initially, the high British hopes of Australia were to be disappointed, as the harsh climate and difficult ground vegetation created problems, as did scurvy.

Moreover, there were concerns about the impact of the policy back in Britain. In 1789, George III was concerned when three convicted felons chose death instead of transportation: 'It is shocking that men can be so lost to every sentiment of gratitude not to feel the mercy shown them in sparing their lives.' George agreed to a proposal made by the Home Secretary, William Grenville, to execute one in order to encourage the other two to choose Australia. To this end, the felons were offered a week's respite to reconsider, and, after they decided that they preferred Australia, George agreed with Grenville that they should make their submission publicly at the next session of the Old Bailey, the king adding this was 'the best method of preventing similar difficulties with future convicts'.

A failure to provide and produce sufficient supplies ensured that until the Second Fleet arrived in 1790 there were grave difficulties. Thereafter, although profit was uncertain, the situation improved: more fertile soils were cultivated, and Port Jackson on Sydney Cove (the latter named after the Home Secretary) became an important calling-place for whalers and sealers. The new colony was rapidly represented on canvas, and there were convict artists, such as Thomas Watling, who depicted indigenous Australians.

The world's leading maritime power, Britain developed its early position in Australia and became the leading power in the South-West Pacific. Economic entrepreneurs followed exploration, when they were not responsible for it. Australia became the key base for this activity. The first British sealing operation off New Zealand was established in 1792, and the first sealing station began operating on the east coast of New Zealand a decade later. The search for seals led to the 'discovery' of sealing islands, such as Antipodes Island in 1800, Auckland Island in 1806, and both Campbell and Macquarie Islands in 1810. Other voyages sought to supply the new colony in Australia until it could feed itself, while traders imported pork from Pacific islands, especially Tahiti.

Mutiny on the Bounty

A great navigator, William Bligh (1754–1817) entered the navy young, sailing from 1761 and becoming sailing master of Cook's *Resolution* in 1776. Commissioned as a lieutenant after serving against the Dutch in the Battle of Dogger Bank (1781), he responded to post-war demobilisation by serving as a captain in the merchant service before, in 1787, being appointed commander of the *Bounty*, an armed transport. A mutiny on the ship near Tahiti in 1789 led to Bligh and eighteen supporters being placed in a 23-foot open boat that Bligh commanded for over 3,500 nautical miles (4,000 miles), to Timor, via the Barrier Reef, in a 47-day voyage in which no one was lost at sea. An earlier attempt to land at nearby Tofua was repelled by hostile indigenous people, and fear of a similar response prevented Bligh from aiming for Fiji. A good commander, Bligh lacked tact. Subsequently honourably acquitted at the court-martial, Bligh returned to the Pacific twice, but in 1808 faced a rebellion as Governor of New South Wales. He won Nelson's approval for his service as a captain in the battle of Copenhagen in 1801. The 1789 mutiny has been represented in five films, but a stronger cultural reference point is the chocolate-covered coconut bar, the

Bounty, introduced in 1951 by Mars as 'The taste of Paradise'.

Those who mutinied sailed to Tahiti where some were later captured by Captain Edwards of the *Pandora*, but, under Fletcher Christian, nine others and eighteen Tahitians took the *Bounty* on to Pitcairn in 1790. Tension between the Englishmen and the Polynesians, particularly over work and women, led to violence, culminating in 1793 in the killing of many of the Englishmen and then of the Polynesian men.

On the opposite side of the Pacific, on the north-west coast of North America, British traders competed with Americans and Russians, and the trade (as elsewhere) was both destructive and enriching for the indigenous people. The traders wanted sea-otter belts, and offered trinkets, beads, copper, iron, firearms, textiles and alcohol in exchange. Trade brought the disruption and suffering that stemmed from alcoholism, firearms and smallpox. The impact was also great in New Zealand where important firearms played a major role in wars between Māori tribes. So also elsewhere, for example on Nauru, where firearms were linked to the civil war that began in 1878, lasting until 1888.

The Napoleonic wars saw the British establish themselves strongly in the approaches to the Pacific. The French possessions in India and the Indian Ocean were captured, the last in 1810, while first Cape Town (1806) and then Batavia (1811) were taken from the Dutch. Not all the hopes of Pacific power were realised. The brief capture of Buenos Aires in 1806 led to speculation of freeing South America for British trade and of spreading power by means of expeditions to Chile and Mexico, but these proved abortive. Instead, Spain became an ally of Britain in 1808. The Congress of Vienna (1814–15) consolidated this position of British maritime dominance.

Paths Not Taken

From the outset, far from colonisation being an inevitable process, there was reluctance and uncertainty about pursuing plans and initiatives, and a mismatch between enthusiasm at the edge of empire for expansion, and reluctance at home. That Britain did not become the imperial power in Tahiti and Hawai'i was to be important to the politics and character of the Pacific to the present, but the same trend was also seen earlier and elsewhere.

Thus, in 1793, Captain John Hayes hoisted the British flag on the north-west coast of New Guinea, which he called New Albion, and Fort Coronation became the first European post on the island. This was a privately funded expedition, backed by two British merchants in Bengal, in search of valuable nutmeg, and the local people were allegedly welcoming, but Sir John Shore, the Governor-General of India, and his council, sceptical about the economic prospects, refused support, and, in 1795, the base was abandoned. In 1790, the East India Company had not persisted in its interest in a base on the Palau islands, to supply ships sailing to China.

Norfolk Island, which seemed to have limited potential compared to Australia, was evacuated in 1807–14, and the settlement by the British in New South Wales might earlier have followed the same route.

In Australia, once a way had been found across the Blue Mountains in 1813, Lachlan Macquarie, the reforming governor from 1810 to 1821, commissioned the surveying and building of a road to the Bathurst Plains, where he established a government settlement in 1815. An active process of land grants helped encourage expansion, and the government sought to control this by organising surveys, under John Oxley and Thomas Mitchell. This served as the basis for an expansion of government structures. Nineteen counties were declared in New South Wales in 1826.

The same process was seen in Tasmania. The British decision to establish a settlement in Tasmania should be placed in the context of bitter competition with France. In 1802, the French explorer Baudin had appeared in Tasmanian waters which excited British concern. Moreover, there was a quest for new sources of timber for British warships. So also with the range of reasons behind British expansion into West and South Australia, and in New Zealand.

In the case of Tasmania, the warship *Calcutta* was sent to establish a base in the Bass Strait to pre-empt the French, but it was recalled when war resumed, and the convict settlers were taken in the storeship *Cloud* down to the Derwent River. The Risdon camp was declared too shady and cramped, so Hobart was established on the opposite shore. The forest came right down to the water's edge, so that the convicts had to fell big trees to make room for their tents and huts. Then the expected store ship from Sydney was wrecked, and the next two years were the 'starvation years' in which the settlers subsisted on kangaroo meat, wiping out the local population of kangaroo. The convicts were entrusted with muskets to hunt kangaroo. Indeed, the convicts played a major role in the development of the colony. Thus, after doing his time, Henry Rice led two expeditions to explore the east coast of Tasmania and was given two land grants for these services, with his name recorded on the imposing centennial monument on the harbour foreshore at Hobart.

William Pitt the Younger, Prime Minister from 1783 to 1801 and 1804 to 1806, and his mentor on the Board of Trade, Henry Dundas, also saw a much bigger picture than both competition with France, with which war resumed in 1803, and the quest for timber. They grasped the potential of a genuinely global empire linked by trade across the oceans as well as the means for holding strategic harbour locations that could contain the ambitions of all Britain's imperial rivals. The vision also provided a trade outlet for the new British manufactured products from the emerging industrial revolution, and would potentially be based on free trade. Having read the economist Adam Smith, Dundas saw free trade as benefiting Britain and as creating a global realm of cooperation. This was a very early version of the *Pax Britannica* that emerged after 1815. Amidst all this, the indigenous population of the colonies could, it was believed, be uplifted by gaining the benefits of civilisation.

Meanwhile, the first American circumnavigation of the world was intimately linked with trading with societies that did not want Western control. Captain Robert Gray obtained furs on the north-west coast of North America, sold them in Canton, and bought tea there which he sold in Boston. This first circumnavigation by an American ship, made in 1787–90, was organised by Boston merchants, and it was followed by a second, in which Gray entered the Columbia River in 1790. Vancouver and Gray met there in 1792. Fifty fur trade voyages to the north-west coast were made by Americans between 1795 and 1804, but this process was not free from tension: in 1792, Gray clashed with the Kwakiuts in Queen Charlotte Sound, while the Russians regarded the Americans as interlopers.

Aside from its activity in Alaska and the Aleutians, not least with the chartering of a Russian-American Company in 1799, Russia was becoming more active in the North Pacific. Russian naval raids and gunboat diplomacy off Hokkaido and Sakhalin from the 1780s had convinced some Japanese commentators about their need for a navy and coastal artillery The first Russian circumnavigation of the world was achieved in 1804–6 and Russian explorers became more active in the Pacific. Arriving in 1815, Russian traders sought to establish a mercantile and imperial presence in Hawai'i, one, Georg Schäffer, an agent for the Russian-American Company, seeking to be the exclusive agent for Kaua'i's sandalwood trade, and to lead Kaua'i's forces in a conquest of O'ahu, thus reversing Kamehameha's success. Fort Elizabeth was accordingly built on Kaua'i in 1817, with two other forts following. However, Schäffer lacked the backing of the Russian government, while the unification of the archipelago by Kamehameha put paid to these hopes, and his supporters gained control of the forts.

Meanwhile, established in Sonoma County in 1812, Fort Ross followed up Russian interest in the Californian coast from 1803. It was founded as an agricultural and commercial base, and farming settlements were founded nearby. Trade, disease and firepower all lessened indigenous opposition. At this point, indeed, Russia appeared best placed after Spain to bestride the Atlantic, but this colony was hit by the overhunting of sea otters and by the ability to buy food instead for Alaska from the British at Vancouver, a process formalised by agreement in 1838. Fort Ross was therefore sold to John Sutter.

Western commercial activity had a very harsh demographic impact, one that went on hitting home. The whalers who came to Hawai'i brought diarrhoea, influenza, measles, smallpox, tuberculosis, venereal disease and whooping cough, decimating the population. Exploitative Western practice (and, possibly, local sexual mores) ensured that syphilis was particularly devastating. The situation with disease became even worse with time as trade increased in the Pacific, and, in 1853, smallpox hit very hard.

In 1800, the *Argo*, an American ship bound from China for Sydney, was wrecked off Fiji and its survivors were responsible for a terrible epidemic. In the Northland of New Zealand, there was a major influenza outbreak in 1808 which may have killed up to half of the population. The infection probably arrived with early traders from Australia. Measles was the other great killer in New Zealand and missionary diaries noted the dates of outbreaks in the 1820s and 1830s. More generally, the European settlement of New Zealand was made much easier by the disruptions and displacements of Māori tribes, and the drastic reduction of population by disease and internecine wars before 1840.

The Māori were enthusiastic early adopters of capitalism. They both traded potatoes and flax to Sydney, often in their own vessels, and fed the first European arrivals in New Zealand. They grew large quantities of wheat, tobacco, potatoes and vegetables, and often had their own mills. However, as they lost land, the Māori economy shrank, and much of it had virtually disappeared by 1900.

New systems of economic activity were often environmentally harmful. Thus, whereas indigenous peoples' whaling in the northern Pacific does not appear to have depleted whale stocks, the situation was very different when European, notably British and French, and Northern American whalers arrived. Whaling and sealing were prime forms of exploitation, with whaling across the Pacific, especially off New Zealand, and sealing particularly off New Zealand, Norfolk Island, and the Chatham, Hawai'i and Marquesas groups. The depletion of Atlantic whale stocks ensured more Pacific whalers from the 1810s; by 1850, America had several hundred whalers there. Without any interest in conservationist methods or ethos, they embraced inefficient methods that killed many whales, but failed to bring in large numbers of those they had harpooned: instead, many died and fell to the floor of the ocean.

The Russian sea otter and seal catch off Pacific North America fell dramatically by the 1820s as animals were hunted to near extinction, while both the bay whaling of whales that came inshore to breed and sealing had been so devastating off Australia and New Zealand by the 1840s that there were few left to hunt. From the late 1820s, there were declining seal numbers due to overhunting. In 1827, the first shore whaling station was established at Te Awati in the Marlborough Sounds. On land, exploitation was seen in the depletion of sandalwood on Fiji in 1804–14. This was to be followed from the 1820s by the important and lucrative *bêche-de-mer* trade of sea cucumbers for sale to East Asia.

WAR OF 1812

Centred in eastern North America and nearby seas, the Anglo-American conflict of 1812–15 also affected the Pacific, which was a clear sign of its growing prominence in the Western world. In the frigate *Essex*, David Porter successfully attacked British shipping in the South Pacific. He captured twelve whalers and their valuable cargo off the Galápagos in 1813, and claimed the island of Nuku Hiva in the Marquesas for America, naming it Madison's Island. This was never acknowledged by the American government and the Marquesas became French in 1842.

The voyage of the 32-gun *Essex* was part of a major extension in American trade warfare, but Porter was forced to surrender after bombardment by British warships off Valparaiso in Chile in 1814. On land, it was not much use for the Americans to advance claims to sections of the Pacific coast of North America if, once they arrived, or sailed there, they were vulnerable to British naval power. On 30 November 1813, Fort Astoria, the base on the south bank of the Columbia River established in 1811 by the *Tonquin*, a ship belonging to John Jacob Astor's Pacific Fur Company, was successfully captured by the *Racoon* and renamed Fort George. The fort had already been sold on 7 October to the Canadian-based North West Company. John McTavish, a company trader, had explained to the Astorians that a British frigate was en route and had successfully suggested such a purchase, but its captain, William Black, insisted on going through the motions of seizing the position.

Latin American Wars of Independence

The Spanish Pacific was ruptured by the Latin American Wars of Independence, conflicts in which British-supported Chilean naval power proved important, notably in the successful invasion of Spanish-held Peru in 1820-1, and in the earlier blockade. However, in 1816, the batteries of the Real Felipe fortress at Callao repulsed an attempt by blockading ships to bombard the port, and, in 1819, an attack on the fortress. It was successfully besieged in 1819-21, recaptured by the Spaniards, and then surrendered by them in 1826. These wars increased the number of Western states with a Pacific seaboard, and, in some cases, islands in the Pacific.

The ending of Spanish rule left four states on its former Pacific coast. Mexico, independent in 1821 and stretching to include California, was also united with Central America down to Panama, which was part of the Republic of Greater Colombia which also included modern Ecuador. Peru and Chile divided the remainder of the coastline. This situation changed rapidly. In 1823, the United Provinces of Central America broke away from Mexico; in 1825, Bolivia, which included a Pacific coastline near Antofagasta but no offshore islands, became independent; and, in 1830, Ecuador followed. The collapse of the United Provinces of Central America in 1838 left Guatemala, Salvador, Honduras and Costa Rica as independent states on the Pacific.

Meanwhile, the commercial logic of Spain's Pacific empire had been lost. In the Philippines, which remained a Spanish colony but one where British capital and trade was important, there was a shift from trade with Mexico to links via the Indian Ocean, including the import of textiles. Spanish coins were melted down and used for Sydney-struck coins from 1814. Spanish warships in the Philippines focused on antipiracy operations and amphibious operations.

Surveying

The Royal Navy played the leading role in surveying the Pacific. Thus, Frederick Beechey and Edward Belcher surveyed the Pacific coast of South America, while in 1837–43, *Beagle* surveyed Australian coastal waters, and, in 1848, *Acheron* began the first systematic survey of New Zealand waters, being succeeded, in 1851–5, by *Pandora*, which produced detailed harbour charts. The two ships covered nearly all the coast and sent 250 charts to the Hydrographic Office. In 1842–7, Belcher surveyed the coast of Borneo, the Philippines and Taiwan, part of the process by which Sir Francis Beaufort, the Hydrographer to the Navy from 1829 to 1855, sought to fill the gaps in his map of the world recording the coast covered by surveys.

In 1845, Henry Kellett was given command of the survey ship *Herald* as part of a survey of the North American coast from Guayaquil to Vancouver, including the Galápagos and British Columbia. Under Henry Denham, the *Herald* from 1852 to 1861 then surveyed the Australian coast and much of the South-West Pacific, notably the Fiji Group, New Caledonia, Vanuatu, and Norfolk Island. This was designed to find safe routes for shipping. Naturalists were carried on such voyages, for example Thomas Huxley and John MacGillivray on *Rattlesnake* when it surveyed Australia and New Guinea in 1846–50.

Others also played a role: Jules Dumont d'Urville, a talented French explorer, began exploring and collecting botanical and zoological material particularly off and on New Zealand. In a circumnavigation in 1826–9, he carried out improved surveys of Marlborough Sound and also showed that what was to be named D'Urville Island was not part of the mainland as Cook had reported. D'Urville also found the site of Lapérouse's shipwreck and mapped many of the islands of the western Pacific. Advancing the terms Malaisia, Micronesia and Melanesia, he differentiated them from Polynesia. The Russians explored the coast of Alaska and made unsuccessful attempts to discover a North-West Passage from the west in 1815–18 and 1820–1, as well as probing Antarctica.

CHRISTIANITY

Motivated by a conviction of the need to offer salvation, Spanish colonisation had from the outset seen Christian prosleytisation, and, from the late eighteenth century, in part driven also by a sense that they had encountered barbarism, the British followed suit. This was the case both with British colonies, such as Australia, and also in areas outside British control, such as New Zealand, where there were missionaries from 1814, Hawai'i where there was large-scale conversion in the 1820s and successful opposition by missionaries to the king marrying his sister, and Tahiti where John Harris, sent by the London Missionary Society, arrived in 1797 and took care to associate himself with the powerful Pōmare clan. On the same voyage, on the *Duff*, William Pascoe Crook travelled to the Marquesas where he spent 1797–8, later producing an account of the islands. Missionary activity at this point was more successful than in East or South Asia which, in turn, encouraged further activity.

William Ellis (1794–1872) of the London Missionary Society left for the Pacific in 1816, spending his time in the Tahiti and Hawai'i groups, transcribing Hawaiian into a Roman alphabet, before returning to England in 1824, at the same time as Kamehameha II came on his visit. Ellis published extensively, most notably *Polynesian Researches* (1829, second edition, 1832). In the Preface, he captured a sense of discontinuity:

All their usages of antiquity having been entirely superseded by the new order of things that has followed the subversion of their former system, the knowledge of but few of them is retained by the majority of the inhabitants, while the rising generation is growing up in total ignorance of all that distinguished their ancestors from themselves.

John Beecham, a Methodist missionary, told a committee of the House of Commons in 1835:

No sooner does the gospel begin to operate in the mind of the heathen than it leads to the first step in civilisation, which was for the people to feel, under the teaching of the missionaries, that a more decent exterior is necessary; and thus the first step is taken in civilization, and clothing is introduced.

Particular missionary societies focused on specific groups, for example the London Missionary Society on the Cook Islands and Samoa, and the Wesleyan Methodist Society on Fiji and Tonga. John Williams of the London Missionary Society set out to the Tahitian archipelago in 1817 and moved on to Samoa in 1830. In 1834, Williams returned to Britain where he oversaw the printing of his translation of the New Testament into Rarotongan. Returning in 1837, he and another missionary, James Harris, were killed and eaten by cannibals on the island of Erromango in the New Hebrides.

Missionaries were very much involved in establishing a British presence. George Pritchard, a missionary for the London Missionary Society, was consul first at Tahiti and then, after being expelled by the French, on Samoa. His son, William, was first consul at Fiji, only to fall foul of the influential Wesleyan missionaries.

In turn, French Catholic missionaries became a major presence in Tahiti from the 1830s in the Gambier and Marquesa groups and encouraged French governmental interests. The deportation of French missionaries from Tahiti Iti in 1836 led to French military intervention and takeover in 1846. The French had enforced toleration for Catholicism in Hawai'i by the threat of attack in 1839. In 1886, a Seventh-Day Adventist converted many of the Pitcairners from Anglicanism. Prosleytisation extended Western norms, but this also involved a degree of local agency and interaction, as earlier in the Philippines.

Judging Harshly from Prejudice

A Dictionary, Geographical, Statistical, and Historical: Of the Various Countries, Places and Principal Natural Objects in the World (1840, 2nd edition, 1849) by John Ramsay McCulloch (1789–1864), Professor of Political Economy at University College London, was an influential work that presented a very harsh view of the Polynesians:

> Cannibalism is still practised in the Marquesas, and some of the other groups. The islanders, however, do not live in the rude independence of savage life, but acknowledge the arbitrary sway of hereditary chiefs ... Some attempts have been made to introduce governments of a more liberal character; but they have signally failed.
>
> The habits of the natives are still in many respects those of barbarians ... the females ... are oppressed and degraded in the last degrees ... The efforts of missionaries have produced little radical change for the better in the morals of the mass of the population.

Pacific Expansionism

The mistake is the assumption that Western powers were the only ones responsible is particularly underlined by the case of Chatham Islands which were invaded by Māori from New Zealand in 1835. The Moriori people, Polynesians of Māori descent, who had settled in about 1500, were largely slaughtered, with the survivors enslaved. To blame the expansionism solely on guns obtained by trade with Europeans is in part to make the means the cause. On the other hand, there was the migration and movement of Māori tribes to avoid attacks by neighbours with muskets. Rather than a deliberate conquest, the tribes Ngāti Tama and Ngāti Mutunga escaped to the Chathams as a gentle peaceful people, and saw the islands as a safe refuge. But after initial good relations, misunderstandings multiplied and the newcomers brutally attacked the Moriori, who were pacifists. There could have been 1,600 of them in 1800 and they were reduced to only 100. In 1842, the islands officially became part of the colony of New Zealand, and in 1863 the slaves were freed by the resident magistrate.

In Fiji, British influence, and then control, was welcome not only as a way to limit American pressure, but also to deter Tongan expansionism, as well as to ensure order within Fiji.

The Oregon Question: Early Stages

Under the Louisiana Purchase from France of 1803, America claimed a vast tract, not least the Oregon Country, which included the modern states of Oregon and Washington, as well as part of Canada. The dispatch, in 1804, of the Corps of Discovery, an expedition under Meriwether Lewis and William Clark that had been planned before the Louisiana Purchase, asserted American interests across the new possessions to the Pacific. The expedition also sought to establish an overland route there, a goal for which it was important to discover the headwaters of the Columbia and then follow it to the Pacific, which was reached at the close of 1805. This was seen by President Thomas Jefferson as a way to thwart the possibility that the British would develop the potential for transcontinental routes shown by Alexander McKenzie, who had crossed the continent in Canada in 1793, and it helped focus attention on the Pacific Northwest as a key area of American interest. Later, there was also a drive to improve relations after an Anglo-American convention of 1818 agreed that the Oregon Country was to be jointly administered for ten years without prejudicing existing claims. The Convention excluded Russia (in Alaska) and Spain and its successor Mexico.

Differing Images

The *Atlas Istorii Geograficheskikh Otkrytt I Issledovanii* [*Historical Atlas of Geographical Discoveries of Russia*] (1959) provided much information on Russian explorers whose journeys were ignored in Western historical atlases, and notably so of the North Pacific.

8

Growing Outside Control, 1840–1898

....

Shipwreck

In 1849, the British survey ship *Rattlesnake* was approached by Barbara Crawford Thompson (1831–1916), who had survived the wreck of a cutter on the Madjii Reef at Horn Island. The captain, her lover, had disappeared, presumed drowned, and she was adopted by a clan leader of the Kuarareg people, a Torres Strait Islander group, who thought her the returned spirit of a recently dead daughter. Called Gioma, she lived on Prince of Wales Island for five years. Less happily, there were murderous reprisals in 1870 against the Kaurareg after their killing of the crew of a schooner.

The major powers proceeded to spread their authority through the establishment of protectorates and colonies. With Spain not using its positions in the Philippines and Micronesia as a base for significant expansion, Britain and France were to the fore and confidently so as part of their wider imperialism. Thus, *Notes to Accompany Mr Wyld's Model of the Earth, Leicester Square* (1851), a sixty-foot-high globe exhibited from 1851 to 1862 in the centre of the British empire, praised it including stating:

What comparisons suggest themselves between the condition of the Pacific region in the time of Cook and now? What was then held by illiterate savages now constitutes the rising communities of New South Wales. There are Tahiti and hundreds of islands with Christian churches and schools.

Control over the whole of Oceania, military, political, economic and cultural, was indeed transformed in the nineteenth century. There was resistance, but it failed. Thus, Tahitian opposition to French control was crushed in 1844–6. In Samoa, civil wars between rival factions in 1886–94 and 1898–9 provided an opportunity for German intervention and Western expansion. The Hawaiian interest in Pacific expansion in the 1880s, including an unsuccessful attempt in 1887 to intervene in the Samoan conflict, ended when America appropriated the sovereign kingdom of Hawai'i. Indeed, Hawai'i next entered military history in 1941 when it was attacked, as America's leading Pacific naval base, by the Japanese in the Pearl Harbor operation.

AMERICA AS A PACIFIC POWER

With the focus generally on Britain and France, there can be a tendency to downplay the growing role of America, one that was of particular importance if the continental coastline is also considered. In 1838, Lieutenant Charles Wilkes was placed in command of the Depot of Charts and Instruments, and also given command of a six-ship expedition to explore the Pacific, which led to sightings of the Antarctic continent. Wilkes, moreover, explored the Pacific coastline of North America, a means of asserting American interests. Returning in 1842, he publicised his work and ambition with a multi-volume narrative appearing in 1844. British humanitarians, who objected to his brutal treatment of the islanders in Fiji, Samoa and elsewhere, took a bleaker view. Wilkes's expedition was related to greater American interest in the Pacific, with the Hawaiian Islands proving a focus of interest.

Abel Upshur, who became Secretary of the Navy in 1841, proposed the establishment of a naval base there, while Daniel Webster, as Secretary of State, announced the so-called Tyler Doctrine in 1842: that America would oppose their annexation by any European power, which was, in part, a response to British and French expansion in the Pacific.

The Oregon Question in the 1840s

The earlier *modus vivendi* with Britain about the coast between California and Alaska was disrupted by growing American interest in the area, not least increasing overland settlement and political pressure for entrenching territorial control. Moreover, there was conviction that a wide-ranging position on the Pacific would benefit America, both as far as the hinterland was concerned and with regard to opportunities for advancement across the Pacific. The trans-Pacific was viewed in terms of trade, rather than land, and there was a powerful sense that East Asia would provide new opportunities for American commerce and industry, not least as Britain's victory over China in the Opium War of 1839–42 encouraged a belief in new possibilities there. President John Tyler (r. 1841–5) sought to develop commercial links with China, leading to the Treaty of Wanghia (1844), by which America gained commercial rights at five ports.

Wilkes's expedition reached Puget Sound in 1841 and he extolled it as a commercial base for America, one that was better than the Columbia River which had a major sandbar near its entrance. American bellicosity over the Oregon Question led to the threat of conflict with Britain but, in 1846, a compromise was agreed, extending the 49th Parallel boundary line to the Pacific, with Britain also receiving Vancouver Island.

Conquering California

California was a different matter as Mexico had succeeded there to Spain's territorial position. San Francisco and San Diego were sought as bases for the exploitation both of the Pacific and of the western littoral of North America. Already, in 1842, American warships under Thomas Ap Catesby Jones, who erroneously believed that war had begun, briefly seized Monterey and San Diego. The 1844 presidential campaign committed James Polk, the successful candidate, to the goal of advancing to the Pacific.

During the Mexican-American war, American forces advanced to the Pacific in 1846, a bland remark that provides little idea of the difficulty of the task for the Pacific littoral was protected by a desert hinterland. Colonel Stephen Kearny, Commander of the Army of the West, advanced from Fort Leavenworth to Santa Fé and then to San Diego.

Meanwhile, California, the sale of which to Britain had been mentioned by Mariano Paredes, the Mexican President, was convulsed in 1846 by the Bear Flag Revolt mounted by American settlers against a weak Mexican administration. The American Pacific squadron played a major role, occupying Monterey, San Francisco, San Diego, Santa Barbara and Los Angeles. Charles Bankhead, the British envoy in Mexico, observed: 'Misgovernment and internal strife have done much to aid them [the Americans] in this enterprise, and to place in their power one of the most vulnerable possessions in the habitable globe, and whose resources are as yet most imperfectly known.' Indeed, gold was discovered in 1849. The Mexican inhabitants in southern California rebelled against American rule in September 1846 only to be defeated that winter.

The Americans went on in the Pacific to attack the west coast of Mexico, ships being joined by others that had sailed round Cape Horn. Guaymas and Matzatlán were captured in late 1847. Intervening in Mexico, France, in turn, captured Guaymas in 1865.

America in the Pacific, the 1850s

America's success over Mexico in 1846–8, combined with the settlement of the Oregon Question, led to bold plans for further expansion and activity. The range was dramatic, and notably so in the Pacific. Both the experience of the value of deployment there during the Mexican War, and the new interests and possibilities that followed the annexation of California, led to greater interest in the Pacific, and this interest was not restricted to the eastern Pacific. Indeed, after the war, when the USS *Ohio* made its final cruise, it visited both Hawai'i and Samoa. More significantly, in 1853, a squadron of four ships under Commodore Matthew Perry anchored at the entrance to Tokyo Bay in order to persuade Japan to inaugurate relations.

A Japanese-American Intermediary

In 1841, in the northern Pacific, an American whaler rescued Nakahama Manjirō, the shipwrecked son of a fisherman. Educated in America, he became an officer on a whaler in 1848 and, three years later, returned to Japan. A teacher there, he was a translator when the American Perry mission arrived to 'open up' Japan.

After presenting a letter from President Millard Fillmore (1850–3), Perry sailed to China, declaring that he would return the following year. Having wintered on the Chinese coast, itself an important display of naval capability, and made naval demonstrations in areas of Japanese interest, namely the Ryukyu and Bonin Islands, which secured a coaling concession from the ruler of Okinawa, competing with British interests there, Perry returned to Japan with a larger squadron of eight warships. He negotiated the Treaty of Kanagawa of 1854, which provided for American diplomatic representation, coaling stations, the right for American ships to call at two ports, and humane treatment for shipwrecked American soldiers. These terms left deep grievances, but reflected the extent to which force underlay America's advancing merchants' frontier around the Pacific, with the developing Pacific trade system seen as a particular national opportunity. Perry returned to America, but, in 1854–5, another American naval expedition, the North Pacific Exploring and Surveying Expedition, greatly expanded hydrographic knowledge of Japanese waters including the Bonins, as well as of the Marianas. In the south-west Pacific, American warships had rarely ventured west of the Hawaiian archipelago prior to the 1850s, but Commodore William Mervine, who took command of the Pacific Squadron in 1854, was keen to champion American commercial interests and instructed his captains accordingly.

Fillmore's successor, Franklin Pierce (1853–7), was interested in acquiring Alaska, Cuba and Hawai'i, albeit without success and, in a context of mounting international competition, the British helped thwart the last. The protection of American interests led to the landing of American forces in East Asia and the Pacific: in Shanghai in 1854, 1855 and 1859, Canton in 1856, and Fiji in 1855 and 1858.

The Pig and Egg Wars, 1859

A boundary controversy over the Suan Juan Islands in Vancouver Sound escalated in 1859 when an American settler shot a pig belonging to the Hudson's Bay Company. Without authorisation from the federal government, General William Harney, the military governor of the Washington Territory, sent troops to the island, and, in turn, the British deployed forces in the archipelago. Thanks in large part to the restraint of British naval officers on the spot, conflict was avoided, and the dispute was ultimately settled by arbitration.

The Egg War followed in 1863, with two people killed on

---

the Farallon Islands off San Francisco as rival companies pursued seabird eggs.

Guano

Due to its high nitrogen, phosphate and potassium content, seabird excrement is useful as manure, and this ensured that islands with many seabirds were a prime target of nineteenth-century entrepreneurs. The Guanay cormorant, Peruvian pelican and Peruvian booby were prime producers, with Peru's Chincha Islands the most productive site.

Nationalisation by Peru in 1840 was followed by large-scale exploitation, with 1870 the prime export year. Chile seized the islands in the War of the Pacific (1879–83) and its revenues thereby increased.

Under the 1856 Guano Islands Act, America claimed to be able to annex uninhabited Pacific and Caribbean islands that contained guano deposits, which led to claims to Enderbury, McKean, Howland, Baker, Canton, Flint, Caroline, Maldens, Jarvis, Starbuck, Fanning, Palmyra, and Clipperton Islands, the Phoenix and Dangerous groups, and Swains, Christmas and Johnston atolls. Britain similarly claimed Kiritimati and Malden islands.

More generally, the guano industry, which saw much environmental damage as well as harsh living conditions for its largely Chinese and Pacific islander, notably Hawaiian, workers, was displaced by the use of synthetic fertilisers from 1913. Whereas about fifty-three million seabirds lived in Peru's guano islands prior to the boom, by 2011 there were only 4.2 million there.

The Eastern Pacific

Ecuador annexed the Galápagos Islands, then essentially a visiting stop for whalers, in 1832. Clipperton Island was annexed by France in 1858, while Mexico also claimed it, establishing in 1897 a colony that lasted until 1917 when lighthouse keeper Victoriano Alvarez, the sole male left after the others had died of scurvy, declared himself king and assaulted the women, one of whom then killed him. The few survivors were evacuated in 1917 and, in 1931, Italy, the agreed arbiter, awarded the island to France. The Americans briefly occupied Clipperton in 1944–5.

Easter Island was occupied by the Chilean navy in 1888 in order to provide a strategic position once a Panama canal was built, for that was seen as likely to transform Pacific geopolitics. The inhabitants were restricted to one settlement and the Williamson-Balfour Company, a Chilean company founded by Scots, ran most of the island for sheep production until 1953.

AMERICA ACQUIRES ALASKA

The American acquisition of Alaska and the Aleutian Islands from Russia in 1867 was scarcely the product of pressure which the Americans were in no position to exert. Instead, for $7,200,000, they bought the territory which the Russians were keen to sell, not least because the Russian-American Company, the finances of which had long been precarious, was close to bankruptcy. At the time, there were only 2,000 white settlers. Critics condemned both the idea and the expense, referring to the episode as 'Seward's Folly', although only a small minority of the American press used this term or even criticised William Seward, the Secretary of State, for making the purchase which was generally supported as another large expansion of territory.

The gain certainly pre-empted the possibility of British acquisition, although that was scarcely an option, and also placed British Columbia and Vancouver Island, which had become British Crown Colonies in 1858, between two areas of American territory. Indeed, disputes over the boundary of the Alaskan Panhandle were only settled in 1903. The new American territory created other issues in relations with Britain, including the transit of cattle through British Columbia en route for the American garrison. In December 1867, the Foreign Office instructed the Governor of British Columbia to help America's authorities in Alaska in their relations with the indigenous people if required. There was no wish to sow or exploit problems for the Americans.

Novo Archangel'sk, the Russian headquarters, was renamed Sitka and the Americans rapidly established forts in order to assert their control. The coastal location of these forts reflected the distribution of population, the possibilities for trade, and the extent to which any attack by other powers would come by sea. The forts included Fort Tongass, on Portland Channel facing British territory, Fort Kodiak, Fort Wrangel on an island at the mouth of the Stikine River (where British efforts to penetrate had been blocked in 1834), and Fort Kenay near the head of Cook Inlet. In 1868, the Alaska force rose to 21 officers and 530 men, but, in 1870, all the posts were abandoned except Sitka from which the garrison was withdrawn in 1877. It was decided that ships would be more effective than troops in maintaining order in a territory without roads. Missionary activity among the local population was also seen as consolidating the American presence.

Alaska was scarcely going to be the basis for expansion into North-East Asia, where the continental land-mass was under the authority of Russia which was also expanding its power offshore into Sakhalin: Northern Sakhalin in 1853 and Southern in 1875. The Kurile Islands only came under Japanese control in 1875, but it would have required a particularly dynamic and risky American policy to have taken pre-emptive steps in the Kuriles or southern Sakhalin. Such a step would have been a challenge for American capabilities, although in 1871 two warships and a small marine force attacked Korea in revenge for the burning, five years earlier, of an armed merchant schooner, the *General Sherman*, that had sought to open up Korea to American trade. In 1871, about 650 Koreans were killed, but the American use of force, particularly superior firepower, yielded them no benefit and their force sailed off.

Russian policy was the key factor in the northern Pacific. Rather than being pushed out by the Americans, the Russians did not wish to retain Alaska and also had accepted the organisation, with successive measures in 1859, 1862 and 1863, of British control nearby in what became Canada. Instead, the Russians were far more interested in the China question. Indeed, the 'Eastern Question' was spreading to Pacific shores. Appointed Commander-in-Chief of the China and East Indies Station in 1854, Rear-Admiral Sir James Stirling feared Russian pressure on China and Japan and American on Japan. He argued, in 1855, that by capturing the coast of Manchuria, Russia would be freed from the constraints of ice and become a threatening Pacific naval power. In response, he pressed for the establishment of 'a maritime empire with all its concomitant adjuncts of naval positions, postal communications, hydrographical surveys, and steam factories and dock yards'. In the Penjdeh Crisis of 1885, the British plans included an amphibious attack on the Russian naval base of Vladivostok which was to be preceded by the establishment of a base in Korea.

The Arrow (or Second Opium) War between China and an Anglo-French alliance provided Russia with the opportunity to make territorial gains, first the Amur region to the north of the River Amur in 1858 and, subsequently, the Ussuri region between there and the Sea of Japan in 1860, the port of Vladivostok being founded that year. This expansion did not encourage Russia to take an interest in the opposite shores of the Pacific, nor indeed in the ocean itself. Instead, other than the Far East and, increasingly, the Chinese province of Manchuria, Central Asia, the Caucasus and the Balkans were the key areas for Russian expansion. Later, the Pacific power that was to be of most concern to Russia was Japan, not America.

Secretary of State Seward had plans for areas other than Alaska. The Midway Islands were annexed in 1867, providing a mid-Pacific base on the way to East Asian waters. Seward suggested gaining Hawai'i and building a canal across Central America, and was reported as wishing to negotiate with Nicaragua 'for the cession of one of her Pacific ports', a measure that would have greatly increased American influence in the Pacific, providing also a forward base from which to exert pressure if necessary on Mexico and Colombia. In 1870, the British government noted the inaccurate rumour that Ecuador would cede the Galápagos Islands to America. In the event, the Americans, instead, pressed forward in the 1890s.

SPAIN

There was a late surge of Spain as a Pacific power, and on both sides of the ocean. In 1864–6, Spain, then the world's fourth naval power, initially in pursuit of reparations over a murderous brawl, eventually fought Peru, Chile, Bolivia and Ecuador (notably Peru and Chile), in a war formally declared in 1865 that included the bombardment of Callao, the port for Lima, and, more damagingly, of Valparaiso. The guano-rich Chincha Islands were occupied. However, it did not persist with the conflict, not least because there were no coaling and provisioning ports available. In the Philippines, Spain extended its power, taking control over the Sulu archipelago from mid-century and using the navy to mount anti-piracy campaigns.

Suppressing Resistance

During this century, indigenous resistance was repeatedly overcome, including in North America and Australia and, although less easily and completely, in New Zealand. In California, the indigenous population was brutally reduced in the 1850s by conflict as well as disease. The federal army did not control the situation there. Instead, local volunteer forces inflicted great damage. They were in a position to do so there, as the settler population in California rose greatly that decade, while the indigenous people lacked unity or a strong military tradition. In contrast, the military played a role in suppressing opposition near Puget Sound in 1856.

In Australia, the indigenous population was hit hard from the outset by Western diseases, especially smallpox and influenza. These not only killed many, but also hit social patterns and morale. Resistance was also affected by the very fragmented nature of the indigenous 'nation', which greatly lessened the prospect of cooperation. The extent to which a failure to adopt firearms on any scale lessened the chances for resistance is controversial. It can be seen as a sign of inflexibility, but also as a response to the limitations of early nineteenth-century firearms and to the difficulty of obtaining supplies. By the second half of the century, the settlers enjoyed an important technological advantage thanks to the spread of breech-loading rifles and were able to make rapid advances, especially in Queensland.

Meanwhile, the government by Britain of eastern Australia changed. With the exception of Van Diemen's Land, renamed Tasmania in 1853, all the Pacific coast was under New South Wales, but its Southern District became Victoria in 1851 and its Northern District Queensland in 1859, leaving the Middle District as New South Wales. Tasmania, Victoria and New South Wales were granted self-government in 1855 and Queensland in 1859.

Changing Environment

The Pacific environment changed in many ways. There were additions. For example, in 1769, prior to the arrival of Cook, New Zealand had had a limited range of mammals: dogs, bats and rats. Cook brought pigs. Later Western settlers added cattle, sheep, horses, rabbits, sparrows, trout and frogs, and, by 1878, there were thirteen million sheep. Sheep were brought into Australia from 1797, seven rams and three ewes being sent in 1804. There was also much depletion, destruction and devastation across the Pacific, both of species, both animal and plant, and of habitats. Pollution was an issue that was not sufficiently appreciated at the time. The first major modern Japanese pollution incident, that at the Ashio copper mine, greatly affected downriver life from 1890. As was so often the case, river pollution flushed eventually into the ocean, which was to be a repeated problem with Japanese mining, industry and construction.

New Zealand

A French colonisation expedition arrived in New Zealand just after the signing of the Treaty of Waitangi in 1840 and the declaration of British sovereignty. The French established a settlement at Akaroa, and the town still has French street names, but a British warship swiftly proclaimed and demonstrated the sovereignty of the British Crown.

The failure of the British to honour the Treaty of Waitangi led to the Northern War of 1845–6, in which Hōne Keke chopped down the flagpole at Waitangi three times.

However, there was a rapid process of British expansion in New Zealand. The settlements founded in the early 1840s, notably

Wellington (1840), Auckland (1841), Nelson (1841) and New Plymouth (1841), were followed by expansion on the east coast of the South Island, particularly with Dunedin (1848) and Christchurch (1850), and then with significant expansion in the 1850s, especially with Gisborne (1852), Invercargill (1855) and Napier (1855). The western side of South Island had little settlement, but Greymouth was founded there in 1865. Separated from New South Wales in 1841, New Zealand was granted self-government in 1852. In 1842, the Chatham, Bounty and Antipodes Islands were transferred by Britain.

The course of conflict in New Zealand indicated the extent to which Western power projection spanned the globe, but also that its progress was far from easy. The Māori used well-sited trench and *pā* (fort) systems that were difficult to bombard or storm, and inflicted serious defeats on the British, for example Ruapekapeka *pā* in 1846 with its underground pits and tunnel. In 1860, in the First Taranaki War, Te Ati Awa Māori were able to inflict heavy casualties on British troops at the *pā* at Puketakauere and Onukwkaitara. Elsewhere the British were more successful in using artillery bombardment to get the Māori to abandon *pā* but the Māori were able to do so without heavy losses. Without either side winning a decisive victory, a ceasefire was negotiated in 1861.

Further north, conflict broke out in 1863 as the British sought to expand their control over land to the south of Auckland, which involved road and fort construction. The British deployed up to 9,000 men, as well as local colonists. The major clash at Rangiriri (1863) saw the outnumbered Māori surrender mobility in order to defend a position in which they were battered by artillery fire from land and sea, but inflicted heavy losses on infantry staging frontal attacks, before leaving their fortifications at night. The following year, at Pukehinahina, the Māori lured British forces into a *pā* before inflicting heavy losses on them and then retreating.

In 1865, conflict spread. The British responded by construct-ing forts at river mouths on the contested west coast of North Island. The following year, *pa* were captured but, in 1868, Māori forces under Titokowaru defeated colonial forces twice at Te Ngutu-o-te-Manu and once at Moturoa. However, Titokowaru's support ebbed in 1869 and the colonists were able to regain ground.

Also on North Island in 1868, another Māori leader, Te Kooti, launched a vigorous attack on colonial settlements. The response was mostly by colonial and pro-British Māori forces as most regu-lar units had now left. A siege of the *pā* at Nga Tapa in 1869 went wrong for the besieged Te Kooti, and he found less Māori support than he had anticipated. Hostilities continued, but, by 1872, Te Kooti had clearly lost. Militarily, the mobility of the colonial forces, including the Arawa Flying Column, was combined with a process of steady entrenchment. Roads, telegraph lines and Armed Constabulary stations were all constructed. As more generally with Western imperialism, local cooperation was crucial to success, while, in military terms, entrenchment and battle were two mutually supporting sides of the same coin.

NEW CALEDONIA

New Caledonia was more similar to Australasia than to the British Pacific islands, as there was a substantial population of European settlers, while the Kanak were moved onto reserves by the French, their resistance greatly weakened in conflicts notably in 1878–9 but also, to a lesser extent, in 1897 and 1901. Moreover, New Caledonia, like Australia, was mineral-rich and therefore of great interest to French elites. While some of the local chiefs cooper-ated with the French, others were subject to the clearances linked to French pursuit of their interests, not least the provision of land for settlers, especially for mining and for cattle stations. This was part of an essentially brutal and violent ruling system.

HAWAI'I

In contrast, Hawai'i retained independence for longer. Indeed, Kalākaua (r. 1874–91) commissioned and fitted out a sometime guano trader as a warship, the *Ka'imiloa*. Intended as a training vessel for the fledgling Hawaiian navy, this was equipped with four brass cannon and two Gatling guns. The captain was British and the standing regulations for the British navy were adopted for its Hawaiian counterpart, which was designed to give effect to the plan for a Pacific confederation of Hawai'i, Samoa, Tonga, and the Cook Islands, intended to prevent Western annexations; to that end, the ship was sent to Samoa in 1887. Germany saw this as interference in its plans and German warships shadowed the *Ka'imiloa* but, faced by serious indiscipline among the crew, the Hawaiian vessel was recalled and mothballed. In 1893, the monarchy was overthrown and, in 1900, Hawai'i became an American colony, which ensured that economic dominance by the 'Big Five' companies was strengthened.

JAPAN

Japan followed a different trajectory. The impact of the West led to a degree of modernisation, in part due to the threat of military attack. The Tokugawa shogunate began a serious effort to remodel its army, but that process had already started with domains such as Choshu and, as a result, the shogunal army was defeated in 1866. This was followed in 1868 by civil war and the overthrow of the Tokugawa shogunate in the Meiji Restoration with control established in Hokkaido in 1869. The civil war demonstrated the strength of Western weaponry, and the political shift made it easier to advocate and introduce a military order. The privileged, caste-nature of military service was replaced by conscription, which was introduced in 1869. The two systems were brought into conflict in 1877 with a substantial samurai force armed with swords and matchlock muskets into combat with the new army of conscripted peasants, individual military prowess and bravery succumbing to organised, disciplined force. Japanese military development was supported by policies of education and industrialisation. A Western-style navy was also developed, looking toward Britain for training and ships.

The pressure for military change in part arose from external challenges. Opportunity as well as concern over the possible ambitions of other Western powers led Russia to occupy Sakhalin in 1853, so brushing aside an earlier Japanese presence. The Japanese feared the Russians would press on to Hokkaido where the Goryokaku Fort was accordingly built in Hakodate in 1865. It can still be visited. The issue was settled, initially, by a condominium over Sakhalin and a partition of the Kuriles and, subsequently, in 1876, by a treaty by which Russia obtained Sakhalin and Japan the Kuriles. These treaties reflected the degree to which military development and territorial expansion led to the loss of control by peoples in what became buffer zones between the major powers, zones that were progressively occupied by imperial powers.

Further into the Pacific, Japan annexed the Bonin Islands in 1875, brushing aside other claims. The uninhabited Volcano Islands were settled by Japanese from the Izu Islands, independent of government direction, in 1889. Government annexation followed in in 1891.

THE WAR OF THE PACIFIC

The War of the Pacific, which began in 1879, was the largest-scale conflict in the New World between the War of the Triple Alliance (1864–70) and the present. This conflict, involving Chile, Bolivia (then a Pacific power) and Peru, and largely waged by regular forces, was, in part, fought over the rich deposits of nitrates in the Atacama Desert. In part, the concern over these deposits reflected the demands of war, as nitrates were of great value for explosives as well as for fertilizers. Bolivia's demand, in breach of a treaty agreement, for more revenue from an Anglo-Chilean company working the deposits triggered the crisis, and Peru backed Bolivia. Overcoming a serious initial lack of preparation, resources and command skills, Chile took the initiative and landed an army at Antofagasta in 1879, advancing, after the sinking of the main Peruvian warship, to overrun the Bolivian Pacific coastline and then to press on to invade southern Peru. The capture of the strongly fortified Peruvian port of Arica in 1880 threw light on the importance, yet also vulnerability, of fortified positions. Exposed to attack as a result of Chilean naval strength, Arica nevertheless resisted a naval bombardment, but the overrunning of the rest of the province left the garrison exposed. Arica still had to be captured, and, as a land bombardment failed to force a capture, the Chileans had to resort to a night-time storming.

This was a conflict in which the availability of Western weaponry including breech-loading rifles, Gatling guns, and steel-barrelled artillery, was important, but there was also a distinctive style of conflict. First, in marked contrast with the Wars of German Unification (1864–71) and even the American Civil War (1861–5), this was a conflict in which amphibious capability helped set the development and tempo of the conflict. Chilean strength in this regard was crucial. Furthermore, Chile's eventual naval success prevented Peru from reinforcing and supplying its forces in what was the world's driest desert, leading them to retreat.

In the autumn of 1880, the Chileans used their naval strength to ravage the Peruvian coast, while, in 1881, they landed and captured Callao and Lima. The Peruvians thus lost their centres of population, but resistance that continued in the interior was not suppressed until 1883, while continued Bolivian opposition only ended when the Chileans invaded the interior. The peace of 1883 left Chile with Bolivia's coastline and Peru's southernmost provinces.

The Mikado

The Gilbert and Sullivan comic opera *The Mikado* (1885) was a brilliant success when it opened. For its inspiration, it drew on the growing fashion for everything Japanese, but was really a satire of British society. Nevertheless, Gilbert and Sullivan did seek a degree of Japanese authenticity as far as costumes and gestures were concerned. There were no public performances in Japan until 1946.

THE PACE OF EXPANSION

As in Africa, the 1880s and, even more, 1890s saw a marked increase in the pace of imperial expansion. This was very much the case with America, Japan and Germany, but was also true of existing powers, Britain, France and the Dutch. The degree of control expected in order to substantiate claims increased after the Congress of Berlin in 1884–5.

Even when existing territories were taken over, there was a drawing of new boundaries, but the process of new control also included the creation of new territories that had had little or no prior unity. This was seen in the Solomon Islands where, in 1893, Britain declared a protectorate, in large part in order to thwart possible French expansion from the New Hebrides, an argument advanced by the expansionist Sir John Thurston, the High Commissioner for the Western Pacific. In 1899, as part of the process in which Germany extended and clarified its position in the Pacific, in large part by purchasing Spain's remaining islands, the Germans ceded to Britain territory they had already annexed in 1893: the islands of Choiseul and Isabel and the atoll of Ontong Java, the last a Polynesian outlier in Melanesia. These islands were added to the Solomons as part of the process by which boundaries were drawn in the Pacific.

THE IMPACT OF THE WEST

The goals and impact of Western powers varied greatly but it was a question of their agendas as the Pacific was increasingly inserted into outside economic, political and cultural strategies, whether with companies, missionaries or politicians pursuing gains, from New Guinea and New Caledonia gold to Tahitian souls. Thus the British annexation of Fiji in part reflected a parliamentary campaign in order to lead to the abolition of slavery; the annexation occurred in 1874. The following year, measles killed about a quarter of Fiji's population.

Under French rule, the Marquesas captured the stark impact of the West. Disease, notably tuberculosis, had led the population to fall from 80,000 to 4,000. Cultural prosleytism by missionaries and officials hit local customs such as total-body tattoos, and were propagated among the young in missionary schools, attendance in which was compulsory until the French government moved against clerical education from 1901. A range of diseases hit home across the Pacific against populations lacking immunity. Thus in California, indigenous peoples, such as the Tongva, had a major drop in numbers.

Violence also played a significant role. In 1882, after the German company Hernsheim persuaded its government to take punitive action against Luf Island in the Hermit group, most of the population was murdered by marines from *Carola* and *Hyäne*, with the islanders driven into the sea, and the huts and boats burned. Only a handful out of the population of 400 survived. The survivors began building the boat referred to in chapter two (page 24), but it was then seized by the company.

The West's impact included a process of classification and standardisation, primarily for governmental purposes, that put indigenous islanders in a secondary position, with major implications not least over political and legal rights, but also over economic contexts. The situation was made more complex by migrant flows, not only of Westerners (including from other imperial powers) but also from Asia and elsewhere in the Pacific. Moreover, the position of people of mixed-race became a growing issue. Different states handled these issues in contrasting as well as overlapping fashions, but the common framework, as for the regulations introduced in New Caledonia in 1887, was racist.

New Empires

The Pacific as the base for new empires was apparent not only with America and Germany, but also as Britain's Australasian colonies launched expansionist projects. Australian confidence was seen in Sydney with the opening of the town hall in 1869 and the international exhibition held in 1879–80. The sense of imperial mission often linked to, or expressed in, cultural arrogance, seen for example with Richard Seddon, New Zealand Prime Minister from 1893 to 1906, drew on a mix of commercial and strategic interest. This encouraged interest in the development of colonial naval power, which owed much to fear of Russian attack, as in 1854–6 and 1885.

In 1881, the Australian colonies pressed for a stronger British naval presence, but were unwilling to pay for it. However, the Colonial Conference held in London in 1887 accepted the idea of cooperative imperial defence and agreed, not only support for a trans-Pacific cable, but also that more British warships should be employed to defend Australasian maritime trade, while Australia and New Zealand, in return, were to provide annual payment. These projects in part reflected the development of Queensland and the sense that the Pacific was no barrier to further growth. The construction of ports was a key element, as with Townsville, founded in 1864 to make it easier to export cattle, and soon offering opportunities for other products, notably gold and sugar. Thus, the Torres Strait Islands were placed in 1879 under Queensland which also developed a strong interest in New

Guinea. Australian, notably Queensland, attempts to seize New Guinea and the New Hebrides reflected interests that threatened international relations and led Britain in 1883 to divide them respectively with Germany and France in order to prevent disputes. British New Guinea was transferred in 1902–6 to Australia which had become a federated Commonwealth in 1901. Similarly, Britain and Spain defined the situation for the Philippines and North Borneo by the Madrid Protocol of 1885.

Japan also became an imperial power, with the 1868 Meiji Restoration followed by a national strengthening and a more assertive stance that none of the smaller island states could have matched. In Hokkaido, control was enforced over the Ainu with the suppression of hunting and fishing rights, assimilation through education in Japanese, and the confiscation of land. Taiwan was conquered from China in the war of 1894–5, and popular resistance treated with great brutality, with many civilians killed.

Like Australia and New Zealand, Chile acted as an imperial power at the expense of indigenous peoples. This was seen in the occupation of Araucania, Mapuche territory, from 1861 to 1881 and notably in 1881 when a Mapuche uprising was overcome. Settlement followed conquest.

Island Traders

Resident Western traders, many Australians, on Pacific islands in the nineteenth century were intermediaries between the world economy and the islanders. They sold Western products, including tobacco and alcohol, and purchased copra (dried coconut flesh) as well as other tropical goods, for example shark fins, which were much in demand in East Asia, and shells. The traders took local women as wives. Prominent ones included Jack Buckland, who was transformed into fiction by Robert Louis Stevenson, and Fred Whibley. This system, however, declined from the 1900s, with resident traders replaced by the supercargo, used by the trading manager on the ship. Thus, the intermediaries exposed to local culture went. Instead, the German company Hernsheim and Company was typical in using trading stations with warehouses, such as on Jaluit for the Marshall Islands, as well as independent agents. That company also came to operate palm tree plantations, for example on New Ireland, using imported labour.

THE VARIETY OF WESTERN CULTURE

Melville, Patteson, Stevenson, Gauguin, Stoddard, and Miklouho-Maclay provided very varied instances of the Western experience of the Pacific.

HERMAN MELVILLE AND *TYPEE*

The American novelist (1819–91) set sail as a whaler in 1841, including off the Galápagos. Jumping ship in the Marquesas in 1842, he wrote *Typee: A Peep at Polynesian Life* (1846) and *Omoo: A Narrative of Adventures in the South Seas* (1847), travel-adventures about his experiences there and later, and sailed home in 1844. *Typee* was sympathetic to the islanders and not so to the missionaries. He followed with *Moby Dick* (1851), the epic of whaling, in which the *Pequod* encounters a typhoon and is finally sunk by the mighty whale. The story drew on the sinking by a sperm whale of the American whaler *Essex* in 1820 in the eastern Pacific and on the 1839 tale of the killing of the gigantic bellicose albino whale Mocha Dick off Chile.

MARTYRDOM IN THE PACIFIC

John Coleridge Patteson, Bishop of Melanesia (1827–71), a well-connected Anglican missionary, sought to develop George

Selwyn's idea of using the education of boys brought, with their parents' consent, to the Melanesian Mission School on Norfolk Island. Using his own funds, Patteson made annual missionary voyages to Melanesia and spent much time there, learning over twenty languages and compiling and printing guides to many. He was killed on Nukapu in the Solomon Islands, probably in revenge for activities by blackbirders (see page 154), but maybe also in opposition to his missionary activity. Punitive action by the *Rosario* led to the death of 20–30 islanders in 1871, and to a question in Parliament the following year about an allegedly excessive response. Patteson's death made a major impact in Britain, greatly increasing interest in missionary activity. He is commemorated as an Anglican martyr, and the church of St Barnabas on Norfolk Island was erected to his memory in 1882, with windows designed by Edward Burne-Jones, important to what is a truly impressive building. An emphasis on Western missionaries, however, should not lead to a neglect of the important role of indigenous evangelists.

ROBERT LOUIS STEVENSON

Dying aged 46 on Samoa in 1894, Robert Louis Stevenson had settled on the island in 1890, only, like Gaugin, to become alarmed by the pace of change arising from the impact of the West. Chartering the yacht *Casco* in San Francisco in 1888, he had sailed the Pacific extensively, notably staying long in Hawai'i and writing extensively about the islanders, with whom he very much identified. Stevenson became a bitter critic of Western colonial exploitation, notably in *The Beach of Falesá* (1893) and *The Ebb-Tide* (1894). He is buried on Mount Vaea on Samoa.

PAUL GAUGUIN

The French post-Impressionist painter (1848–1903) visited Tahiti in 1891 in a quest to break free of European civilisation and 'everything that is artificial and conventional'. Returning to France in 1893, he remained fascinated by Tahitian subjects. After his journey back to Tahiti in 1895, he never left Polynesia. Financial and health problems pressed hard, while he continued his earlier pattern of sexual relationships with teenagers. Deciding that Tahiti had become too Europeanised, Gauguin moved to the Marquesas in 1901 and died there. His ability to capture Polynesian faces remains powerful.

CHARLES WARREN STODDARD

Stoddard was an American author, who helped popularise Polynesia which he first visited in 1864. This proved the basis for *South Sea Idyls* (1873), which presented the islands in a very attractive light. Stoddard (1843–1909) also wrote *Lazy Letters from Low Latitudes, The Island of Tranquil Delights, Summer Cruising in the South Seas, A Trip to Hawaii, Hawaiian Life*, and *The Lepers of Molokai*, the last about Father Damien, a Jesuit who tended to the leper settlement on Hawai'i, dying of leprosy in 1889, and was canonised in 2009. The willingness of Polynesian society to accept homosexuality was of considerable personal appeal to Stoddard.

NIKOLAI MIKLOUHO-MACLAY

An idealistic Darwinian scientist (1846–88), he based himself on the north-eastern coast of New Guinea pressing for its independence or for a sympathetic protectorate. Arguing the need to understand the humanity of the New Guinea people and not to treat them as a separate species, he failed in his political quest.

Blackbirding

Known as blackbirding, the seizure of local people as slaves became an insistent part of the Western presence in the nineteenth century from the slave raid on Easter Island in 1805 on. To a degree, enslavement reflected notions of civilisational superiority, but crude equations of need and opportunity were more significant. This was especially so in 1863 as Peru sought labour to collect guano on the Chincha Islands. This led to widespread depredation as in the seizure of much of the population of the Tongan island of 'Ata, a step followed by the removal of the surviving population to 'Eua in order to protect them from subsequent seizures. The same year, most of the able-bodied men on the Tokelau atolls were seized, with very few returning. The enormous scale of this horrendous episode was accentuated by the extremely small number of returnees then (re) introducing smallpox and other diseases to their home islands, horribly depopulating most of them. Many of the blackbirded Polynesians were also used for domestic labour in Peru.

Whereas the slave trade from Atlantic Africa depended on sale by African rulers, in the Pacific there was more straightforward seizure of islanders, as well (separately) as hiring by means of contracts that were not then honoured, the latter a process still seen, for example in some of the fishing factory ships in the Pacific. In the later nineteenth century, a large number of Melanesians were 'contracted', or in practice impressed, to work Queensland's sugar plantations. This was devastating for many Western Pacific islands and archipelagos.

MIGRATION

The Pacific saw many migrant movements, some voluntary, some involuntary and some in-between. The influxes of Americans to California and of British settlers to New Zealand were key instances of the first, and by 1860, when the settler population was over 100,000, Europeans outnumbered Māori in New Zealand. Gold rushes were important in California, Australia and New Zealand from 1848, 1851 and 1861 respectively. Land was also of value. In the 1850s, Germans colonised Valdivia and nearby areas of Chile.

Involuntary migration was most clear in the case of convicts, with British convicts sent to Australia and Norfolk Island, and, after the British movement had finished, French, from 1864, to Noumea in New Caledonia. So also with the seizure of islanders for slavery, most obviously in 1862–3 to Peru, but also more generally. The Pacific Islanders Protection Act of 1872, the annexation of Fiji in 1874, and the establishment of the Western Pacific High Commission in 1877 were regarded as ways to protect the indigenous people. Such protection was on terms. Taxation for example could force islanders into wage labour. Partly as a result, islanders continued to work as indentured labour, for example in Queensland.

Indentured labour was voluntary, but could involve coercion and/or deceit. East and South Asia were the major sources. China produced labour for the Americas, Australia and Pacific Islands, including Hawai'i; the 1,000 Chinese brought to Tahiti to work cotton plantations in 1865–6; and the indentured Chinese labour brought in to work plantations in German New Guinea. India was significant in Fiji from 1874, with over 60,000 Indians moving there from 1879 to 1916, particularly to work in the sugar industry, and Japan and the Philippines were important sources of workers for Hawai'i from mid-century.

Nativist sentiment was particularly focused on the Chinese, as in Australia, the United States, and Canada. In Australian Papua New Guinea, there was a ban on Asian labour and the requirement that vessels be manned by white crew. A head tax was levied on every Chinese person entering Canada. There was also concern about immigration from Japan, which was greatly restricted in America in 1907–8 and totally stopped in 1924, as part of a broader pattern of American restrictions.

Shipping Infrastructure

Steam had advantages over sail, not least being more predictable and enabling ships to proceed in the face of winds. However, steam was more expensive and not inevitably faster, not least due to the development of fast clippers. There was also the need to provide coaling facilities and boiler maintenance. Both Australia and New Caledonia produced coal, but the quality of the latter deteriorated in humidity. British coal was regarded as being particularly good quality. Hong Kong and Singapore, and, later, also Shanghai and Yokohama, were major coaling stations. Hong Kong and Sydney, both part of the British system, were key ports for ship repairs, but, from 1866, France developed the Saigon shipyard for major ship repairs. However, in comparison to Britain, Germany and America, France in the Pacific was weak in terms of commitment, capital, entrepreneurs and mercantile shipping lines. Other areas, notably North Africa, attracted far more French attention. French Polynesia depended on Australia for supplies.

Rail Work on the Central Pacific Railway 1866

'Almost the entire work of digging is done by Chinamen . . . They are found to be equally as good as white men, and less inclined to quarrels and strikes. They are paid $30 per month and boarded, and a cook is allowed for every twelve men.'

Sacramento Daily Union, 18 June 1866.

PORT-CITIES

The extent to which Pacific history should include Pacific shores becomes more significant from the mid-nineteenth century, not least with the development of new port cities, particularly Auckland, San Francisco, Vancouver, and Yokohama, as well as of existing cities, such as Callao (the port for Lima), Valparaiso, and Manila, and the creation of major Pacific navigational links between them. That port cities also acted as the termini of railways greatly increased their significance as transhipment points.

Capital accumulated, expertise developed, and credit was offered at these cities, and the Pacific was more insistently linked into wider commercial patterns, the demands of which pulsed from these ports into and across the ocean. The construction of lighthouses and other navigational aids was a crucial support to shipping. In Sydney, where there was initially reliance on lighting bonfires, the first lighthouse was finished in 1818, and its replacement in 1883. The treacherous Farallon Islands off San Francisco were made safer by a lighthouse built in 1855.

In the case of Vancouver, a stipulation when British Columbia joined the Canadian Confederation in 1871 was that a rail route was built from coast to coast, and one was opened in 1885, overcoming the north-south nature of the topography which, it was feared, would increase American influence. The ocean-to-ocean rail route in Canada was followed by the establishment of a steamship route from Vancouver to Sydney and Melbourne, which reflected the degree to which communication routes that did not focus on London were opened up between parts of the British empire. So also with telegraph routes, and the Pacific Cable was opened in 1902. To that end, Britain had annexed Fanning Island in 1888, using explosives to drive a shipworthy gap through the atoll.

Rail links brought out a key contrast between North and South America, one that was environmental and political. Coast-to-coast rail routes were developed in America and Canada, with railways also serving to link the interior to port cities. San Francisco and Vancouver were the most important, but Seattle, Portland, San Diego and Long Beach were to follow.

In contrast, there were not comparable economic links in South America, in large part due to the terrain, the Andes being more formidable than the Rockies, and forest cover, but also as a result of political division. The interiors of Brazil and Argentina look to Atlantic, and not Pacific ports.

The network of shipping links thickened with economic development. Thus, at the close of the century, the largest business in New Zealand was the Dunedin-based Union Steam Ship Company. Founded by Dunedin and Glasgow entrepreneurs in 1875, its shareholding was predominantly British from the 1880s. Aside from British capital, the company benefited from the demands and opportunities provided by the empire. In addition to links with Australia, there were also routes to Fiji and Calcutta from 1881 and 1887 respectively, while routes from Melbourne to Fiji and Brisbane to Vancouver began in 1882 and 1901 respectively. By 1914, shortly before it was bought by P&O which owned it until sold to New Zealand investors in 1971, with its seventy-five ships, the company was the largest shipping line in the southern hemisphere.

The role of the port cities was to be changed by the opening of the Panama Canal, which established a new route between Europe and the Pacific, but, prior to that it was crucial, not least to Pacific exchanges of technology and know-how. For example, the Californians who went down to the Victoria gold rush brought with them devices and methods unheard of in Australia, and then brought them to New Zealand for the Otago and West Coast rushes. After the devastating 1906 San Francisco earthquake, shiploads of kauri timber from the Northland of New Zealand were shipped from Auckland to help rebuild the city.

Canadian Totem Poles

Made from untreated cedar logs, totem poles told clan stories and were erected at great feasts known as *potlach* ceremonies. The practice of carving human-sized wood or stone figures was also seen in Hawai'i, New Zealand, and Easter Island. Metal tools obtained from trade with Westerners made it easier to carve totem poles, and these were particularly seen amongst the Haida of the Queen Charlotte Islands of the Pacific North-West. However, smallpox epidemics, especially that of 1862, and measles, cut the population dramatically, that of the islands falling from about 7,000 in 1835 to 800 in 1885. Moreover, missionaries mistook totem poles for pagan symbols, and converted indigenous people were encouraged to burn poles; while a collecting rampage by museums led to the loss of many traditional items from about 1870. There has been a revival since World War Two, with many totem poles erected for the public.

Canada's First Nations

Aside from the harsh blows of infectious disease picked up from Europeans, particularly the 1862 smallpox epidemic which helped lead the Haida to abandon the village of Sgan Gwaii on Moresby Island (now a UNESCO World Heritage Site), the position of the First Nations deteriorated with Canadian nationhood as government regulation was established and enforced, notably by the Indian Acts of 1876, 1880, and 1884. In 1884, the *potlatch* ceremony central to the coastal cultures was banned, a measure not reversed until 1960. Tribal governance was overthrown, resources seized, and European systems of marriage, parenthood and land tenure all enforced. Reserves were regulated by the Department of Indian Affairs. Indigenous children were forced into residential schools in order to break traditional links, and indigenous communities were sometimes moved. There was no right to vote in federal elections until 1960.

Conclusion

A vivid demonstration of the Western impact in the Pacific can be found in what became the French Polynesian coral atoll of Makatea, 150 miles north-east of Tahiti. From 1908 to 1966, eleven million tons of phosphate-rich sand was dug out, and a dock was built at Temao. The population expanded to about 3,000 only to fall to fewer than 100 after mining stopped in 1966 leaving over a million deep circular holes caused by the mining. The British had done the same from 1900 with phosphate on Banaba Island, which is between Nauru and the Gilbert Islands. Between 1900 and 1979, about 90 per cent of the surface was stripped away and from 1945 to 1983 much of the population was relocated to the Fiji island of Rabi.

Yet, a somewhat different impression is left from the career of Charles Morris Woodford, a naturalist who learned local languages and became the first Resident Commissioner of the Solomon Islands Protectorate, serving from 1896 until 1914 and trying, with few resources, mostly Fijian policemen and episodic help from the Royal Navy, to stop headhunting, fight smallpox, support Anglican missionaries, and create a civil administration. The contrast between lines of imperial control on the map and small administrations was more generally apparent. Thus, in Bougainville, the first permanent Christian mission station was not established until 1901, and the first colonial administration station in 1905. Even if willing, colonial administrations were not in a good position to regulate companies. Instead, they tended to share power: with the companies, as with the British on the Solomons; with existing chiefs, as with the British on Fiji; and with the local representatives of the Western military.

Changing Pacific Cities

Both founded in the late eighteenth century, San Francisco and Sydney were instances of Pacific cities that greatly expanded from the mid-nineteenth. Annexation by America and, more particularly, the California Gold Rush which began in 1848, saw the population of San Francisco, a settlement of fewer than 100 buildings, rise from 1,000 to 25,000 by the close of 1849 and about 70,000 by 1859.

Brick and stone buildings were hastily built to provide facilities and housing, while wharfs and piers served shipping. More prosperity brought grander buildings, such as the enormous Palace Hotel with its 755 guest rooms, built in 1875, in which king Kalakawa of Hawai'i died in 1891. Hit very hard by the 1906 earthquake and subsequent fire, the city was rebuilt with more thoroughfares, broader streets, Beaux-Arts style building, and a new civic complex. The new city was celebrated by the Panama Pacific International Exposition of 1915 which was held to celebrate the opening of the canal.

The opportunities offered by California drew in large numbers of Asian immigrant labourers, but although they were initially encouraged, not least in order to build the railways, discriminatory laws were passed from the 1870s in order to push them out. Chinatowns were depicted as dens of depravity, criminality and insanitary conditions as in the map of San Francisco's Chinatown produced by the Board of Supervisors in 1885. This map used colour coding to denote uses, including for gambling, prostitution and opium, and resembled those used to identify epidemic hotspots.

The dynamism of Sydney reflected that of Australia but also its oceanic role. In 1874, the world's first iron wharf was built there for coal loading. The 1888 panorama produced there by M. S. Hill showed many steamships as well as others reliant on sails alone. The busy coastline was backed by harbour facilities, warehouses and factories including the Australian Steam Navigation Building built in 1884.

Meanwhile, the mythic account of the Pacific islands was given another Western interpretation by anthropologists. Sir James George Frazer, a Scottish anthropologist, proved particularly important. His *The Golden Bough: a study in magic and religion* (1890), a widely read comparative study of mythology and religion, made several mentions of the cultures of New Caledonia and other Pacific islands, although he had not visited them and, instead, was reliant on questionnaires. Frazer saw these cultures as primitive. Such attitudes, underlined by later works on the cargo cults or millenarian beliefs springing in particular from exposure to World War Two outsiders of New Guinea and

Melanesia, such as that by Peter Worsley in 1957, helped encourage the imperialist mind, and certainly a sense of relative Western superiority. In contrast, beginning on Fiji in 1885, the Tikka Movement sought to recover ancestral potency in reaction to the challenge of Western control. The instability was contained, but this was an instance of the sense of crisis created by this control. If that was not to the fore, nevertheless the realities of disturbance and disruption were aspects of this and the succeeding period that should not be forgotten.

9

The Struggle of Empires, 1898–1945

Running Out of Options

A sense of the tropics as a onetime, but past, source of opportunity was presented by the narrator in Margot Bennett's *The Widow of Bath* (1952):

If he had made his gesture forty years earlier . . . he could have found redemption planting sugar-cane or coconuts in some empty island where the natives would rapidly have learnt to worship him. But there was a waiting list now for all islands.

While politics and war reflected and created divisions in the Pacific world, ships sailed the ocean in order to establish and sustain links. A key figure was John Diedrich Spreckels (1853–1926), an American of German antecedents whose father Adolph was crucial from the late 1860s to the sugar trade between Hawai'i and San Francisco and from 1878 a key producer of sugar there, notably with Spreckelsville, the biggest sugarcane plantation in the world. Founding the Oceanic Steamship Company in 1881, John developed a major fleet, which played a key role in shipping between San Francisco and Hawai'i, especially in the early twentieth century with the *Sierra*, *Sonoma* and *Ventura*, and also a passenger, freight and mail route on to Tahiti, Samoa and Australasia. In 1926, Oceanic became a subsidiary of the Matson Navigation Company. John also was key to the development of San Diego, where he was crucial in property, transport, and newspapers, not least in establishing a rail link to the east that, once finished in 1919, was important to San Diego's development into a major port. The base there, established in 1922, also became the principal homeport of the Pacific Fleet.

America was now the Pacific great power, politically, militarily and economically. Albeit against a weak empire, America had demonstrated its power in a war with Spain in 1898 that reflected wide-ranging geopolitical interests and capabilities. The conquest of Cuba and Puerto Rico and the arrival of American troops in the Philippines followed rapid and decisive naval victories. The peace treaty with Spain left Puerto Rico, Guam and the Philippines to America, but, in the last, control was enforced only after national- ist opposition from 1899 was suppressed in a bitter counter-insur- gency war. The Americans found it hard to fix their opponents for combat, and their methods were often brutal. The inability of American commanders to understand local situations was a major handicap. The Americans were eventually victorious, in part thanks to a blockade which limited the insurgents' ability to resup- ply and to coordinate operations. The presence of the pro-Ameri- can Filipino Federal Party was also a help. The Philippines were not to have the possibility of becoming an independent oceanic power, indeed a post-colonial one on the pattern of those in former Spanish America. In 1915, the Americans pressed on to take control of the Sultanate of Sulu.

In 1899, Spain sold its remaining Pacific colonies, the Caroline and Northern Mariana islands and their dependencies, to Germany. The loss of Spanish warships in 1898 and of the administrative centre of Manila removed the logic of Spain's Pacific presence. The spread of American and German power encouraged other imperial powers to consolidate their position. Thus, in 1904, Portugal agreed with the Dutch to divide Timor, and settled the border, which was followed, in 1912, by the Portuguese suppression of the independent Timorese nobles. The Dutch imposed control on their side of the border, just as they overcame resistance in Sulawesi and Bali in 1905–6. The Dutch expansion of control included the Talaud Islands north-east of Sulawesi and to the south of the Philippines. However, whereas the Dutch rapidly took over what eventually became Indonesia, there was no Portuguese expansion in the region other than in what became East Timor.

The American achievement against Spain was thrown into greater prominence by the problems Britain encountered in defeating the Boers in South Africa in 1899–1902, and by the serious defeat Russia suffered at the hands of Japan in 1904–5; although these wars were far from comparable. President Theodore Roosevelt's successful mediation of the Russo-Japanese War, for which he won the Nobel Peace Prize, was a testimony to America's importance and influence, and both were demonstrated in 1907–9 when the sixteen battleships of the 'Great White Fleet' sailed round the world in a major show of strength, albeit one that in practice depended on British help with coaling. By 1914, America was a major power in the Pacific, with Hawai'i, Midway, Johnston, Palmyra, Tutula and Wake islands, as well as Guam and the Philippines, and was also increasingly assertive in Mexico and Central America, which provided a different purchase on the Pacific.

Madame Butterfly

This opera by Giacomo Puccini, set in Nagasaki, Japan, was based on a 1887 French novel by Pierre Loti, a 1898 short story by John Luther Long, and the 1900 dramatisation of the latter, and premiered in 1904. The theme of Western exploitation is driven home repeatedly in a powerful opera of broken love and self-sacrifice. Silent film versions appeared from 1915, while the musical *Miss Saigon* (1989) drew heavily on it.

American power was dramatised in the new geopolitics of the Panama Canal, which provided a link for warships and merchantmen between the eastern and western seaboards of America, helping integrate their economies. A project originally and unsuccessfully begun with French capital had ended in 1914 as a triumph for American engineering and influence, for, in 1903, adding another state to the Pacific, Panama became an independent state carved out from Colombia under American protection, and, under the Hays-Bunau-Varilla Treaty, America gained control over the land zone, providing a parallel to British control over the Suez Canal. The construction of the canal owed much to the American army which played a major role in its planning and organisation, as well as in providing protection from disease.

Another indicator of American power was provided by the settlement of the Alaskan frontier dispute between Canada and America largely on American terms, because Britain was more conciliatory over this and over seal fishing rights in the Bering Sea than the Canadians would have liked. The naval strength of any Asian state did not become a factor until the rapid development of that of Japan. Pacific power changed as a result of the rise of Japan that was demonstrated by its defeat of China in 1894–5. This led to an Anglo-Japanese treaty in 1902 which reduced British defensive commitments in the Pacific, and the alliance was renewed in 1905 after Russia had been heavily defeated by Japan in the war of 1904–5. In January 1905, Sir Ernest Satow, the perceptive British envoy, observed: 'The rise of Japan has so completely upset our equilibrium as a new planet the size of Mars would derange the solar system.'

Once Anglo-Japanese relations had deteriorated in the 1920s, this abruptly changed the assumptions of British naval power. Prior to that, however, the focus of naval conflict for Britain was likely to be in European waters, for, if their opponents could not prevail there, at least to the extent of maintaining communications, they would not be in a position to sustain a serious challenge to the British in more distant waters.

Indeed, thinking of Australasia and Canada in 1902, Halford Mackinder, the leading British geopolitician, wrote:

> The whole course of future history depends on whether the Old Britain besides the Narrow Seas have enough of virility and imagination to withstand the challenge of her naval supremacy, until such time as the daughter nations shall have grown to maturity, and the British Navy shall have expanded into the Navy of the Britains.

Japan's rise concerned Australia, encouraging the formation of the Australian National Defence League, and, earlier in the decade, leading an Australian naval conference to conclude:

> Within the last half-dozen years the keen attention of the political world has been concentrated on the Pacific. There is every indication that it will play the part of the Mediterranean in the past century as the arena of national contending forces. France, Russia and Japan have established naval bases and possess powerful fleets in the north of the Pacific. Nearly every other European power has effected a lodgement in the seas to our north.

In 1913, Billy Hughes, an influential Australian MP, later Prime Minister from 1915 to 1923, declared when the Australian Fleet Unit steamed into port for the first time:

> Australia has assumed the toga of nationhood ... The Australian Fleet Unit is a formal notification to the outside world that we have recognised our responsibility, our danger, and our duty to ourselves, to the Empire, and to the cause of civilisation.

The imperial power of the Western states served as the basis for the further spread of Western economic interests. These focused on the extraction and use of resources. Established land use and agricultural patterns were transformed with the development of plantation economies. These included the large-scale diversion of water as on Hawai'i.

World War One saw a German squadron sail east from Chinese waters en route to a planned return to Germany via the Atlantic. One warship was detached to destroy the British cable station at Fanning Island, and soon after the Germans attacked the port of Papeete on Tahiti. The Germans pressed on to defeat a weaker British opponent in the battle of Coronel off Chile on 1 November 1914, with two British cruisers sunk, but instead of exploiting that victory in the Pacific, where supplies were scanty, the squadron entered the South Atlantic en route to Germany, being destroyed by a swiftly dispatched British squadron off the Falklands on 8 December. The *Dresden* escaped, but sought coal in March 1915 in the harbour of Robinson Crusoe Island in the Chilean-ruled Juan Fernández archipelago. This was neutral, but the British attacked and sank the ship. Drawing on long patterns of anxiety, Britain claimed that the *Dresden* had planned to use the island as a base for attacking British shipping.

German commerce-raiders were a major challenge. They were also the basis for C. S. Forester's *Brown on Resolution* (1929), a story which, being in the local library, I read as a child, about a lone British seaman, survivor of a sunk warship, who delays the *Zeithen*, a repairing German cruiser, on the fictional uninhabited island of Resolution in the Galápagos, until the Royal Navy is able to arrive and destroy the cruiser. The island is presented not as a tropical paradise but as a lava and cactus wilderness.

Germany's Pacific colonies fell rapidly in 1914, the Japanese taking the islands in the north-west Pacific, the Australians New Guinea and nearby islands, including Nauru, and the New

Zealanders Samoa. British and French forces also played a role in the Pacific conflict with Germany.

There was no equivalent in the German Pacific to the ability of forces in German East Africa (Tanzania) to hold out until the end of the war. This encouraged the dispatch of large Pacific forces to fight in Europe and the Middle East. The Australian and New Zealand contributions are well known, but there were also men from the smaller islands, for example both settlers and Kanaks from New Caledonia. Japan sent warships to the Mediterranean, but not army troops.

Unlike in the Islamic world, the Germans were not successful in winning support or tapping into disaffection as they did in British, French and Italian colonies. However, the war helped increase economic tensions as well as encouraging a sense of volatility. This was particularly so in northern Caledonia, where, in 1917, Kanaks fought European settlers and French forces in a struggle that brought to the fore already existing tensions and fears arising from colonial control. The French treated the Kanaks as rebels.

The war enabled Australia, New Zealand and Japan to pursue their territorial interests in the Pacific; and they all gained territory in the eventual peace settlement. These were all League of Nations mandates, but the limitations represented by that were very modest. German New Guinea, including the Bismarck Archipelago, was handed to Australia, Nauru to Britain, Australia and New Zealand, the German possessions north of the Equator to Japan, and German Samoa to New Zealand. The end of Germany's Pacific empire, and the resulting expansion of these other powers, removed buffers to future conflict between them. New Zealand continued to expand with the transfer in 1926 from British colonial rule of the Tokelau Islands. In 1923, Britain had also transferred the Ross Sea Dependency in Antarctica.

Spanish Flu

A very different sign of the removal of buffers was the worldwide spread of the Spanish flu pandemic in 1918–19. This could be devastating. New Zealand had taken control of German Samoa in 1914, but its military administration failed to quarantine the ship *Talune* in November 1918. This resulted in one of the world's worst death tolls in that pandemic. A fifth of the population perished. The loss of young adults disrupted the agricultural economy, causing a famine in 1919, and by 1920 the population had been reduced by one third since 1917. Other islands also suffered serious losses, Tahiti coming next in Polynesia with 3,500 deaths from a population of 21,000, followed by Fiji with 9,000 from 164,000. New Zealand Māori lost 2,500 from 51,000. The severe second wave was brought to New Zealand by shiploads of sick and wounded troops returning from camps in southern England. In contrast, the governor of American Samoa imposed a strict maritime quarantine, and there was not a single case nor death.

The Invincibles

The New Zealand rugby team, usually known as the All Blacks, that toured the British Isles and France in 1924–5 were called 'The Invincibles' because they won every game. The All Blacks had their international debut in 1903, beating Australia, and in 1905 had a tour of Europe and North America in which they lost only one of thirty-four games. They were wearing all black, hence the nickname.

Margaret Mead

An American cultural anthropologist (1901–78), Mead reported on liberal attitudes to young sex in the South Pacific in *Coming of Age in Samoa* (1928) and *Growing Up in New Guinea* (1930) and on attitudes to violence and gender in the New Guinea-based *Sex and Temperament in Three Primitive Societies* (1935). Her scholarship was a matter of fierce later controversy, not least due to her emphasis on nurture rather than nature, as well as claims that she had presented Samoan culture as more relaxed sexually than the West, claims that have also been rejected in Samoa.

INTERWAR DEVELOPMENTS

The 1920s saw the development of new possessions, alongside revived interest by the existing colonial powers, and investment by, and in, independent countries, for example in Californian agriculture. For France, trade in the Pacific grew, and there was a greater commitment to the possibilities of the colonies there, while the newly founded *Revue du Pacifique* focused public attention. The British, however, had so many calls on their resources that attention was more patchy. Independence movements were very limited, but there could be disaffection. In 1929, protest in Samoa owing to the suppression of the Fono of Faipule, Samoa's democratic assembly, and organised by the Mau movement, led to an armed police response in which the High Chief was killed, and to the deployment of New Zealand troops.

Alongside the emphasis on the use, indeed rage, of power, there was the story of the people, their suffering, contributions, altered economies, and social upheaval, often with permanent repercussions that have lasted to the present. After the influenza epidemic, the next key disruption during the interwar years was the Great Depression, which hit the plantation economies hard, as with the impact of low sugar prices on Hawai'i in 1929–33, and also greatly reduced the ability to fund social capital in the Pacific, both from local resources and from colonial governments that had to balance the requirements of the distant metropole with problems locally. In turn, these local problems in part arose from the need to reconcile the very different assumptions of indigenous people and settlers. Law and order, education and taxation were particular areas of disagreement. In Hawai'i, there was the additional role of the navy as a cause of change.

Schemes for development continued across the Pacific. Thus, in the British empire, the Phoenix Islands Settlement Scheme sought to move people from the Southern Gilbert Island, where there was population pressure, to atolls in the Phoenix Islands, where copra was to be cultivated. The project lasted until the settlements were evacuated in 1963.

Very differently, after legislative contention within America and the Philippines in 1932–3, the Philippines in 1935 were granted Commonwealth status, a stage toward the independence gained in 1946. The colonisation of Mindanao was part of the policy of the new government.

An Anglo-American Condominium

The Anglo-French condominium in the New Hebrides from 1906 is well-known, but not so the Anglo-American one over the coral atolls of Canton and Enderbury in the Phoenix Islands. Claimed by both powers from the mid-nineteenth century, the issue was pushed by both from 1936 with hostile steps, before an agreement of 1939 led to joint administration without prejudice to the claims of either. In 1979, control passed to Kiribati. There was a separate dispute over Hull Island, but it was also brought under the condominium and eventually transferred to Kiribati.

Pacific Images

Waikiki Wedding was a 1937 American comedy set in Hawai'i, with Bing Crosby offering popular songs such as *Blue Hawaii* and *Sweet Leilani*. A volcano and Walford the pig each provide somewhat different action. The American film industry was dominated by the Pacific in the shape of Hollywood.

PLANNING FOR THE PACIFIC

In the case of naval warfare, speculation about the likely role of carriers, and of carriers as opposed to battleships, focused on the Pacific. Preparation for conflict affected all powers; Chile, for example, investing in submarines and a submarine depot ship. Japan, the United States and Britain planned for war. Indeed, in 1919, an Admiralty memorandum warned that the British navy was likely to be weaker than that of Japan in the Far East, and that using Hong Kong as a base would expose the fleet to overwhelming attack from Japan.

A collision of American and Japanese interests in the Pacific region had been building since Japan's stunning victory in the Russo-Japanese War eliminated her sole naval threat in the region. America strengthened its fleet in the Philippines as an element in the event of war with Japan while, in 1911, Battery Randolph was constructed to defend O'ahu's southern coast and protect Pearl Harbor. The two 14-inch guns it was to contain were the largest in the entire Pacific.

Both countries now recognised each other as a potential threat to their respective interests and ambitions. Japanese naval commanders, fearing Japan would lose in a sustained war, hoped that quick decisive naval battles would enable it to establish a defensive perimeter against the American navy, as Japan had done against Russia in 1905.

There were specific American interests in the western Pacific, including the territories of the Philippines, Guam and Samoa, trade, and a strong commitment to the independence of China and to an 'open door' allowing other powers that had no territorial bases there, notably America, to share in Chinese trade. This concern led to American planning for war with Japan, which was correctly seen as menacing all these interests.

The likely character of a major future war in the Pacific resulted in a new geography of commitment and concern that was reflected in the development of naval bases or the consideration of alternatives. The switchover from coal to oil as the power source of major warships helped ensure that the previous system of coaling bases was obsolete. In addition, the expansion in the size of battleships from the deployment of the dreadnoughts in the mid-1900s had made the existing imperial harbours inadequate. The British Chiefs of Staff urged that Singapore should be not only a modern naval base but also the location of troops able to act as a strategic reserve forward of India, a measure aimed at Japan and to protect India, Malaya and Australasia.

In turn, the strategic value of Pearl Harbor, the American base in Hawai'i, for controlling the eastern Pacific and advancing across the Western Pacific, was clear to the American Joint Army and Navy Planning Committee in 1919. More than any other navy, the American one got the war it expected in the 1940s. Naval exercises that were a bridge from the naval thought of the pre-1914 Mahanian period to the American strategy in the Second World War were pursued. War Plan Orange of 1924 called for the 'through ticket'. This was a rapid advance directly from Pearl Harbor to Manila in order to relieve the Philippines from Japanese attack, followed by a decisive naval battle, and then starving Japan by blockade.

Changing Sydney

H. E. C. Robinson's *Map of Sydney* (1922) was different in that it provided what was intended as an aircraft view. The scale of the city was clear, as was the significance of the rail links that ran to wharves. The geography of the city was soon to change with the opening in 1932 of the Sydney Harbour Bridge, which was even more iconic than the Union Ferry Station, with its imposing clock tower, completed in San Francisco in 1898.

Pearl Harbor would be crucial for the planning that, by the mid-1930s, superseded the 'through ticket', a planning in which there was now greater interest in a slower, three-year process of seizing the Japanese islands in the Pacific – the Marshalls, Carolines and Marianas, which they had gained from Germany as mandates in the Versailles peace settlement. The capture of these islands would provide the Americans with forward bases en route to the Philippines and also deny them to the Japanese. Without control of this area, it was argued, a naval advance to the Philippines would be unsuccessful.

The American navy was experienced in large-scale movements, the Atlantic Fleet regularly joining the Pacific Fleet for manoeuvres: in 1925, the Pacific Fleet engaged in manoeuvres with the Atlantic Fleet off Panama. Both fleets then went up the West Coast of the United States for 'fleet week' events, after which they engaged in manoeuvres from California to Hawai'i and then, while the Atlantic Fleet went home, the Pacific Fleet went to Australia and New Zealand. By 1940, no other fleet had as much experience in such large-scale movements.

The logistical challenge of projecting power into the western Pacific was formidable. It included an erosion of efficiency as warships addressed fouled hulls and reduced speeds. American naval leaders responded to the lack of adequate bases in the western Pacific by favouring technological, operational and force structure solutions, including warships of greater range, underway replenishment and aircraft carriers. The Americans and Japanese made major advances with naval aviation and carriers, in part because they would be key in any struggle for control of the Pacific. The Japanese commissioned six carriers between 1922 and 1939, some converted, but others purpose-built. In 1927, as part of his graduation exercises at the Japanese Naval War College, Lieutenant-Commander Tagaki Sokichi planned an attack by two Japanese carriers on Pearl Harbor, although, in the evaluation, he was held to have suffered heavy losses. In 1929, the American *Saratoga* launched eighty-three aircraft in a simulated raid on the Panama Canal. At sea, however, air power was restricted by the difficulty of operating aircraft in bad weather and the dark, by their limited load capacity and range, and by mechanical unreliability.

Flying the Pacific

In 1928, Charles Kingsford Smith, with Charles Ulm as relief pilot, both Australian World War One veterans, in the first trans-Pacific flight, flew from Oakland, California, to Hawai'i, and then on, via a tropical storm, to stop first at Suva before arriving at Brisbane, a distance of 7,187 miles. In 1934, Kingsford Smith successfully made the return flight, but he was lost in the Andaman Sea in 1935.

Options were tested in fleet exercises and in war games. In one of 1933, Captain Ernest King chose a northern attack route on Japan, via Hawai'i, Midway, Wake and the Marianas, while the President of the Naval War College, Rear-Admiral Harris Laning, who had served in the Philippines, preferred a southern route. A decade later, King put his plan into action, while Douglas MacArthur put Laning's plan into action, but they each took far longer than expected. Moreover, practicalities such as fuel and ammunition were underplayed in the planning and exercises. When operating at peak performance, carriers need to refuel very often.

There was also a focus on increasing the range, size and speed of submarines. The American S class of 1918-21, with a range of 5,000-8,000 miles at a surface speed of 10 knots, was replaced by the B class (12,000 miles at 11 knots), and then by the P-boats of 1933-6, which were the first American submarines with a totally diesel electric propulsion. These were followed by the *Gato*-class introduced in 1940, with a range of 11,800 miles and a surface speed of 20-25 knots. By the time of the Japanese attack on Pearl Harbor, the American navy had 111 submarines in commission although their cautious use in the first year of the war reflected deficiencies in interwar doctrine and poor torpedoes.

The Japanese had sixty-three ocean-going submarines. Their *Sen-toku*-type I-400 submarines had a range of 37,500 nautical miles, a surface speed of 18.7 knots, a submerged speed of 6.5 knots, and carried two seaplanes and supplies for sixty days. In the event of war with the United States, the Japanese planned to use them to sink American warships steaming from Hawai'i into the western Pacific. In the event, Japanese submarines repeatedly failed to fulfil expectations.

The need to plan for conflict with Japan accentuated the problems for Britain and the United States, powers with major commitments in both Atlantic and Pacific, for they had to think about how best to distribute naval forces, and how vulnerabilities would affect policy. There was a *de facto* division of spheres of activity, with the United States dominant in the Pacific, and the British more prominent in East Asian waters, although the

Americans had a small Asiatic Fleet to defend the Philippines and their interests in China.

The British failed to agree among themselves, or with the Americans, on how best to contain the Japanese threat. In response to Treasury opposition in 1934 to sending a fleet to the Far East and, instead, concern about Germany and support for air power, the Admiralty and the Dominions Office argued that this was an unacceptable stance due to the impact on Australia and New Zealand of leaving them without support. The Admiralty was ready to consider a forward policy of projecting a battle-fleet into Far Eastern waters (and thus protecting Hong Kong), to provide support against Japan, but that policy required an American willingness to move naval units to East Asian waters as an aspect of a coordination that did not yet exist. Fearing that this would leave Hawai'i vulnerable, the Naval Department, which anyway included anglophobes, was unwilling to support such a scheme.

In 1935–6, in the Second London Naval Conference, Japan demanded equality of tonnage with Britain and the United States, which would have meant Japanese naval superiority in the Pacific and Far East. British attempts at negotiating compromise failed, and the Japanese left the talks in January 1936. Already, in December 1934, Japan had provided the necessary two years' notice under the treaty regime to end their commitments. Launching the Marusan Programme of shipbuilding, which was designed to prepare for victory over American and British fleets, Japan focused on the force structure of a large navy based on battleships and on the goal of victory stemming from a decisive battle, the lesson the Japanese had taken from their victory over Russia at Tsushima in 1905.

The build-up of their navy included the largest capital ships in the world, the 'super-battleships' *Yamato* and *Musashi*, ordered in 1937, each displacing 72,000 tons and carrying nine 18.1-inch guns. Their size and gunnery were designed to compensate for

Japan being heavily outnumbered by American battleships, but they were to be sunk by the Americans in 1944 and 1945; airpower, or rather the lack of their own airpower, proving the nemesis of this class.

'The *Titanic* of the Pacific'

In 1940, a recently laid German minefield sank RMS *Niagara* in Hauraki Gulf off Auckland. No lives were lost, but eight and a half tons of gold, en route to Vancouver to buy American munitions, went down. Built on Clydebank, Scotland in 1913 for New Zealand's Union Steam Ship Company, and owned from 1931 by its partly owned subsidiary, the Canadian Australasian Line, the ship was a 525-foot long liner on the Vancouver-Honolulu-Suva-Auckland-Sydney run, known as 'the *Titanic* of the Pacific'. Fuel oil has leaked from the wreck ever since, although all but five of the 585 gold bars were later recovered.

The larger sister ship, the *Aorangi*, (1924–53), ran on the same route, helping to provide a regular service. Subsidised American competition, from San Francisco and Los Angeles, to Australasia was provided by the *Mariposa* (1932–74), *Monterey* (1932–2000), and *Lurline* (1933–80). Their owner, the Matson Line, helped develop tourism in Hawai'i, where, in 1932, it had acquired the Moana and Royal Hawaiian hotels, with the *Malolo* (1927–73), playing a key role on its San Francisco to Honolulu run. The company had made a lot of its early money bringing sugar from Hawai'i.

JAPAN ATTACKS

In turn, the passage of the Two-Ocean Naval Expansion Act in July 1940 was designed to produce a fleet that would enable the United States to wage naval war against both Germany and Japan. It provided for the building, at a cost of $4 billion, of a truly massive additional complement that was designed to increase the authorised total tonnage of American warships by 70 per cent, including 18 fleet carriers, 11 battleships, 6 battlecruisers, 27 cruisers, 115 destroyers, and 43 submarines, although most of these ships were not due for completion until 1946–8. Keels were laid down for four 45,000 ton *Iowa*-class battleships in 1941, and seven were projected at over 60,000 tons each. The Act served notice that the Americans were going to be in a position to back up their hostility to Japanese expansionism.

PEARL HARBOR

On 7 December 1941 (8 December on the other side of the International Date Line), Japan attacked Pearl Harbor without any prior declaration of war. Thanks in part to total radar silence, it achieved a degree of surprise that indicated considerable deficiency in American intelligence gathering and assessment, and that has led to a morass of conspiracy theories. The Americans had considered the prospect of a Japanese pre-emptive strike, but thought the more vulnerable Philippines the most probable target, while the Pacific Command in Hawai'i focused on the threat from the nearest Japanese territory, the Marshall Islands, and not from the north, the direction from which the Japanese came. The defences on O'ahu were manned for sabotage, not air attack, which helped the Japanese greatly.

In Japan, in place of separating vulnerable carriers, there was a conviction of the value of massed air power at sea, and thus of a carrier group. The attack was a dramatic assault that was tactically successful, but also an attack that indicated the problems with achieving strategic results. It was a classic case of an operational-tactical success, but a strategic failure. Operating from six Japanese carriers, 353 aircraft totally destroyed two American battleships and damaged five more, while, in an attack on the naval air station at Kaneohe Bay, nearly 400 American aircraft were destroyed or damaged on the ground.

The attack, however, revealed grave deficiencies in Japanese (and American) planning, as well as in the Japanese war machine. Only 45 per cent of naval air requirements had been met by the start of the war, and the last torpedoes employed in the attack were delivered only two days before the fleet sailed. Modifications of aircraft to carry both torpedoes and heavy bombs were last-minute and there was a lack of practice. Furthermore, the Japanese target-prioritisation scheme was poor, attack routes conflicted, and the torpedo attack lacked simultaneity.

Because of the focus on destroying warships rather than strategic assets, there was no third-wave attack on the fuel and other harbor installations. Had the oil farms (stores) been destroyed, the Pacific Fleet would probably have had to fall back to its Californian base at San Diego, gravely hindering American operations in the Pacific. Had the Japanese invaded O'ahu, the Americans would have had to do so, but the logistical task facing the Japanese in supporting such an invasion would have been formidable.

The Japanese had embarked on an attack that was not essential. Their fleet was larger than the American Pacific and Asiatic Fleets, which were not in a position to have prevented the Japanese from overrunning British and Dutch colonies, their major expansionist goal. In addition, the devastating nature of the surprise attack encouraged a rallying round the American government. Moreover, the damage to America's battleships (some of which were to be salvaged and used anew), forced an important shift in American naval planning toward an emphasis on their carriers, the *Lexington*, the *Yorktown* and the *Enterprise*, which, despite Japanese expectations, were not in Pearl Harbor when it was attacked.

Across the Pacific (1942)

Directed by John Huston, and with a dream team of Bogart, Astor and Greenstreet, this film was originally scripted to confront a Japanese attack on Hawai'i, but the real attack led to a rescripting so that the Japanese threatened the Panama Canal, only to be thwarted.

THE JAPANESE ADVANCE, 1941–2

Naval strength was crucial to the Japanese conquest of South-East Asia, although it was the army which had the key experience, equipment, doctrine and responsibility for amphibious operations. Fear of Japanese air power and concern about the relative ratio of naval power led the American navy, mindful of the wider strategic position, to fail to provide the support for the Philippines requested by the commander of the American Forces in the Far East, Douglas MacArthur, who had not taken the necessary precautions. A convoy of reinforcements turned back, the navy refused to fly in aircraft, and the submarines were evacuated, which left the defenders in a hopeless position. Superiority in the air (over the poorly prepared American local air force component) and at sea enabled the Japanese to land where they pleased. The main force landed in Lingayen Gulf in north-west Luzon, with supporting units landing in south Luzon at Legaspi and Lamon Bay, threatening Manila with a pincer attack.

Further east, American islands in the western Pacific were captured, Guam falling on 10 December 1941 to an expedition from the Mariana Islands. Wake Island was attacked on 12

December, but the Marine garrison drove off the attack, sinking two destroyers. However, an American failure to relieve the island ensured, that, on 23 December, a second attack, supported by carriers from the Pearl Harbor operation, was successful, although only after heavy casualties.

Allied naval forces tried to protect Java, unsuccessfully attacking a Japanese invasion fleet in the battle of the Java Sea on 27 February 1942, which was the first fleet action of the Pacific War. The two fleets were relatively balanced, with five cruisers and ten destroyers in the Allied fleet, and four and thirteen in that of the Japanese, but the latter was well coordinated, enjoyed superior air support, and benefited from good air reconnaissance and better torpedoes. In contrast, the American, Australian, British and Dutch warships lacked an able commander or unified command structure, experience of fighting together, air reconnaissance and air cover. Heavy Allied losses, then and subsequently, including all of the cruisers, left the Japanese in a dominant position, and, on the night of 28 February – 1 March, they landed in Java, which surrendered soon after.

As an aspect of a panicky defence-in-depth, 110,000 Japanese-Americans and 22,000 Japanese-Canadians were interned and moved from the Pacific coast. In contrast, about 22,000 Japanese-Americans served in the American forces. The internment has been criticised, but was as nothing compared to the repeated brutality of Japanese occupiers towards indigenous peoples, as on Nauru and the Solomon Islands, as well as to Western civilians.

Japan's entry into the war encouraged also coastal fortifications, as at San Pedro, California, which included 16-inch guns, and Stony Batter on the island of Waiheke to control the approaches to Auckland. Concern about a possible amphibious invasion, notably of Queensland, led Australia to defensive preparations. Japanese submarines sowed mines off Great Barrier Island near Auckland, while the coast watch there listened for the diesel engines of the submarines recharging their batteries at night.

War in the Pacific, 1942

The Japanese planned to press on to fix and strengthen the defensive shield with which they wished to hold the western Pacific against American attacks, but initial successes led to interest in a more extensive perimeter, which proved a serious mistake in terms of the eventual loss of units. The Naval General Staff considered an attack on Australia, but the army was unprepared to commit the troops required, and, instead, favoured a more modest attempt to isolate Australia. Having captured Rabaul on New Britain in January, the Japanese decided, in order to do so, to seize Port Moresby, as well as New Caledonia, Fiji and Samoa.

Their plan, however, was thwarted as a result of the battle of the Coral Sea on 7–8 May, the first battle entirely between carrier groups in which the ships did not make visual contact, which indicated the failure of the Pearl Harbor attack to wreck American naval power. The Americans had intercepted and decoded Japanese messages, and, in a major forward-deployment of American naval power that demonstrated the challenge it posed to Japan, were waiting in the Coral Sea. In the battle, the Americans suffered serious losses, especially the carrier *Lexington*, but the Japanese, who had failed to achieve the necessary concentration of strength and had an overly rigid plan, also suffered, not least with the loss of aircraft and pilots. Crucially, the Japanese, whose naval commanders were divided over strategy, failed to persist with the operation and lost momentum, while American pilots acquired experience in attacking Japanese carriers. It was necessary to develop carrier warfare techniques, a formidable task, including cooperation with other surface warships.

Rather than focusing on Australia, where Darwin and parts of the north were being repeatedly attacked from the air, and on the south-west Pacific, Yamamoto preferred a decisive naval battle aimed at destroying American carriers. The decision was made in

February, but the Doolittle raid, a symbolic American air attack on Tokyo on 18 April launched from the carrier *Hornet*, both raised American morale and, by demonstrating Japanese vulnerability, further encouraged the Japanese to act. Yamamoto proposed to seize Midway and other islands that could serve as support bases for an invasion of Hawai'i, which, he thought, would lead to such a battle. Yamamoto hoped to lure the American carriers to destruction under the guns of his battleships, in what would therefore be a decisive battle.

The continued capacity of the American navy, however, was shown clearly, on 4 June, with the American victory in the battle of Midway, a naval-air battle of unprecedented scale, which reflected the superiority of American repair efforts and intelligence, while the combination of fighter support with carriers (in defence) and of fighters and bombers (in attack) were crucial. The Americans encountered serious problems, and contingency and chance played a major role, but, at Midway and, increasingly, more generally, the Americans handled the uncertainty of war far better than the Japanese. The Japanese navy, which had doctored its war games for Midway, was affected by the tension between two goals: those of decisive naval battle and of the capture of Midway, which ensured that the Japanese had to decide whether to prepare their aircraft for land or ship targets, an issue that caused crucial delay during the battle.

While the American ability to learn hard-won lessons from Coral Sea was highly significant, the dependence of operations on tactical adroitness and chance played a major role in a battle in which the ability to locate the target was crucial. The American strike from the *Hornet* failed with the fighters and dive-bombers unable to locate the Japanese carriers. Lacking any adequate fighter support, the torpedo-bomber attacks suffered very heavy losses – forty-four out of fifty-one aircraft – but the result of these attacks was that the Japanese fighters were unable to respond, not least because they were both out of position to intercept the dive-bombers which, in only a few minutes, in a triumph of dive bombing, wrecked three carriers, a fourth following later; once wrecked, they sank. Added to the loss of pilots and maintenance crew, these minutes shifted the arithmetic of carrier power in the Pacific.

Yamamoto's inflexible conviction of the value of battleships in any battle with the Americans had served him ill, as the American carriers prudently retired before their approach, and the Japanese had lost their large-scale offensive capacity at sea, at least as far as carriers were concerned. Nevertheless, battleships and cruisers were very important for night-fighting and for shore bombardment in support of amphibious operations. In an early demonstration of the potential political significance of the Pacific, Midway ensured that the Congressional elections that November took place against a more benign background than if earlier in the year.

GUADALCANAL, 1942–43

Midway did not mark the end of Japanese advances as they sought to strengthen their perimeter. The advance on Port Moresby in New Guinea was now mounted overland from the northern shore of New Guinea, but, on 7 July 1942, the Japanese landed at Guadalcanal in the British-ruled Solomon Islands in the south-west Pacific. The island had strategic importance, being seen as a key forward base to cut off the American re-inforcement and supply route to Australia and New Zealand, but the American attempt to regain it launched a month later took on a significance to contemporaries that exceeded both this and the size of the Japanese garrison. It was important to the Americans to demonstrate that the Japanese could be beaten not only in carrier actions, but also in the difficult fighting environment of the Pacific islands. It was also necessary to show that air and sea support could be provided to amphibious forces, both when landing and subsequently. In addition, Coral Sea and

Midway had been defensive successes, but, at Guadalcanal, the attack, or rather counter-attack, was clearly taken to the Japanese in what was the first American offensive operation in the south-west Pacific.

Eventual American naval success in the naval battles off Guadalcanal compromised the ability of the Japanese to support their force on the island, and indicated the key role of warships other than carriers, which could play little role in night-time surface actions. Destroyer torpedo attacks could be highly effective, as when used by the Japanese, while their submarines were responsible for important American losses. In mid-November 1942, however, in what was to be a turning-point in the conflict off Guadalcanal, success was won by the Americans in a three-day sea action focused on surface warships fighting by night. For example, on 14 November, the radar-controlled fire of the battleships *Washington* and *South Dakota* hit hard the battleship *Kirishima*, which capsized on 15 November. Japanese battleships lacked radar-controlled fire. The Americans inflicted important losses on the Japanese in the Guadalcanal campaign in what was attritional fighting at sea and on land. There was an equal loss of warships, but the build-up of American naval resources ensured that they were better able to take such losses. Victory offshore was crucial to the American success in driving the Japanese from Guadalcanal in January 1943, while the Americans developed a degree of cooperation between land, sea and air forces that was to serve them well in subsequent operations.

Mapping For War

Facing the need to operate in the poorly mapped Pacific, much of which had been in British or Japanese hands prior to the conflict, the Americans made extensive use of photo-reconnaissance, not least for mapping invasion beaches. Amphibious attacks required maps both of the islands and of the coastal waters. The American navy had the old Royal Navy Admiralty charts but most dated from the late nineteenth or early twentieth century. While the charts were pretty good, their use posed problems, such as shoals created by subsequent storms. For the Solomon Islands, there were some Australian maps and charts (nautical maps) but relatively few.

Indeed, the American landing force on Guadalcanal lacked adequate maps, including landing maps, a problem that indicated the need for special amphibious landing maps. Moreover, the American naval raid in 1943 on Wake, which before the war had been an American possession, encountered the problem of inadequate charts for the surrounding waters. So also for the Australians with northern Australia, New Guinea, and the Solomon Islands. As the islands, bar New Guinea and the Philippines, were small, however, aerial reconnaissance allowed the army and marines to make up maps quickly to issue to the troops, and this was done down to platoon level.

In contrast, the Philippines, an American colony prior to the war, had been surveyed by the Coast and Geodetic Survey, a civilian agency under the Department of Commerce. Its 1933 map of the Philippines as a whole, a map with depths shown by soundings, which greatly clarified sailing routes, was reissued in 1940. The Survey's data and charts were used for the successful American invasion of the Philippines in 1944–5. In 1944, moreover, the Army Map Service published maps of the individual islands and cities, for example Cebu with the necessary depths of the coastal waters and location of the coral reef, both important to amphibious operations. The Service also published maps for other areas of potential operations, notably Southeast China, West Java, South Borneo, and North Borneo. The Australian Navy Hydrographic Service surveyed

New Guinea from 1939, pressing on to produce surveys for elsewhere in the South Pacific, in part using material from U.S. Coast and Geodetic Survey mapping, notably of the Philippines.

More generally, there was a widespread use of fathometers for inshore navigation. In addition, the heavy costs incurred by the Marines in the capture of Tarawa in November 1943, a landing greatly hindered by the coral reef, the depth of which had been misunderstood in part due to aerial reconnaissance, exposed the need for proper advance reconnaissance and beach surveys. As a result, the Americans created Underwater Demolition Teams for the Pacific, pressing forward an initiative begun in late 1942. The recent development of the open-circuit scuba system allowed divers to swim in and out and actually go ashore at night to do the surveys, collect sand samples, plot the location of reefs, obstacles and defensive arrangements such as mines, and determine the beach gradient, all prior to the landings.

War in the Pacific, 1943

In July 1942, the Australian War Cabinet cabled Winston Churchill: 'superior seapower and airpower are vital to wrest the initiative from Japan and are essential to assure the defensive position in the southwest Pacific Area'. Due to their greater industrial capability, the Americans were able to build up their naval strength far more successfully in late 1942, and this success proved crucial both in 1943 and to the key 1944 campaign. This build-up included not only the carriers and submarines that tend to dominate attention, but also other classes of vessel, including destroyers, which played a key role in escort, patrolling, and amphibious support tasks.

Moreover, the Americans developed important organisational advantages, from shipbuilding to the use of resources. Their advance across the Pacific would have been impossible without the ability to ship large quantities of supplies and to develop the associated infrastructure, such as harbours and oil-storage facilities, and the ships of the support train. Processes for transferring fuel and ammunition and other supplies from ship to ship at sea were developed. In addition, the use, from 1944, of shipping as floating depots for artillery, ammunition and other *matériel*, increased the speed of army re-supply, as it was no longer necessary to use distant Australia as a staging area for American operations. In some respects, this was a war of engineers, and the American aptitude for creating effective infrastructure was applied to great effect in the Pacific. Large numbers of men were deployed accordingly in order to develop facilities, for example in Queensland and at Bora Bora in Tahiti, providing, as on Guadalcanal, an important postwar infrastructural legacy.

As the Americans advanced, the vast extent of their Pacific warzone moved even further from mainland America, underlining unprecedented problems of warmaking and infrastructure. Substantial fleets had to operate over great distances, and required mobile support and maintenance. The scale of planning was large in resources, space, and time, but a problem-solving, can-do approach to logistics permitted a rapid advance.

Naval and air superiority were fundamental to the American advance, permitting the identification of key targets and the bypassing of many of the islands the Japanese continued to hold, which was a sensible strategic and operational decision given the time, effort and casualties taken to capture Guadalcanal. Thanks to this superiority, the Japanese would be less able to mount ripostes and any bypassed bases would be isolated. Thus, the Pacific War was to become one that was far from linear. Bypassing at the strategic level was not matched at the tactical level where the navy and marines attacked island defences frontally, frequently taking heavy casualties.

The process of island-hopping in the Solomon Islands began in June 1943, with an attack on New Georgia; there was a landing on Bougainville in November, losses to the latter, in the first battle fought entirely by radar, and the Solomons advance culminated with the capture of Admiralty Island at the end of February 1944.

In the central Pacific, the Americans opened up a new axis of advance, capturing key atolls in the Gilbert Islands in November 1943 in hard-fought amphibious attacks in which well-prepared and highly motivated defenders fought to the death inflicting heavy casualties notably on Tarawa. Clearing the Gilberts prepared the way for operations against the Marshall Islands in early 1944. This route revived the pre-war American Plan Orange, and represented the shortest route for an advance on the Philippines. The army wanted a southern drive, the navy a central Pacific drive; but the key point was that the Americans had enough resources to do both.

WAR IN THE PACIFIC, 1944

The Japanese continued building warships, but their numbers were insufficient and their navy lacked the capacity to resist the effective American assault. It also suffered from poor doctrine, including a lack of understanding of the naval air war, and an inadequate grasp of respective strategic options, including an inability to understand American policy and to respond to earlier deficiencies in Japanese strategy and operational planning.

The Japanese aimed to destroy the spearhead of the advancing American fleet by concentrating their air power against it. There was the hope, even conviction, that the decisive success of the Japanese fleet at Tsushima in 1905 could be repeated, which reflected a more general conviction, also seen in the Midway operation, that a decisive victory could be obtained on one front, which could overcome the more general role and impact of Allied resources.

Aside from the lack of political understanding underlying the assumption that this would wreck American morale, it was anachronistic militarily. Defeat in 1944 on one front would have delayed the Americans, but nothing more; and, by concentrating a target for the Americans, Japanese strategy made it more likely that the American attack would succeed in causing major casualties. The Americans had a better and more mobile fleet, a far greater ability to replace losses, and far more capable leadership than the Japanese. There were now sufficient American aircraft both for a carrier battle and for protecting an amphibious assault, and the fast-carrier task forces, combined with surface escorts, constituted a major operational-level weapon with the necessary tactical cohesion. In the Pacific, air power could be applied from the sea as never before, and as part of an effective and well-supported modern, combined-arms, force.

The campaigning in 1944 saw the collapse of the Japanese empire in the Pacific. In January–February 1944, the Americans successfully attacked the Marshall Islands. American success reflected the lessons learned at Tarawa, notably the need for closer and sustained inshore bombardment from appropriate ships and the use of underwater demolition teams to clear man-made and natural obstacles, particularly routes through coral reefs. In turn, success there made it easier to strike at the Mariana Islands – Saipan, Tinian and Guam – in June, which led to the battle of the Philippine Sea on 19–20 June, the major battle the Japanese had indeed sought. American Task Force 58, with fifteen carriers and over 900 aircraft, was attacked by the nine carriers and 400 aircraft of the Japanese First Mobile Fleet, but, located by American radar, Japanese air attacks launched on 19 June were shot down by American fighters and by anti-aircraft fire from supporting warships, with no damage to the American carriers. The Americans also benefited from radio interception. The following day, a long-range American air attack in the failing light sank the carrier *Hiyo* and damaged three others. The

Japanese carriers were protected by a screen of Zero fighters, but, as a clear sign of growing Japanese weakness in the air, this was too weak to resist the fighters escorting the American bombers. Although the Japanese still had a sizeable carrier fleet, once again the loss of pilots and carrier-based maintenance crew was a crippling blow. As part of the combined capability of the American navy, its submarines sank two large carriers, *Shokaku* and *Taiho*.

This victory enabled the Americans to overrun the Marianas, a decisive advance into the western Pacific. The determination of the Japanese resistance was shown on Saipan where nearly the entire garrison died in a strong defence in the jungle-covered mountainous terrain or in costly frontal counterattacks. The Marianas provided not only sites for American airfields, but also an important forward logistical base for the navy and for subsequent amphibious operations. The cumulative nature of warfare was readily apparent. Looked at differently, there was acute environmental disruption and devastation.

The Americans used their naval and air superiority, already strong and rapidly growing, to mount a reconquest of the Philippines from October, which led to Leyte Gulf of 23–26 October 1944, the largest naval battle of the war and one that secured American maritime superiority in the Pacific. The availability of oil helped determine Japanese naval dispositions and, with carrier formations based in home waters and the battle force located just south of Singapore, any American movement against the intervening Philippines presented a very serious problem for Japan. There was growing pessimism in Japan and losing honourably became a goal for at least some Japanese naval leaders, the head of the Naval Operations Section asking on 18 October that the fleet be afforded 'a fitting place to die' and 'the chance to bloom as flowers of death'.

In Operation *Sho-Go* (*Victory*), the Japanese sought to intervene by luring the American carrier fleet away, employing their own carriers as bait, and then using two naval striking forces, under Vice-Admirals Takeo Kurita and Shoji Nishimura respectively, to attack the vulnerable American landing fleet. This overly complex scheme posed serious problems for the ability of American admirals to read and control the tempo of the battle, and, as at Midway, for their Japanese counterparts in following the plan. In a crisis for the American operation, one of the strike forces was able to approach the landing area and was superior to the American warships there. However, instead of persisting, the strike force retired, its exhausted commander, Kurita, lacking knowledge of the local situation, not least due to the difficulties of identifying enemy surface ships. The net effect of the battle, which, overall, was dominated by American naval airpower, was the loss of four Japanese carriers, three battleships including the *Musashi*, ten cruisers, other warships and many aircraft.

The Collapse of Japan, 1945

The horrors of war were fully on display in February–March 1945, as many Filipino civilians were slaughtered by Japanese forces during their unsuccessful defence of Manila against American attack. Separately, in the closing months of the war, as American operations neared the Japanese Home Islands, the Japanese increasingly turned to *kamikaze* (suicide) attacks in order to counter overwhelming American naval superiority: aircraft were flown into ships, making them manned missiles, although they had little or no penetrative power against large warships. Such attacks were a product not only of a fanatical self-sacrifice, but also of the limitations, by then, of the Japanese naval air arm. First mounted in October 1944, these attacks led in 1944–5 to the sinking of forty-nine ships, with another 300 damaged, and were designed to sap American will, which they totally failed to do.

The fighting on the islands of Iwo Jima and Okinawa was fierce, a bland remark that gives no sense of the difficulty of the conquests and the heavy casualties involved in defeating the well-positioned Japanese forces. They fought to the death with fanatical intensity for islands seen as part of Japan, although under heavy pressure from the attacking Marines with their massive air and sea support. The skilful Japanese exploitation of the terrain, not least by tunnelling into Iwo Jima, ensured that the bombing and shelling that preceded the landing of the Marines there in February inflicted only nominal damage. As a consequence, the conquest was slow and bloody.

So also with Okinawa which was invaded in April 1945. The Japanese sent their last major naval force, led by the battleship *Yamato*, on a *kamikaze* mission, with only enough oil to steam to Okinawa. However, it was intercepted by 380 American carrier-based aircraft, and sunk.

Japan's position in 1945 indicated the great value of Allied naval power, most of which, in these operations, was American. Although the Japanese still occupied large areas in East and South-East Asia, for example much of China, Malaya, Sumatra and Java, these forces were isolated, while American submarines operated with few difficulties in the Yellow and East China Seas and the Sea of Japan, carrier-borne aircraft attacked Japan, dominated its air space, and mined its waters, and warships bombarded coastal positions.

American naval and amphibious operations and planning benefited from their mastery of logistics, not least in ensuring the availability of sufficient oil, a key instance of the Pacific being part of a global economy. The Americans could plan where they wanted to mount an invasion. Cumulative experience proved important, not least in the development and testing of capabilities. The transfer of ammunition between ships at sea was tested during the Iwo Jima operation, following success earlier with fuel. The development of service squadrons by the navy, and the supporting structure of floating dry docks, was important to American forward movement, not least as existing harbours tended to be distant, exposed to the sea, and limited in their facilities. Despite logistical limitations, the British Pacific Fleet played a successful role, but the attack on Japan and the planning for the invasion were very much American triumphs, and this looked toward post-war American naval dominance.

The Soviet Union entered the war against Japan on 8 August 1945. Most of its attack was a land invasion of Manchuria. However, the invasion of northern Korea was supported by amphibious operations from the Sea of Japan, as was that of southern Sakhalin. The Kurile Islands were also successfully invaded. Whereas earlier in the war against Germany, the Soviets had suffered from a lack of preparation in their amphibious operations, the 1945 operations were ably conducted and supported by much naval infantry.

1945 saw the American crushing of the Japanese empire and the bringing thereby to fruition of one trend in this and the previous chapter – the rise of American power, and to an end that of another – the growth of Japanese power. The inverse duality involved was the product not of any inevitability but of a profound failure of Japanese strategic culture, processes and decisions.

The likely consequences of American power, however, were unclear. Japan had surrendered and was occupied, brought low as China had never been despite frequent defeats by Japan. The end of the Japanese empire meant the restoration of rule by the other empires, but the extent to which this rule would be readily accepted was unclear, and notably so in the Dutch East Indies and French Indo-China. Yet, there was no comparable lack from 1945 of Western control in the islands of Polynesia, Melanesia and Micronesia, in large part because both political context and political content were very different. The anti-Western movements the Japanese had sought to foster in the Philippines, the Dutch East Indies, China and Burma lacked an equivalent in these island groups. Again, however, it was unclear what this would lead to.

Economic Trends

The twentieth century saw the Pacific affected by global economic trends as well as those specific to the region. Thus, both World Wars witnessed major disruption to economic links and the need accordingly as part of import substitution to rely on local production. The revival of the 1920s was followed by the Great Depression, which hit primary producers hard. From the Korean War to the early 1970s, there was the long boom, and, after the disruption of the oil shocks, renewed growth focused on the development of the economies of East Asia.

10

The American Age, 1945 to the Present

······················

Power Politics

In the second half of the twentieth century, the Pacific showed many of the characteristics seen elsewhere in the world, notably decolonisation, the Cold War, population growth, and growing environmental disruption. Yet, as in other periods of Pacific history, there were also significant differences within the region. In particular, decolonisation was not seen in the Eastern Pacific. In part this was a reflection of the earlier fall of the Spanish empire, which had left a series of independent states on the American margins of the Pacific. In addition, far from granting independence to Alaska and Hawai'i, America incorporated them, while, in addition, maintaining control over some (but not all) of its smaller colonies. Chile, Ecuador and Peru also retained control of islands in the eastern Pacific, and Australia, New Zealand, Russia and Japan of western Pacific counterparts.

The degree of control involved in this process varied greatly. A democratic mandate delivered through referenda kept New Caledonia under France which also continued to rule much of Polynesia. The referenda verdicts would have been very different had only the indigenous population been consulted, which underlined the difficulty of determining not only whose voices should be heard but also whose history, and on what terms. This was a problem across much of the Pacific, for example in both

Hawai'i and Tahiti, and also lay behind controversies over the histories of Australia and New Zealand.

In contrast, there was no comparable controversy in Japan and none of note in the Russian Far East, or on the coastline of the Pacific United States. In part this reflected a far greater demographic mismatch between the original inhabitants and later settlers, but respective political cultures were also very significant.

At any rate, there was a potential continuum between history wars about a contested past and political dissension about present rights and future policies. This was very much seen in both New Zealand and New Caledonia, albeit being expressed differently due to the particular constitutional situation. Independence, the pressing issue in New Caledonia, was not an option for the Māori of New Zealand.

As in the Caribbean, there was also the question of the consequences of independence, notably whether federations would work and on what terms. This was not so much a problem with islands with tiny populations, not least as they had to cooperate, but the situation was different where populations were larger and senses of distinctive interests more strongly developed, as in New Guinea, the Solomons and Vanuatu. These issues are ongoing and the future situation remains unclear.

The Cold War

World War Two left the Pacific very much under the sway of America. Whereas the previous world war had been followed by Britain, Australia and Japan, but not America, making gains from the German Pacific empire, now the Japanese Pacific empire went to America which gained the Caroline, Mariana and Marshall groups as the Trust Territory of the Pacific, while also becoming the occupying power in Japan. The Soviet Union gained the Kuriles and southern Sakhalin, but not the share in the occupation of Japan it sought. Former President Herbert Hoover in 1945 suggested that Japan be rebuilt as an anti-Soviet bulwark and, to that end, keep Korea and Taiwan. That end was not followed, but, alongside American military facilities, Japan was recast as a non-threatening ally, while in 1951 America entered into a defence pact with Australia and New Zealand.

The Philippines gained independence in 1946 as part of the process by which America (unlike France in IndoChina) abandoned its principal position in the western Pacific but without having to face a war of independence, and the Americans then provided help in suppressing the Communist-led Hukbalahap insurrection in 1946–54. In 1946–7, the conservative government failed to defeat the insurrection but from 1948 and, even more, 1950, the American-run Joint Military Advisory Group received more American military assistance so that the Philippine army was able to take the war to the Huks, a policy powerfully supported by land reform.

America's commitment to the region greatly increased with the Korean War of 1950–3, and the Pacific became crucial to the infrastructure of America's Cold War power, a process increased by the lengthy Vietnam War. The Korean War resulted in the maintenance of American army, navy and air power in Japan, where important bases were preserved after the American occupation was ended as a result of peace and security treaties in 1952. This infrastructure remains significant to the present, as with the American-Philippine mutual defence treaty and their 1998 Visiting Forces Agreement and, in a display of military hardware, Operation *Pacific Iron* in 2021 in which America moved twenty-five F-22As and ten F-15Es to operate from Guam and Tinian. The Korean War also led America to commit to Taiwan where, in 1949, the Nationalist Chinese government fled having lost control of the mainland to the Communists who pressed on to seize the island of Hainan.

There was no equivalent in the Pacific to the Soviet development of naval potential in the Atlantic. The Soviets did have a naval presence in the Far East, with Vladivostok as the principal base, and Japan, accordingly, was of geopolitical significance as providing a block on movements from there, a situation accentuated by the shallow waters of the Sea of Japan. This was first of importance as a base for American naval forces, but the subsequent development of the Japanese navy, and, in particular, of its anti-submarine capability, was vital.

Yet, for the Soviets, there was no access to the Pacific comparable to that to the Atlantic from their submarine bases on the White Sea. Nor was there a regional counterpart to Cuba. Opportunity was one factor, but so also was doctrine and strategy. Neither the Soviet government nor the Soviet navy devoted much attention to the Pacific as a whole, and certainly not in comparison with the commitment to North Vietnam, where Cam Ranh Bay, a deep-water bay on the South China Seas, became an important base from 1979 to 2002. This served as a counterweight to China as well as a potential threat to the Philippines; but the Soviets were not interested in ranging further afield.

China did not have a significant ocean-going navy until the 2000s and, still more, 2010s. Its military was dominated by the army, and as far as maritime issues were concerned in the second half of the twentieth century, they focused on Taiwan, Korea and Vietnam, but with overland power-relationships crucial for the last two. Nor did China at this stage have distant Pacific links prefiguring those they were to seek to develop in the 2010s, notably with the abortive plan to establish maritime facilities in Samoa.

The other Pacific powers fitted into the standard Cold War alignments. Australia and New Zealand signed the Anzus Treaty with America in 1951, and fought together in the Vietnam War. Japan and the Philippines provided America with key bases, and Britain, France and Canada were allies of America, which also generally had the support, or at least quiescence, of the Pacific states of South and Central America. Indonesia, which followed an anti-Western policy, notably in the early 1960s in both Borneo and Western New Guinea, as its government moved toward the Communist bloc, changed direction in 1965–6 with the Americans encouraging the military to destroy the Communist movement and move in a pro-Western direction. This was a more significant defeat for the Communist bloc than their success in Vietnam. In Chile, the left-wing government of Salvador Allende was overthrown in an American-backed military coup in 1973.

American hegemony was not used for further gains or to encourage other powers to decolonise, but rather served in a passive role to protect existing interests, as with help in the defeat of the Communist insurrection in the Philippines in 1946–54. The Maritime Zone declarations in 1952 by which Chile, Ecuador and Peru extended their territorial waters claim to 200 miles were no threat to the United States.

In another light, the consolidation of American power in Alaska and Hawai'i, a consolidation of late-nineteenth century imperial expansion, was a crucial victory for America, and one of its most important in the Cold War. An alternative of pro-American independence might in time have led to differences, not least over the maintenance of military bases, as for the Americans in Japan and, even more, the Philippines, and for the Russians in Vietnam. Another alternative, that of separatist political movements, on the model possibly of that in Puerto Rico, might also have caused difficulties, especially if benefiting from foreign sponsorship. This is yet another instance of the significance of paths not taken, a point that bears reiteration.

DECOLONISATION

From the 1960s, in addition, decolonisation became a major theme of Pacific history, but it was affected by the problems of the same process elsewhere and also began later than in other parts of the world, notably Asia, the Middle East and Africa. Instead, the nearest comparison was with the Caribbean, but decolonisation in the Pacific was largely later and more limited. There was little in the way of independence insurgencies, with the Mau in Samoa in the 1920s and the Maiasina Ruru (Marching Rule) on Malaita in the Solomons in the 1940s having scant success, and certainly not leading the British to decolonise as rapidly as they did. The independence of Nauru in 1968 from a joint Anglo-Australian administration showed that independence for small Pacific states was possible, as opposed to the earlier British view of a moral responsibility to rule in such cases.

The first indigenous Pacific state to achieve full nationhood was Samoa, gaining independence from New Zealand in 1962. In 1946, the new United Nations had renewed the authority New Zealand had wielded in (Western) Samoa under a League of Nations mandate for the territory, and Western Samoa became independent in 1962 after a plebiscite sponsored by the United Nations. New Zealand's earlier moves toward self-government for Samoa alarmed France as a dangerous precedent. The Cook Islands followed in 1965. After initial reluctance, Australia proved willing to press on, Papua New Guinea gaining independence in 1975. Britain withdrew from rule over Fiji and Tonga, both in 1970, the Solomon Islands and Tuvalu in 1978, and Kiribati in 1979. Formal independence, however, was not always co-terminous with its economic and cultural counterparts. Thus, indigenous believers had to gain control of the churches from Western missionaries. Informal controls often related to resource exploitation by foreign companies, as with logging companies on Papua New Guinea and the Solomons, although such logging companies were also influential in, for example, Tasmania.

A Godly Royal

Prince Philip, the husband of Queen Elizabeth II, was a godlike spiritual figure in the villages of Yakd and Yaohnanen on Tanna island of Vanuatu, where it was thought he fulfilled a prophecy that an islander would leave in his spiritual form to find a powerful wife overseas. Philip was seen as a recycled descendant of a very powerful spirit or god who lived on one of their mountains. Prince Philip memorabilia, notably photos, were kept from the 1960s, and the Prince Philip Movement saw daily prayers for his blessing of banana and yam crops.

The problems of the Anglo-French condominium and the differing views off the two powers ensured that the New Hebrides did not follow into independence, as the new state of Vanuatu, until 1980. The United States provided statehood to Alaska and Hawai'i in 1959, the federal government transferring to the state government 1.8 million acres seized from the Hawaiian kingdom. The Marshall Islands and Micronesia gained independence from American rule in 1986 and Palau, having split off from the Federal State of Micronesia in 1978 under a referendum, in 1994.

This, however, left much of the Pacific under the rule of imperial powers and/or their heirs. Some did not see themselves in that light, for example New Zealand, the ruler of the Auckland, Chatham and Kermadec islands; Australia of Norfolk Island, where separatism was overawed by a forcible response; Chile of Easter Island and the Juan Fernández islands; Ecuador of the Galápagos; and the United States of Midway, Wake, Guam, the Northern Marianas, Jarvis, Baker and Howland Islands, the Aleutians, and atolls or reefs, such as Johnston, Palmyra and Kingman. Indonesia continued to control the western portion of New Guinea which it had seized from the Dutch in 1962, the

French remained rulers of the extensive French Polynesia and New Caledonia, and Britain of the Pitcairn Islands. The United Nations list of non-self-governing territories includes Tokelau, a New Zealand dependent territory that holds elections and has voted against independence. Others on the list include American Samoa, French Polynesia, Guam, New Caledonia, and the Pitcairn Islands.

Political issues emerged from some instances of continued imperial rule, with separatism on New Caledonia, notably with the *Front de Libération Nationale Kanak et Socialiste*, many of the families of which had been involved in the conflict of 1917. The movement formed a provisional government in 1985. In 1984–8, particularly 1987, separatist conflict, which led to a violent response by settlers and police, led to an agreement on eventual referenda that so far have found for continued French rule, but also, as a result of agreements in 1988 and 1998, for the establishment of a power-sharing executive and a customary senate, both of which were requirements of the indigenous Kanak. The French also began to spend more on majority-Kanak regions. In 2018 and 2020 referenda, New Caledonia voted to remain part of France, on the latter occasion by 53 per cent to 47 per cent. Alongside the *Front de Libération Nationale Kanak et Socialiste*, there is *L'Éveil Océanien* (Oceanic Awakening), a party backed by migrants from the French Pacific, that has proved willing to consider independence. In Tahiti, there were demands for a different deal from France, and the election of a pro-independence party in 2004 was followed by more internal autonomy.

Having seized East Timor (Timor-Leste) from Portugal in 1975, Indonesia faced a secessionist movement there. Armed resistance had little success against a powerful military determined to maintain control and willing to employ large-scale violence as in the killing of hundreds of unarmed demonstrators at a cemetery in the capital, Dili, in 1991, the destruction of crops, and the internment of much of the population in disease-ridden camps. The role of the military in running Indonesia from 1966 to 1988 ensured that this approach was maintained, and East Timor won independence in 1999 with Australian and United Nations support, only after this role ceased. Given the choice of independence or regional autonomy, the people overwhelmingly chose the latter despite serious pressure from militias supported by the army. After the election, the coercion was stepped up, but international anger finally led the Indonesians to accept the popular verdict.

There were also tensions within other new states, the far-flung nature of which helped ensure separatist activity as in Bougainville in Papua New Guinea, Espiritu Santo in Vanuatu, and Mindanao in the Philippines; as well as the more commonplace divisions between areas, as in the Solomons. The difficulty of grounding new political orders in consent could interact with systems of corruption and favouritism.

In 1980, New Guinea forces, with Australian logistical support, ended the Espiritu Santo separatism of Jimmy Stevens and the Nagriamel Movement. The separatism drew on support for the customary ownership of land rather than land nationalisation. While the separatism stopped nationalisation, the tension over land control was part of a broader issue, one also seen with pressure to retain indigenous political, social and cultural practices, for example on the Solomons. There, anger on the island of Guadalcanal, where the capital is located, toward settlers from the most populous province, Malaita, led, in 1999, to an uprising in the former in which about 25,000 rural settlers from Malaita were evicted. Each 'side' established militia, and, in 2000, Malaitan forces overthrew the government. Peace was brokered that year by the Australian government, but conflict continued in remote parts of Guadalcanal, with some encouragement from Bougainville militants, in a dangerous instance of interacting crises. Moreover, the militias divided and also increasingly engaged in criminal activity.

Instability in the Solomons, in which about 200 people were killed in 1999–2003, mostly in revenge killings, encouraged action under the auspices of the Pacific Islands Forum's Biketawa Declaration of 2000 authorising intervention 'in time of crisis'. Beginning in 2003, a long-term military and police deployment by Australia (which bore 96 per cent of the cost and provided most of the personnel), New Zealand, and a number of the Forum members, including New Guinea, Fiji and Tonga, helped restore order; although, after the mission was ended in 2017, divisions remained. From 2019, dissension increased anew, with a growing secessionist movement in Malaita and competition to acquire commercial opportunities. In response to China's wooing of the Solomons, Taiwan and America sought to give funds directly to the provincial government of Malaita. Complicating matters, corruption remains a problem in the Solomons.

Fiji began a process of coups in 1987, but coup leaders such as Frank Bainimarama, who seized power in 2006, then sought to become democratic. Indeed, Bainimarama was able to win general elections in 2014 and 2018 and to move toward an inclusive politics, declaring all citizens Fijian, which thus included ethnic Indians. Bainimarama won Indian support as well as that of much of the indigenous people. Since 1987, many Fijians of Indian descent have moved to Australasia and North America, and this has reduced the challenge they might seem to pose to those of indigenous descent whose Great Council of Chiefs was abolished by Bainimarama.

From the outset of independence in 1975, resource-rich Bougainville has seen separatism from Papua New Guinea, with the reliance of the latter on support from Australia, until 1975 the former colonial power, unpopular in Bougainville. An Australian company was the majority owner of the large Panguna copper and gold mine, and the distribution of its profits was a major issue. A civil war in 1988–98, in which there were many casualties and the displacement of over half the Bougainville population, was followed by a 2001 agreement. In 2019, a non-binding Bougainville referendum saw 98.3 per cent of the votes cast for independence as opposed to greater autonomy.

In the Philippines, although there is a significant and persistent Islamic separatist movement in Mindanao, a movement accompanied by terrorist activity, the tendency has been towards on the whole more peaceful politics. There has also been a different political tone; after the fall of Ferdinand Marcos in 1986, provincial and local authorities gained greater power in the Philippines, which weakened national political parties.

The Philippines government is in dispute with China over the South China Sea. Less centrally, in 2013, about 200 men invaded Sabah in the Malaysian-ruled northern part of Borneo. Part of the Sultanate of Brunei, it had been ceded to the Sultan of Sulu in the Philippines in 1658, but, in 1878, when Sulu was weak, was leased by the Sultan of Brunei to the British North Borneo Company, and thus became part of Malaysia in 1963. Descendants of the Sulu sultans received a nominal rent, but in 2013 the Sultan's brother invaded, only for the force to be defeated by the Malaysians.

Marcos was an instance of the tendency in some Pacific states for democracies to become one-party fiefdoms with strongmen-governors, as with Samoa which was under Tuilaepa Sailele Malielegaoi as Prime Minister from 1998 to 2021. The crisis surrounding his difficult peaceful ousting underlined another aspect of political culture that can make politics complex, the role of traditional chiefly leaders. Thus, in 2021, Tuilaepa was replaced by Fiame Naomi Mata'afa, who held one of Samoa's paramount chiefly titles, as does the current head of state, who backed Tuilaepa.

The situation on the Pacific perimeter varied, although, generally, without any particular reference to that perimeter. However, American President from 1981 to 1989, Ronald Reagan, a former Governor of California, appeared particularly appropriate for a country that was increasingly aware of the pull of its Pacific rim and the declining influence of Europe and the East Coast. Yet California had a maverick character in American culture and politics, and Reagan's success was not that of a narrowly regional candidate. Instead, he benefited greatly from reaching out to wider constituencies.

The Last Voyage

Advertised as '91 Minutes Of The Most Intense Suspense In Motion Picture History', *The Last Voyage* (1960) was not a film to encourage crossing the Pacific by liner. The fictional SS *Claridon* en route to Tokyo suffers an engine fire that leads to an explosion and the eventual sinking of the ship. Filmed off Japan, the American disaster movie used the iconic liner *Ile de France*, which had been sold to a Japanese scrapyard. As part of the filming, its forward funnel was sent crashing into the deckhouse and the Art Deco interiors destroyed by explosives.

Liners of that period sailing from Britain to Australia via the Panama Canal included P&O's *Orcades* (1948–72), which could carry 1,635 passengers. A more common route to Australia was via the Suez Canal, as with the *Orcades*'s sister ships *Himalaya* (1949–74) and *Orsova* (1954–74), although the latter sometimes sailed via Panama.

The variety of political outcomes helped alter the context for the exploitation of the Pacific that had been such a prominent feature of its history from the nineteenth century. The removal of raw materials continued to be a significant trend, but a very different new form of exploitation was seen with the use of the Pacific for nuclear testing.

NUCLEAR TESTING

Territorial control was made more of an issue due to the anxieties and anger arising from this testing. Undertaken by America, Britain and, eventually, only France, this was initially not largely understood in terms of environmental damage but, instead, very much as a matter of Cold War preparedness. Indeed, this was an aspect of imperial control as well as the degree to which the Pacific was part of the Western sphere during the Cold War. The testing reflected an attitude of disposability for even entire islands, and also for the fishing they represented. In some cases the islands were uninhabited, but there was also a willingness to move people to vacate them.

In 1946, the Americans began nuclear testing in Micronesia, at both Enewtak and Bikini atolls. In Operation *Crossroads*, 242 ships were assembled at Bikini Atoll for the experimental detonation of nuclear weapons over a fleet. This assault on the Marshall Islands compromised them for the islanders. The Americans also used Johnston Atoll and, jointly with Britain, Christmas Island, while the British separately used Malden Island. Later, from 1963, no longer able to use their test sites in the Sahara due to Algerian independence, the French developed sites in their quest for nuclear self-sufficiency. These sites employed large numbers of French expatriates and local people. In 1966, they began testing nuclear bombs in the Tuamotu Islands, destroying the islands of Mururoa and Fangataufa. This became a big issue for New Zealand in the 1970s, not least due to the atmospheric and oceanic pollution arising from atmospheric explosions. In 1973, New Zealand and Australia took France to the International Court of Justice at The Hague, only for France to ignore the court's order to cease testing. As a result, New Zealand, from 1973, stationed a frigate to observe the tests and continue protesting. The French finally agreed to transfer their testing underground at Mururoa. Very differently, in 1968 the

Soviet submarine K-129, which contained nuclear weapons, sank in the Pacific.

Mounting environmental criticism in the 1980s led the South Pacific Forum, the annual meeting of heads of government, to declare a nuclear-free Pacific in 1985, only for France and the United States to reject this. Also in 1985, a converted trawler, the *Rainbow Warrior*, on its way to the test zone on a Greenpeace mission to protest about the tests, was sunk in Auckland Harbour by mines placed by French secret agents. A Portuguese photographer was killed. Two of the French agents were arrested, convicted and imprisoned, but the French government demanded their release, threatening trade sanctions, and they were returned to France where they went free. This affair caused great outrage and resentment.

Independence for Micronesia and the Marshall Islands, both in 1986, affected the situation, but both Johnston Atoll (American) and French Polynesia remained under the control of nuclear-testing powers, although America last carried out tests at its Pacific Proving Grounds in 1992. Rioting against nuclear testing in Tahiti in 1995 was followed by the series being completed in 1996 and the site dismantled. Probably over 100,000 people in the French Pacific were affected by fallout from at least 175 underground and atmospheric nuclear tests in 1966–96.

CONTESTING AUSTRALASIAN HISTORY

The Western legacy is under assault in many areas and respects. Thus, in Peru in 2021, the new left-wing President declared that he would not use the presidential palace which was built on the site of the house of Pizarro, the Spanish conqueror. The current situation of indigenous peoples makes their history more particularly contentious, and notably so in Australasia. Indigenous Australians, Torres Strait Islanders, and Māori, on average have far more difficult living circumstances, with less wealth and poorer health and education. They are disproportionally unemployed, in prison, the victims of crime, and commit suicide.

On Australia Day, 26 January, in 2018, monuments to Captain James Cook and to other British explorers of Australia were defaced by indigenous Australian activists. A statue of Cook in Melbourne was covered in pink paint with the words 'no pride' painted beneath his feet alongside the indigenous Australian flag. Paint was thrown on a monument to an expedition across inland Australia in the nineteenth century and the word 'Stolen' was added. Statues of Lachlan Macquarie, the most prominent colonial Governor of New South Wales, have also been defaced. Alan Trudge, the Citizenship Minister, declared on radio, 'These people are trashing our national heritage.' The date of Australia Day is that when, in 1788, the 'First Fleet' of British convict ships arrived and Captain Arthur Phillip claimed the land for George III, some compensation for the loss of the Thirteen Colonies. To some, it is what they term 'invasion day' and a celebration that whitewashes earlier history.

In 2011, new tensions arose when the left-wing Sydney City Council, after pressure from its Aboriginal and Torres Strait Islander Advisory Panel, insisted that the words 'European arrival' were to be replaced in official documents with the term 'invasion or illegal colonisation', and Qantas, the national airline, issued instructions to its staff that they were to refer not to the settlement of Australia but to its invasion.

In 2017, a statue of Cook in Hyde Park in Sydney erected in 1879 had already been given the addition 'no pride in genocide'. Politics as ever are involved. Malcolm Turnbull, the Prime Minister, criticised activists, while his Labour opponent, Bill Shorten, backed a change to the inscription which claims that Cook discovered 'this territory'. In 2018, indigenous Australian protestors unsuccessfully sought to disrupt the opening of the Commonwealth Games on the Gold Coast in Australia, referring to it as the 'Stolenwealth Games'.

It is necessary to reconcile a colonial past with a continuing indigenous presence. In place of beginning Australian history in 1788 has come an interest in the long human occupancy of the country. Moreover, there is now a presentation of this occupancy as more sophisticated and adaptable than in terms of a simple and static description of the early inhabitants as 'hunter gatherers' who, therefore, were unable to develop unless confronted by the example of Western rule. That approach gives all agency to the settlers.

A major cause of contention is that of control over land. Bound up in those disputes were issues over the moves and treaties by which this control had been obtained by settlers or by their descendants. In New Zealand, this contention has made the Treaty of Waitangi (1840) an issue. Although presented as a means by which Māori and Pakeha (Europeans) jointly founded modern New Zealand, and by means of an agreement, this treaty has since been rejected as a misleading account that sought to sanitise settler colonisation. As a result, sparked by the Māori Affairs Amendment Act (1967), which aided the compulsory acquisition of land, there were protests on Waitangi Day from 1971.

Charges of racism and a lack of recognition were issues in the questioning of the purpose and implementation of historical treaties in New Zealand. There was an attempt to give greater voice to Māori accounts of the past, as part of a national reconciliation that has been sought on the basis of equality, an attempt that has been challenged from both 'sides'. In 1996, the term 'holocaust' was used by the Waitingi Tribunal which investigated Māori grievances. This was in *Taranaki Report: Kaupapa Tuatahi*, its report on Taranaki, a district in the North Island which saw conflict, land confiscation, protest and dispossession in the nineteenth century:

> As to quantum, the gravamen of our report has been to say that the Taranaki claims are likely to be the largest in the

country. The graphic *muru* [plunder] of most of Taranaki and the *raupatu* [confiscation] without ending describe the holocaust of Taranaki history and the denigration of the founding peoples in a continuum from 1840 to the present.

In 2000, Taria Turia, a prominent Māori and the Associate Minister of Māori Affairs, gave a 'Māori holocaust' speech and, in the resulting furore, referred to the report. This clashed with the decision by Helen Clark, the Prime Minister, that the word 'holocaust' must never again be used in a New Zealand context, not to deny the Māori their place in history, but rather to address the sensitivities of New Zealand Jews. Moreover, many other New Zealanders were deeply offended by the use of the term. The Taranaki War had started with Māori killing settlers and their families, there was no large-scale massacre of Māori, and no deliberate policy of extermination, but their land was confiscated and redistributed to British settlers.

In Australia, where there were not such historical treaties, the focus was on the challenging of colonial doctrines, the dispossession to which they had led, and the erasure, both real and alleged, of the indigenous Australians from the national memory. The latter responded with complaints, as in 1938 when a 'Day of Mourning' for indigenous Australians was held in Sydney by the Australian Aborigines' Progressive Association at the same time that the sesquicentennial celebrations for the original British landing were being held. Formed in 1925, the Association pressed for full citizenship rights and for land as a compensation for dispossession. There was a pronounced trend from the 1960s, through legislation and judicial rulings, to abandon discriminatory practices, recognise original occupancy, and concede land rights, notably a High Court ruling of 1992 and the Native Title Act of 1993.

From the 1990s, the longstanding issue of indigenous Australian claims became more central, with a conservative position strongly advanced by John Howard, the Prime Minister from 1996 to 2007, who argued that a positive interpretation should be advanced in contrast to what he presented as the 'Black Armband view', which, he claimed, under the goal of offering a multicultural account that accepted indigenous Australian perspectives, was negative about Australian achievements. In turn, Howard's Labour-Party replacement Kevin Rudd issued a formal apology to the indigenous peoples in 2008.

The impact of changing views can be seen by comparing the centenary of the beginning of British settlement in Tasmania in 1803 (the city of Hobart itself was founded in 1804) with the bicentenary. For the centenary, in front of several thousand spectators, the Governor unveiled a monument to the founder of the colony and praised the settlers. No indigenous Australian people are known to have been present, and no mention was made of the subsequent 'massacre' of indigenous Australians on 3 May 1804, in practice most likely the shooting dead by troops of probably three indigenous Australians found molesting a settler and his wife at their hut.

In 2003, in contrast, no formal ceremony was held to mark the landing at Risdon Cove, the site of both the landing in 1803 and the killings in 1804. Indeed, on 3 May 2004, the latter were commemorated from an indigenous Australian perspective, a monument covered with a white sheet splattered with blood, while the Secretary of the Tasmanian Aboriginal Centre, the representative group of the northern Tasmanian people, declared, 'They killed us off in this place 200 years ago, stole our land, took away our people and imposed their religion on us. But our presence here today shows they have not destroyed us.' After indigenous Australian pressure, including the disruption of a re-enactment of the 1803 landing held in 1988 to celebrate the bicentenary of the establishment of the first British colony in Australia (in New South Wales), Risdon Cove was declared an indigenous Australian historic site and transferred to the Tasmanian Aboriginal Land Council. The southern Tasmanian people, the Lia Pootah community, adopted a more conciliatory approach.

The transfer of land rights has continued. Thus, in 2021, the Daintree tropical rainforest, including its coastal section, was handed over to the Eastern Kuku Yalanji people so that they could manage the national park jointly with the Queensland government.

HAWAIIAN CONTENTION

Such issues could be seen across the Pacific. Thus, the complex interweaving of law and politics with ethnic issues was clearly demonstrated on Hawai'i. A strong sense of ethnic consciousness among much of the indigenous population led, from the 1970s, to political pressure: the assertion of cultural identity, especially from the 1960s, was followed, in the 1970s, by debate over land rights and self-determination. As with the mainland Native Americans, land rights were a major issue, and indigenous advocates argued that ceded land was in fact stolen. Pressure led to the State Constitutional Convention of 1978 creating an Office of Hawaiian Affairs. Furthermore, under the Carter administration, the US Congress created a Native Hawaiians Study Commission. The Reagan government that took office in 1981 changed the direction of policy, and the membership of the Commission. In place of the six Hawaiians and three Mainlanders, there were now three and six respectively. As a result, the Commission's draft report of 1982 denied that there was an issue, as it found American policy in the overthrow of the Hawaiian monarchy in 1893 acceptable. The majority final report, published in 1983, supported this view, but the three Hawaiians produced a conflicting version.

Tension, however, continued, and 1993, the centenary of the overthrow, saw much public debate and dissension. The Hawaiian state's flag, that of the old monarchy, was widely flown without that of America, and the state legislature issued a resolution condemning the events of 1893, and thus the legitimacy of current arrangements. It declared that 'the United States military committed the first overt act to overthrow the independent nation of Hawai'i, an overt act of military aggression against a peaceful and independent nation'.

These were not abstract issues. Claims of dispossession continue to serve as the basis for sectional demands on behalf of those of Hawaiian descent, for example for special educational provisions, that exclude the large numbers, in fact a majority of the population, with non-Hawaiian antecedents. Like other controversies about race, however, this issue at the same time highlighted problems of definition, which, in 2003, included the case of Brayden Mohica-Cummings, an 'Anglo' adopted by a Hawaiian. He was excluded on the grounds of race from Kamehameha Schools, Hawai'i's well-funded guardian of indigenous culture and customs, but this was overturned by the US District Court of Hawai'i. The court's earlier views on the issue of race and discrimination – a 1997 ruling – had been overturned by the Supreme Court in 2000, and in 2003 the District Court followed the Supreme Court. Aside from the relationship between federal and state courts, the dispute revealed the extent to which a perception of historical wrongs clashed with constitutional prescriptions of uniformity. One of the Kamehameha Schools trustees, Douglas Ing, declared that the Trust sought 'to rectify past imbalances to the Hawaiian people', and another that the 2003 court decision ignored 'centuries of injustice to the Hawaiian people'; while the Supreme Court's minority in 2000 argued that the majority had failed to recognise 'a history of subjugation at the hands of colonial forces'.

Mapping

The mapping of submarine morphology developed from the late 1940s, first with the Atlantic, but with a map of the Western Pacific published in 1981 by the Geological Society of America. Two years earlier, the *National Geographic Magazine* published a map of the Pacific Ocean floor. Satellite altimetry subsequently produced more information, leading, in 1995, to a *Gravity Field Map of the World's Oceans*. Digitising records offered a significant advance with algorithms for digital hill shading being developed. However, much of the Pacific seabed continues to lack detailed mapping.

New Tensions

Partly as a result of American hegemony, the end of the Cold War with the Soviet Union proved of limited significance. Yet, looked at differently, this end, and at a time of good American-Chinese relations, left the Americans relaxed about at least some of the changes in their political and/or military relationships in the western Pacific, notably the pressure in the Philippines to remove American bases, as well as independence for American territories in Micronesia.

The situation might have been less relaxed had China been a serious challenge in this period, still more a serious naval challenge, but that situation did not become a clear prospect until the 2000s. Even then, American commitments in Afghanistan from 2001 and in Iraq from 2003 were such that the American government and military remained focused on the Middle East. The navy war-gamed conflict with China; but its views did not come to the fore until the early 2010s when, under President Obama, there was a 'pivot to Asia', in the shape of confrontation with China. This encouraged a new geopolitics, with revived military cooperation with Australia and Japan, and a strengthening in American navalism. The backwash was that of a new competition in the Pacific, and that represented a break with that covered in this chapter which is thereby defined as a period of American hegemony.

The other aspect of this hegemony was clearly that of economic dominance. That analysis may appear problematic given the challenge from Japan and later the major significance of China as a source of goods and a market once it industrialised, and notably so for Australian minerals. By 1987, the trade deficit with Japan had reached $60 billion while in 2000 close to 40 per cent of Japanese car exports went to America. Doubling in 2001–5, the trade deficit with China was $202 billion by 2005. These imports sustained activity in Pacific ports such as Los Angeles, where, by 2021, there were dozens of large ships waiting to dock and unload containers. However, for a long time this significance was within a geopolitical and geomilitary American dominance, such that, in the 2000s, there was reference to 'Chinerica' or 'Chinamerica'. With Chinese industry in part a matter of offshoring production by, and for, American companies to cheaper and more flexible labour suppliers, a process also (differently) seen with South Korea and Vietnam, trans-Pacific trade routes and shipping became of greater importance.

This shipping represented cooperation, a cooperation seen with the queues of container ships off the Pacific end of the Panama Canal, with East Asian, notably Chinese goods, en route to America's East Coast ports such as New York and Philadelphia. Complementing the major development of trade to the American West Coast, this route was an aspect of the significance of technological change, in the shape of the container, for the Pacific. Indeed, containerisation was of more significance for the Pacific than for any other ocean, in part due to goods and distances, but also because of the importance there of new integrated harbour facilities. The economic cooperation of America and China of that period was in part a matter of America bearing the protection cost for Chinese exports, although the relatively low cost of these exports helped sustain the living standards of Americans and the profits of many of their companies. Again as a sign of a change in direction, it was unclear how far this economic model would be sustainable in the context of growing animosity between the two states from the 2010s. Indeed, in 2021, the Chinese Foreign Minister Wang Yi declared that the rise of China was unstoppable, which certainly appears the case as far as naval strength, shipbuilding, and finance are concerned.

POLITICAL DISPUTES

There is a variety of political disputes in the broader Pacific. The most serious are those on the Asian fringes involving in particular China, Taiwan, Japan and the two Koreas, as well as the broader issues of navigation in the East and South China Seas. But these are not all. Despite losing 250 miles (400 kilometres) of coastline in the War of the Pacific in 1879–84, a loss accepted in a peace treaty of 1904, Bolivia still has an annual 'Day of the Sea' and tries to negotiate sovereign access to the Pacific that the constitution adopted in 2009 calls an 'irrevocable' right. In practice, Chile provides Bolivia's goods with tariff-free access and allows Bolivia to have its own customs officials in the ports of Antofagasta and Arica. The two powers broke off diplomatic relations in 1978.

For all the South and Central American countries, however, the prime issues are domestic – political, social and economic – rather than international. Thus, Colombia, El Salvador and Peru were greatly affected by rebellious movements, which long proved difficult to suppress, let alone contain.

Governing from 1990 to 2000, Alberto Fujimori, however, was able to defeat the Shining Path guerrillas in Peru. Such challenges were exacerbated by economic strains and social divisions. Population growth does not help. In 2018, when the populist Andrés Obrador easily won the presidency, about half of Mexico's 126 million people lived in poverty. In turn, economic downturns accentuated the situation.

A New Geography

The context for the Pacific therefore changes, although, barring pollution, the direct impact on most of the islands of the transit of container ships is minimal. The situation is very different with factory fishing. A similar point about trade could have been made about trans-Pacific steamships from the mid-nineteenth century, but now it is more so. The relationship between transit and islands has therefore changed.

So also with air services that are now able to overfly the entire Pacific, rather than needing to stop at intermediate points for refuelling. The trans-Pacific route from Europe via Los Angeles to Auckland became an important alternative to the route via Asian intermediate stops, notably Singapore. Subsequently, longer trans-Pacific direct routes developed, including Newark to Singapore. The Pacific ceased to be an obstacle, instead becoming the chore of hours of travel alleviated by videos. This was a very different experience of Pacific travel and one where LAX or Tokyo's Narita were the prime hubs. More people came to the Pacific, but to its peripheries rather than to the islands. Moreover, the web of links developed very unevenly. There was an important growth in Japanese air links to New Zealand but not, comparably, in air links from East Asia or the United States to Pacific Latin America.

Environmental Pressures

Over-fishing in the Pacific had already hit major catches, such as the anchoveta in the 1970s and the chub mackerel in the 1980s.

America aimed the Magnuson-Stevens Fishery Conservation and Management Act of 1976 at over-fishing but pressure on stocks continued. A form of exploitation that became more general and prominent in the 2010s was that of factory-fishing. In part, this reflected the overfishing already of waters near major fishing powers, notably China, South Korea, and Japan, but there was a more specific development of Chinese fishing capacity to over 12,000 vessels fishing beyond its waters by 2018 and its use for industrial-scale exploitation, an overfishing that depleted stocks. Fishing boats take more fish than they are permitted, misreport species caught, and use illegal drift nets. Forced labour is used by ships, while on-board fisheries observers are murdered, handicapping the efforts of the Western and Central Pacific Fisheries Commission, notably in trying to control tuna fishing.

There has been considerable pressure in western Pacific waters, including the South China Sea. In 2021, there was a row over a Chinese fishing fleet of about 200 boats in the Spratley Islands, with human waste from the fleet allegedly causing an increase in bacteria and problems for the coral. Another form of damage from fishing comes from fishing nets that are lost or cast adrift. They lead to the death of marine creatures, for example the dugong and turtle in the Torres Strait.

Yet, the far distances of the ocean were also under threat, as with those around the British dependency of Pitcairn Island, for where in 2016 Britain announced a marine reserve. As a result, in 2021, the British admiralty proposed to deploy warships to protect the latter. In 2017, Mexico banned fishing around the Revillagigedo Islands and tourism on them.

There is certainly a major challenge. In 2020, nearly 300 Chinese vessels, including refuelling vessels and fish processing plants, were stationed off the Galápagos, fishing for squid, tuna and billfish, and dropping plastic waste overboard. Plastic bottles and equipment packaging washed up on the islands. The Chinese fishing fleet, described as like a 'city' at sea, then moved to the Peruvian coast and on towards Easter Island. The Chinese pose a major challenge to local fishermen, not least those of Peru and Chile which are major fishing states.

Environmentalism itself has an imperial character in that local communities can have their interests protected from depredation by major powers, but on terms set by their protecting imperial power. The treatment of animals reflected the myriad tensions within individual societies, as well as the differing values between states shown in the criticism of Japanese whaling. In America in 1999, the Macaw Native Americans decided they would hunt the grey whale in the Pacific in order to develop an appreciation among the younger members for traditional hunting methods. Due to the enormous outcry against this, the Macaw, when out practising and then hunting, were protected by the Coast Guard and the Washington National Guard. Critics claimed that even as the Macaw claimed tradition, they hunted the whales with the far from traditional .50 caliber rifle. Macaw culture was attacked with calls for the acceptance of American norms. Pilgrim Congregational, a very liberal United Church of Christ church in Seattle, that was normally quite supportive of indigenous culture, argued that the whales' rights took precedence over those of the Macaw.

The Deeds of Cession for American Samoa preserved indigenous, village-based, governance there, but, after 1945, American federal marine fisheries and sanctuary policies, including the expansion of the National Marine Sanctuary and federal minimum wages, affected Samoan practice and did not draw on Samoan ideas and values. Instead, Western environmental practices prevailed, although, in the case of the community-based Fisheries Management Programme, this was in accordance with Samoan views. Nevertheless, Samoa's autonomy and GDP are both increasingly dependent on federal views and grants.

Hawai'i Five-O

The American television series set in Hawai'i and broadcast in 1968–80 was then the longest-running police series in American television history. Beginning with very popular theme music, largely shot on location in Hawai'i, which was realised for many by that means, it focused on a fictional state police force headed by Jack Lord as Steve McGarrett. The title refers to Hawai'i being the 50th state. Wo Fat, a Chinese intelligence agent, was the lead villain. The first run and syndication were seen by maybe 400 million people.

Population Flows

Already very significant in the nineteenth, movements within, into and from Polynesia became more large-scale anew in the late twentieth century, in part because, helped by much better healthcare, the size of populations grew and outstripped the local capacity for livelihood and jobs, a process accentuated by agriculture requiring less labour. In part, labour movements were within current or former imperial systems, notably to Australia, New Zealand and the United States, for example of Samoans to New Zealand, mainly to provide cheap factory labour in the 1970s: 182,721 in the 2018 census, making up 3.9 per cent of the New Zealand population, and an increase of 39.4 per cent since the 2000 census, living mostly in Auckland. There were smaller groups from Tonga and Niue. In the 1970s, many Polynesian overstayers in New Zealand were forcibly sent home after dawn raids. The military coups in Fiji brought large numbers of migrants of Indian ancestry, who now run most of the corner shops in Auckland. The Polynesians mostly live in South Auckland, in the suburbs of Mangere and Otahuhu, where unemployment and overcrowding in poor-quality housing have created major health problems and social issues with gangs.

More recent immigrants have been wealthy Chinese who bought upmarket houses as investments and helped push up prices. By 2021, Auckland had an acute shortage of housing, and an overheated property market with record high prices.

In 2010, 37,463 (2–3 per cent of the population) Hawai'i residents claimed Samoan ancestry, but, in contrast, in 2021, 16 per cent of Hawai'i's population was Filipino, a key element of the very significant East Asian population there.

American Pacific islands, past and present, provide a source of migrants, both within the Pacific, for example from Guam to Hawai'i, and to continental America. About 30,000 people from the Marshall Islands have moved to America, mostly over the last two decades and principally for jobs, education, and healthcare. There has also been a major movement of mainland Americans to Hawai'i for work, notably in the military, and retirement.

Significant Chinese and, to a lesser extent, Vietnamese diasporas in the wider Pacific both build on earlier links and involve escaping Communist control, which were particularly seen with movement to Canada, the United States and Australasia. Thus, Chinese money and immigrants, notably from Hong Kong, transformed central Vancouver, while the rest of the city did less well, which helped foster anti-East Asian sentiment. Immigration from Asia and South America helped alter the character of nearby Victoria, which had hitherto been Canada's most English city.

More generally, economic opportunities encouraged movement to Pacific coastal cities , such as Shanghai, from within America, Canada, China and Japan. California gained

1.1 million residents between 1955 and 1960, Long Beach becoming known as 'Iowa-by-the-Sea', and was the most populous state in the country by the 1960s, as jobs and the sun attracted new residents, ensuring that its representation in the House of Representatives rose by twenty-two seats between 1950 and 1990. In turn, higher taxes and the tarnishing of the earlier Californian dream helped lead to a significant outflow from California to other states from the mid-1990s.

Some large-scale migrations were more surprising, for example of Venezuelans in the 2010s fleeing the collapse of their economy and moving to Peru. There was also government-sponsored movement in order to strengthen support, as from Luzon to Mindanao in response to the Communist Hulbalahap insurrection of 1946–54.

Climate change may lead to other population movements, as some islands become uninhabitable. Kiribati and Tuvalu have discussed plans to move people to Fiji. Whether states can still exist if they disappear under the water or become uninhabitable (or inhabited in exile) is unclear, but would lead to discussion about rights to large economic zones.

South Pacific

Based on James Mitchener's *Tales of the South Pacific* (1947), this musical, composed by Richard Rodgers with lyrics by Oscar Hammerstein II, was a tremendous hit on Broadway in 1949, winning a Tony Award for Best Musical in 1950, and opening in London in 1951. It addresses racial prejudice in the romances depicted, and includes songs that made the cast album the best-selling record of the

1940s and that have lasted the course, including 'Some Enchanted Evening', 'There is Nothing Like a Dame', 'Bali Ha'i' and 'I'm Gonna Wash That Man Right Outa My Hair'. A dangerous reconnaissance mission in which one of the leading characters is killed by the Japanese forms part of the plot. The 1958 film was a great commercial success, the third highest-grossing film in 1950s America, and the highest in Britain prior to *Goldfinger*.

ECONOMIC STRAINS

The economic strains of the early twenty-first century hit many Pacific countries, albeit differently and with contrasting political consequences. Thus, Australia, Canada, Japan and New Zealand did not have the strained stability seen in a number of states including Chile, Peru and Mexico. Chile had been a major economic success after the end of the Pinochet dictatorship in 1990, and this had helped produce a great decline in poverty and significant expansion of the middle class, as well as enabling Chile to join the OECD in 2010. However, from 2014, economic growth there slowed down, while the ability of the political system to deliver results lessened, which helped cause a lack of confidence in institutions and a populist assault on what was seen as an unequal society run to the benefit of the élite who indeed dominated much of the economy. Public order collapsed with rioting in 2020.

Ecuador's economy contracted by 9 per cent in 2020, while Covid gave Peru, which had had significant free-market economic growth in the 2000s and early 2010s, a very high fatality rate and an economic crisis that pushed 20 per cent of Peruvians back into poverty. In 2021, Pedro Castrillo, a left-winger, narrowly won the presidency on the slogan of 'no more poor in a rich country'. The poor rural hinterland provided him with his core support, but it was not clear whether he had viable policies and in 2022 he lost power. Peru certainly needs investment in its Pacific infrastructure as Callao, the leading port, is antiquated, not least with insufficient cranes.

Yet, California in 2021 appeared scarcely better in confronting problems, although it avoided the severe public order crisis of Portland, Oregon. Typhus and typhoid were found in Los Angeles and Long Beach, with homeless people camping permanently on beaches, and many drug addicts, both also major issues in San Francisco. In Oakland, there are homeless encampments under the Chester Nimitz Freeway, an instructive comment on the after-effect of a World War Two hero.

Although some avoided Covid, for the smaller Pacific islands, the Covid pandemic posed serious demographic and economic challenges that interacted with more general problems stemming from climate change, population growth, poverty, international crime, corruption and geopolitical competition.

The Revival of British Columbia's First Nations

The percentage of the province's population defining itself thus was only 3.8 in 1996, and they had long suffered from difficult social circumstances and governmental regulation, but, from 1969, the situation had improved, not least over land rights and education. A treaty with the Nisg'a in 1996, giving them land, fishing and logging rights, and self-government, was resisted by the provincial government, but was upheld by the courts in 2000.

11

Where Goes the Pacific World?

....

Climate change is a general threat. To a degree, there has been adaptation to sea-level rises, with atolls adapting by changing shape as sediment is eroded and moved. This, however, will be a defence mechanism that does not last, as the sea-level rises at a faster rate, while there are also both stronger waves and high tides that are more damaging and move further inland. The seawater driven inland can affect groundwater as well as hitting crops. Climate change affects marine life in a variety of ways. Grey whales, walruses and eider ducks moved into the northern Bering Sea as it warmed up.

Aside from rising sea levels and damage to coral, there are also more severe fires that in part are a reflection of high heat as well as strong winds. In 2021, the Big Island faced the biggest fire in Hawai'i's history, with over 62 square miles burned out. 2020–2 also saw terrible fires in the Pacific west of America and Canada.

Climate change takes the headlines, but other factors play a major role in environmental transformation, notably those relating to a rapidly rising population, both globally and round much of the Pacific, especially in the Philippines, although not in Japan. This population has requirements for food, fuel and other resources that press hard on the various interrelated environments that compose the Pacific.

One of these requirements has led to an expansion of the Pacific somewhat different to that due to the continental drift. This other expansion is that of the movement of salt water as the fresh water in littoral areas decreases due to the extraction of groundwater locally and the greater upriver extraction of river water. Such salination is a particular issue in California.

Exploitation is a key theme at present, and in very many forms. Factory-fishing, a major one, is affecting species' ability to sustain numbers, and is both part of a wider global crisis and one that is hitting the Pacific hard, and increasingly so.

A different form of exploitation is that provided by the global race for rare-earth elements, which are crucial for a range of new technologies, including wind turbines, electric cars and batteries. A range of states, including China, Japan, South Korea, Belgium, Germany, France and Britain, were involved in deep-sea mining projects in the Pacific. The British government sponsored a project by UK Seabed Resources, a subsidiary of the American defence company's Lockheed Martin's British division. By 2030, the British project seeks an annual output of three million tonnes of the tennis-ball-sized mineral-rich nodules on the ocean floor. As with trawling on the ocean bottom, there was a concern for the damage to the ocean floor. A different form of damage arises from the movement into the ocean of plastic, usually by straightforward dumping. This is a particular problem in the north-east Pacific.

A different form of pollution occurred in the north-west Pacific where the tsunami-caused catastrophe at the Fukushima nuclear plant in Japan in 2011 led to the melting down of three reactors. Used to cool the aftermath, 170 tonnes of water are contaminated by them daily, and, in 2021, Japan announced that it would pump over a million tonnes of treated contaminated water into the Pacific from 2023. The water would still contain traces of the radioactive isotope tritium; both local fishermen, whose fish has been shunned by many customers since 2011, and South Korea are opposed to the process.

Oil spills have been a major problem in Pacific waters, notably off Alaska and California. In August 2021, an oil slick was created off the Japanese port of Hachinohe when a ship carrying woodchips there from Thailand ran into trouble in bad weather before breaking up.

The *Exxon Valdez* oil spill

The risks of Pacific navigation were fully demonstrated in 1989 when the tanker *Exxon Valdez*, en route from Alaska to Long Beach, California, ran aground in Prince William Sound, Alaska on Bligh Reef off Bligh Island, both of which were named after William Bligh who had served as Master on Cook's third Pacific voyage. 10.8 million US gallons of crude oil, out of the total 53.1 million carried, were spilt. Deaths included at least 100,000 seabirds and 2,800 otters, with others affected, including seals, fish, whales and mussels. Much of the oil-ruined coastline remains damaged.

Covid

As with previous epidemics, the vulnerability of Pacific people was compounded by a lack of hospital facilities. In 2021 for its nine million population, Papua New Guinea had only 500 doctors, fewer than 4,000 nurses and no more than 5,000 hospital beds. Fortunately, the low median age, only 22, reduced vulnerability. By July 2021, Fiji had run out of morgue space. Covid hit both tourism and also seasonal migration in search of work. Pacific trade was also affected, not least in 2021 due to Covid at Chinese ports.

The ability to respond to exploitation and environmental change is limited. The Pacific contains many microstates, the significance of which has been enhanced by sovereignty which includes a place in the United Nations and other bodies and by issues such as the struggle between China and Taiwan. This provides the microstates with a role and can offer an opportunity to win economic support. Thus, in 2002, Nauru switched from recognising Taiwan to following the Chinese line and received help accordingly, as did Panama in 2017, and the Solomon Islands and Kiribati in 2019.

The implications of microstate status have become more apparent as independence has ceased to be a novelty. Decolonisation came late to the Pacific and is incomplete, but is now well-established. Nevertheless, these states have scant ability to confront major powers, lacking for example the aerial, let alone satellite, surveillance necessary for fishery supervision. For these and other reasons, the microstates have to rely on backing from major states, but are then affected by their agendas as well as the rivalries between them. This became more of an issue as Chinese-American relations worsened in the 2010s. Moreover, China sought a more distant impact in the Pacific, one that made it a possible patron, but also an issue. Thus, in the early 2020s, there was Chinese interest in a 'fixed aircraft carrier' on the island of Canton, 1,800 miles south-west of Hawai'i, within Kiribati. Its long runway had been important for American bombers in World War Two, and since then the atoll has been used by America for space and missile-tracing operations. In 2018, there were reports that China was in talks to build a military base in Vanuatu. China developed facilities at both ends of the Panama Canal and discussed the construction of a cruise ship terminal on Panama's Pacific coast. Separately, the melting of the Arctic ice has led to greater Chinese interest in the routes thither which has underlined Japan's blocking position across Chinese maritime routes.

The role of great-power competition and, more specifically, the question of whether China was a legitimate security and development partner, has threatened to divide regional agencies, such as the Fiji-based Pacific Forum (founded in 1971 as the South Pacific Forum and with South only dropped in 1999). The Forum itself has shown growing divisions that reflect differences and tensions, notably within Polynesia and also between it and Micronesia. The latter relates to a more general geopolitical contrast between islands near and north of the Equator which look to the United States, notably for aid and migration, and a South-West Pacific where Australia and New Zealand are far more influential. Reflecting the significance of aid, they are also the biggest contributors to the Pacific Islands Forum. The contrast between these two parts of the Pacific is also seen in air links, with those in the South-West Pacific looking to Australasia, and those further north to Hawai'i.

Tourism

Prior to the Covid pandemic, tourism to the Pacific had been steadily increasing. Beach holidays were, for long, largely within perimeter coastal regions, notably Americans to California and Acapulco, or Australians to the Queensland coast. However, jet aircraft and entrepreneurialism led to the development of Hawai'i as an American destination. The Hawaiian Village Hotel was opened in 1955; Conrad Hilton, who proved a key developer, purchased half of it in 1961, and that year Elvis Presley filmed the successful musical romantic comedy *Blue Hawaii*, providing beach-life, seaside romances, and tourism.

Greater wealth and longer-distance long-haul flight changed the situation from the 1990s. Tourism to Polynesia increased. So also did Pacific cruises. Alongside tourism from the West, there was a major growth in that from Japan and, later, China, with Hawai'i and New Zealand becoming major Japanese tourist destinations, although much Japanese tourism remained within the extensive archipelago.

This increase was despite the extent to which tourism posed environmental challenges. Most obviously, these were to the area itself, not least pressure on reefs and beaches, as well as sewage outflows; but also the impact on the atmosphere of long-distance flights. Yet, there were also environmental challenges to tourists, notably earth-quakes, as on Lombok in 2018, and volcanos, as with Mount Agung on Bali the same year.

Moana: Into Fantasy

The continuing ability of the Pacific to call forth fantasies, as well as the repackaging of old myths, was seen in the computer-animated Disney film *Moana* (2016). Set in Polynesia, it links myth, gods and journeys. This successful film grossed over $645 million worldwide. Set on the fictional Polynesian island of Motunui, it featured a volcanic demon, demigod of the wind and sea, the brave daughter of a Polynesian chief, a blight that hits the island, killing vege-tation and reducing the fish catch, a powerful reef, a past history of Pacific voyaging, navigation on a *camakau*, the traditional watercraft of Fiji, a typhoon, pirates, a magical fishhook, a monstrous coconut crab, the Pacific as a living force, and the resumption of voyaging by the islanders.

Imperial Relicts?

Britain and France are the imperial powers of note in discussion of the Pacific, and the latter, in particular, still rules an extensive area from which it obtains considerable mineral resources, which helps explain the significance of retaining control of New Caledonia. Moreover, the yield from the French Pacific may increase, as with the plans in the early 2020s to renew phosphate extraction from Makatea, a plan that led to disputes. However, in terms of population, it is more appropriate to focus on America, Australia and New Zealand.

In turn, east of 120° the key powers are Chile, Ecuador and Mexico, although France rules uninhabited Clipperton Island, a coral atoll which is closest to Mexico. Chile has a range of islands, notably San Felix, San Ambrosio and Easter Island, Sala y Gómez and the Juan Fernández Islands; Ecuador has the Galápagos, and Mexico Guadalupe, Rocas Alijos and the Revillagigedo Islands. There are no signs of imminent territorial change to any of these. Whereas the Galápagos has many tourists, access is restricted to the Mexican islands and there is a military presence. America continues a territorial power, although, in 2011, Guam, the Northern Marianas and American Samoa became associate members of the Pacific Islands Forum.

Influence is not only by formal rule, and Australia in particular wields considerable informal control, with its currency used in Kiribati, while Nauru is fiscally dependent on providing a detention centre for asylum-seekers to Australia, and there is another in Papua New Guinea.

Pacific Geopolitics

The extent and pace of international attention have increased greatly in recent years, in part in response to real or alleged moves by China, which has offered its Belt and Road Initiative of infrastructure investment. For example, it has proposed to integrate this initiative into Kiribati's development plan, and has specifically offered to develop port facilities and fish-processing in the Line and Phoenix archipelagos. In 2019, a Chinese company sought to lease Tulagi Island, which had been a Japanese naval base, only for the Solomon Islands government to reject the idea.

American and Australian interest and activity have risen in response. In 2018, an annual 'Pacific Security Cooperation Dialogue' of America, Australia and New Zealand was established, while Australia announced its 'Pacific Step-up' policy of economic and military commitment, and New Zealand its 'Pacific Reset'. The following year, America followed suit with its 'Pacific Pledge', while the joint statement from AUSMIN, the Australian-American ministerial consultations, emphasised 'the need for an increasingly networked structure of alliances and partners' across the region, a view restated in 2020. The Kwajalein Atoll in the Marshall Islands has the Ronald Reagan Ballistic Missile Defense Test Site, and the American regional presence is designed to expand further under the 'Pacific Deterrence Initiative' outlined in the 2021 defence budget which included provision for an improved Guam Defence System and a multi-mission over the horizon radar in Palau. The American navy had earlier undertaken to locate 60 per cent of its forces in its Asia-Pacific region. Moreover, in 2013, America agreed to base surveillance drones and reconnaissance aircraft in Japan in order to patrol nearby waters.

Japan has repurposed its defence strategy, away from the Cold War emphasis on defending Hokkaido against possible Soviet attack and, instead, towards opposing China. As a result, there has been (notably with the National Security Strategy and Mid-Term Defence Programme formulated in 2013, when the defence budget was increased), a geographical resetting, with Japan's southerly islands to the fore, and also a development of the Japanese navy, as part of a new Pacific naval race. In 2015, Japan took delivery of the *Izumo*, which, in designation, was a 'helicopter-carrying destroyer', but, in practice, is as big as the World War Two carriers and can take aircraft. Mobility and flexibility are now emphasised.

In July 2021, on his first official visit to French Polynesia, President Macron declared that France would help South Pacific nations to launch a coastguard network to counter 'predatory' behaviour by China including with its use of paramilitary fishing vessels. In May 2021, French, American and Japanese troops carried out their first joint-military exercises off Japan. That June, France sent fighter and troop transport aircraft and air-to-air refuellers to Tahiti to show that its forces could intervene in the region in less than forty-eight hours. In August, America, Australia and Britain entered into an agreement to build a new generation of Australian submarines.

Not only military deployment is at issue. Somewhat differently, the Papua New Guinea Electrification Partnership established in 2018 is a partnership between America, Australia, Japan and New Zealand to increase the proportion of Papua New Guinea's population connected to electricity from 13 to 70 per cent by 2030.

So also with submarine cables, which remain a major form of geopolitics. In 2020, there was competition over the route of the first fibre-optic cable between South America and East Asia. China, Chile's largest trading partner, wanted to have Shanghai as the terminus for the route from Chile, but American pressure helped lead to the adoption of the Japanese plan for a 13,000-kilometre (8,700-mile) link via Auckland to Sydney where it could connect to the cable to Tokyo completed in 2020. Separately, the Chinese plan for links from Hong Kong to Los Angeles and Guam was thwarted by American pressure and in 2020–1, instead, proposed routes were announced from America via Guam to Taiwan, Singapore, Indonesia and the Philippines.

CONCLUSION

Considering both present and future is one way to conclude a book, but to do so risks underplaying the complexities of the past and the variety of paths they can suggest for the future. The very different nature of societies and states across the wide expanses of the region, both ocean and continental shores, guards against simplistic accounts of past and present, and should do the same for the future. There are trends that suggest an overarching commonality of experience, notably so with environmental change, and in particular in the shape of rising sea levels. Yet, the impact of that experience can vary, not least depending on the particular topography, economy and settlement patterns of individual islands. So even more with economic, social and political trends, such as mechanisation, population growth and populism. Contingencies are highly significant but so also is the strength of pre-existing patterns of behaviour, not least in so far as they have expression and continuity in institutional practices and social cohesion. As a consequence, it is not terribly helpful to think of the Pacific as a unit, or indeed of the Pacific islands, or even only of Polynesia. Each see too much variety for any such conclusion.

Yet, that situation also contributes to the great fascination of the subject. Behind the sand and the surf, there is a profound diversity in circumstances and developments. Alongside the substantial and growing importance of the Pacific, that helps make its history of significance. This is a history that is too vital to dismiss in terms of ready patterns and pat conclusions.

Turtles under Threat

Rising plastic pollution in the Pacific affects juvenile sea turtles who swim into the Great Pacific Garbage Patch between California and Hawai'i where, already in 2020, there was nearly 90,000 tonnes of rubbish covering an area over twice the size of Texas. There is far more plastic found in Pacific than in Indian Ocean turtles. Aside from ingesting the plastic, turtles also suffer from being entangled in plastic waste and get caught in fishing nets. Seas warming at an accelerating rate and the longer, more frequent and hotter marine heatwaves they cause, have also meant that turtles have to swim further north to catch prey, using extra energy that, in turn, leads them to lay fewer eggs on beaches, contributing to the decline of some species. The biodiversity of the Pacific is being lost, and that is a warning to us. We are only another species; not a form of deity.

Island Sanctuaries

A 2021 survey published in *Sustainability* sought to identify places best positioned to carry on when, or if, others fell apart as a result of climate change. The emphasis was on self-sufficiency and New Zealand was foremost notably because of its renewable energy capacity (particularly geothermal), its ability to produce its own food – a situation helped by a small population – and its island character ensuring that it could be isolated from other countries. The top four runners-up were Tasmania, Ireland, Iceland, Britain; and the next two, the United States and Canada.

The ranking for New Zealand and Tasmania, the latter increasingly being a part of Australia, attractive for internal migration and foreign and domestic tourism represented a different vision of the Pacific to that of sandy tropical islands. In part, a heating of life has been accompanied by a cooling of the imagination. In the case of New Zealand, it has benefited from the visual attention it received through being used for the filming of the *Lord of the Rings* (2001–3) on both islands.

The Covid pandemic also had an impact in that New Zealand, at least initially, was seen as a successful example of how best to respond, and therefore as a refuge, which was not the case with tropical islands such as Fiji. So also with the hot weather extremes of 2021 which hit Pacific America and Canada, but not New Zealand. Images certainly change.

There are many other Pacific territories, but their food and energy self-sufficiency are generally very limited. Indeed, nearly half of the most aid-dependent countries in the world are Pacific islands.

Selected Further Reading

....

The *Journal of Pacific History* is a very valuable periodical.

Abulafia, David, *The Boundless Sea: A Human History of the Oceans* (London, 2019).

Adler, Antony, *Neptune's Laboratory: Fantasy, Fear, and Science at Sea* (Cambridge, Mass., 2019).

Aldrich, Robert, *The French Presence in the South Pacific, 1842–1940* (London, 1990).

Anderson, Atholl, *Prodigious Birds: Moas and Moa-Hunting in Prehistoric New Zealand* (Cambridge, 1989).

Anderson, Atholl, *The First Migration: Maori Origins 3000 BC – AD 1450* (Wellington, 2016).

Andrade, Tonio, *How Taiwan Became Chinese: Dutch, Spanish, and Han Colonization in the Seventeenth Century* (New York, 2008).

Arista, Neolani, *The Kingdom and the Republic* (Philadelphia, Penn., 2019).

Behlmer, George, *Risky Shores: Savagery and Colonisation in the Western Pacific* (Stanford, Calif., 2018).

Belich, James, *The New Zealand Wars and the Victorian Interpretation of Racial Conflict* (Auckland, 1986).

Belich, James, *Making Peoples: A History of the New Zealanders from Polynesian Settlement to the End of the Nineteenth Century* (London, 1996).

Belich, James, *Paradise Reforged: A History of the New Zealanders from the 1880s to the Year 2000* (Honolulu, Ha., 2001).

Bennett, Judith, *The Wealth of the Solomons: A History of a Pacific Archipelago, 1800–1978* (Honolulu, Ha., 1987).

Bonnemaison, Joel, *The Tree and the Canoe: History and Ethnogeography of Tanna* (Honolulu, Ha., 1994).

Borofsky, Robert (ed.), *Remembrance of Pacific Pasts: An Invitation to Remake History* (Honolulu, Ha., 2000).

Bougainville, Louis-Antoine, *The Pacific Journal of Louis-Antoine de Bougainville, 1767–1768*, translated by John Dunmore (London, 2002).

Brunt, Peter and Nicholas Thomas (eds), *Oceania* (London, 2018).

Buschmann, Rainer, Edward Slack and James Tueller, *Navigating the Spanish Lake. The Pacific in the Iberian World, 1521–1898* (Honolulu, Ha., 2014).

Calder, Alex, Jonathan Lamb and Bridget Orr (eds), *Voyages and Beaches: Pacific Encounters, 1769–1840* (Honolulu, Ha., 1999).

Campbell, Ian, *World's Apart: A History of the Pacific Islands* (Christchurch, 2011).

Chapell, David, *The Kanak Awakening: The Rise of Nationalism in New Caledonia* (Honolulu, Ha., 2013).

Connell, John, *New Caledonia or Kanaky? The Political History of a French Colony* (Canberra, 1987).

Craig, Barry et al., *Art and Performance in Oceania* (Honolulu, 1999).

Crosby, Ron, *The Forgotten Wars: Why the Musket Wars Matter Today* (Oratia, 2020).

Crowe, Andrew, *Pathway of the Birds: the Voyaging Achievements of the Māori and their Polynesian Ancestors* (Honolulu, Ha., 2018).

Cushman, Gregory, *Guano and the opening of the Pacific world: a global ecological history* (Cambridge, 2013).

Dening, Greg, *Mr Bligh's Bad Language: Passion, Power and Theatre on the Bounty* (London, 1992).

Dening, Greg, *Beach Crossings. Voyaging Across Times, Cultures and Self* (Melbourne, 2004).

Denoon, Donald and Philippa Mein-Smith, *A History of Australia, New Zealand and the Pacific* (Oxford, 2000).

Dunmore, John, *French Explorers in the Pacific* (2 vols, Oxford, 1965, 1969).

Eisler, William, *The Furthest Shore: Images of Terra Australis from the Middle Ages to Captain Cook* (Cambridge, 1995).

Fausett, William, *Writing the New World: Imaginary Voyages and Utopias of the Great Southern Land* (Syracuse, NY, 1993).

Firth, Stewart, *New Guinea Under the Germans* (Melbourne, 1983).

Fischer, Steven, *Island at the End of the World: The Turbulent History of Easter Island* (London, 2005).

Fischer, Steven, *A History of the Pacific Islands* (2nd edition, Basingstoke, 2013).

Fraenkel, Jon, *The Manipulation of Custom: From Uprising to Intervention in the Solomon Islands* (Wellington, 2004).

Gell, Alfred, *Wrapping in Images: Tattooing in Polynesia* (Oxford, 1993).

Godelier, Maurice and Marilyn Strathern (eds), *Big Men and Great Men: Personifications of Power in Melanesia* (Cambridge, 1991).

Graham, Wade, *Braided Waters* (Berkeley, Calif., 2018).

Grossman, Derek et al., *America's Pacific Island Allies: the freely associated states and Chinese influence* (Santa Monica, Calif., 2019).

Gunn, Michael (ed.), *Atua: Sacred Gods from Polynesia* (Canberra, 2014).

Harrison, J. A., *Japan's Northern Frontier* (Gainesville, Fl., 1953).

Hau'ofa, Epeli, *Tales of the Tikongs* (Honolulu, Ha., 1994).

Hau'ofa, Epeli, *We Are the Ocean: Selected Works* (Honolulu, Ha., 2008).

Howarth, Crispin (ed.), *Myth and Magic: Art of the Sepik River, Papua New Guinea* (Canberra, 2015).

Howe, Kerry (ed.), *Vaka Moana, Voyages of the Ancestors: The Discovery and Settlement of the Pacific* (Auckland, 2006).

Hughes, Robert, *The Fatal Shore* (London, 1986).

Hunt, Terry and Carl Lipo, *The Statues That Walked* (New York, 2011).

Igler, David, *The Great Ocean: Pacific Worlds from Captain Cook to the Gold Rush* (Oxford, 2013).

King, David, *Food for the Flames: Idols and Missionaries in Central Polynesia* (San Francisco, Calif., 2011).

Kirch, Patrick, *On the Road of the Winds: An Archaeological History of the Pacific Islands Before European Contact* (Berkeley, Calif., 2001).

Küchler, Susanne and Andrea Eimke, *Tivaivai: The Social Fabric of the Cook Islands* (London, 2009).

La Croix, Summer, *Hawai'i. Eight Hundred Years of Political and Economic Change* (Chicago, Ill., 1954).

Lewis, David, *We The Navigators: the Ancient Art of Seafinding in the Pacific* (Honolulu, Ha., 1994).

Lineham, Peter (ed.), *Weaving the Unfinished Mats: Wesley's Legacy – Conflict, Confusion and Challenge in the South Pacific* (Auckland, 2007).

Macdonald, Bruce, *Vancouver. A Visual History* (Vancouver, 1992).

Manning, Patrick, *A History of Humanity: The Evolution of the Human System* (Cambridge, 2020).

Mar, Tracey, *Decolonisation and the Pacific: Indigenous Globalisation and the Ends of Empire* (Cambridge, 2016).

Matsuda, Matt, *Pacific Worlds: A History of Seas, Peoples and Cultures* (Cambridge, 2012).

McAleer, John and Nigel Rigby, *Captain Cook and the Pacific* (New Haven, Conn., 2017).

McIntyre, W. D., *Winding Up the British Empire in the Pacific Islands* (Oxford, 2014).

McLean, Gavin, *The Southern Octopus: The Rise of a Shipping Empire* (Wellington, 1990).

McLynn, Frank, *Captain Cook: Master of the Seas* (New Haven, Conn., 2010).

McMaster, John, *Sabotaging the Shogun: Western diplomats open Japan, 1859–69* (New York, 1992).

Miller, Sally, A. Latham and Dennis O'Flynn (eds), *Studies in the Economic History of the Pacific Rim* (London, 1998).

Moore, Peter, *Endeavour: The Ship That Changed the World* (New York, 2018).

Muckle, Adrian, *Specters of Violence in a Colonial Context. New Caledonia, 1917* (Honolulu, Ha., 2012).

Nechtman, Tilman, *The Pretender of Pitcairn Island: Joshua W. Hill – The Man Who Would be King among the Bounty Mutineers* (Cambridge, 2018).

Nelson, Hank, *Black, White and Gold: Gold Mining in Papua New Guinea, 1878–1930* (Canberra, 1976).

Newell, Jennifer, *Trading Nature: Tahitians, Europeans, and Ecological Exchange* (Honolulu, Ha., 2010).

Newell, Jenny, *Pacific Art in Detail* (London, 2011).

Notehelfer, F. G. (ed.), *Japan through American Eyes: the journal of Francis Hall, 1859–1866* (Princeton, NJ., 1992).

Okamura, Jonathan, *Ethnicity and Inequality in Hawai'i* (Honolulu, Ha., 2008).

Padrón, Ricardo, *The Indies of the Setting Sun: How Early Modern Spain Mapped the Far East as the Transpacific West* (Chicago, Ill., 2020).

Paine, Lincoln, *The Sea and Civilization: A Maritime History of the World* (New York, 2013).

Pickles, Katie and Catharine Coleborne (eds), *New Zealand's Empire* (Manchester, 2015).

Place Names of the Ancestors. A Maori Oral History Atlas (Wellington, 1990).

Poblete, JoAnna, *Balancing the Tides. Marine Practices in American Samoa* (Honolulu, Ha., 2020).

Rice, Geoffrey, *That Terrible Time: Eye-witness Accounts of the 1918 Influenza Pandemic in New Zealand* (Christchurch, 2018).

Richardson, Brian, *The Journal of James Macrae, Botanist at the Sandwich Isles, 1825* (Honolulu, Ha., 2019).

Rodman, Margaret, *Houses Far from Home: British Colonial Space in the New Hebrides* (Honolulu, Ha., 2001).

Salmond, Anne, *Between Worlds: Early Exchanges between Māori and Europeans 1773–1815* (Honolulu, Ha., 1997).

Salmond, Anne, *The Trial of the Cannibal Dog: Captain Cook in the South Seas* (New Haven, Conn., 2003).

Salmond, Anne, *Aphrodite's Island* (Berkeley, Calif., 2010).

Salmond, Anne, *Bligh: William Bligh in the South Seas* (Berkeley, Calif., 2011).

Saranillio, Dean, *Unsustainable Empire: Alternative Histories of Hawai'i Statehood* (Durham, NC, 2018).

Sherman, Daniel, *French Primitivism and the Ends of Empire, 1945–1975* (Chicago, Ill., 2011).

Shineberg, Dorothy, *They Came for Sandalwood: A Study of the Sandalwood Trade in the Southwest Pacific, 1830–1865* (Melbourne, 1967).

Skaggs, Jimmy, *Clipperton: A History of the Island the World Forgot* (New York, 1989).

Spate, Oskar, *The Spanish Lake: The Pacific Since Magellan* (Minneapolis, Minn., 1979–84).

Thomas, Nicholas, *Entangled Objects: Exchange, Material Culture and Colonialism in the Pacific* (Cambridge, 1991).

Thomas, Nicholas, *Islanders: The Pacific in the Age of Empire* (London, 2010).

Thompson, Christina, *Sea People: The Puzzle of Polynesia* (New York, 2019).

Tumarkin, Xa (ed.), *Nikolai Miklouho-Maclay, Travels to New Guinea* (Moscow, 1982).

Walker, Brett, *The Conquest of Ainu Lands: Ecology and Culture in Japanese Expansion, 1590–1800* (Berkeley, Calif., 2001).

Williams, Glyndwr, *The Great South Sea* (London, 1997).

Williams, Glyndwr, *Buccaneers, Explorers and Settlers: British Encounters and Enterprise in the Pacific 1670–1800* (London, 2005).

Winchester, Simon, *Pacific: Silicon Chips and Surfboards, Coral Reefs and Atom Bombs, Brutal Dictators, Fading Empires, and the Coming Collision of the World's Superpowers* (London, 2015).

Index